AMERICAN BOMBER AIRCRAFT VOL. II

Boeing B-29 Superfortress

John M. Campbell

AMERICAN BOMBER AIRCRAFT VOL. II

Boeing

B-29

Superfortress

John M. Campbell

Schiffer Military/Aviation History
Atglen, PA

Cover Artwork by Steve Ferguson, Colorado Springs, CO

Book Design by Ian Robertson.

Cover Artwork by Steve Ferguson, Colorado Springs, CO

Library of Congress Catalog Number: 97-66913

Printed in China.
ISBN: 0-7643-0272-8

We are interested in hearing from authors with book ideas on related topics.

Published by Schiffer Publishing Ltd.
4880 Lower Valley Road
Atglen, PA 19310
Phone: (610) 593-1777
FAX: (610) 593-2002
E-mail: Schifferbk@aol.com
Please write for a free catalog.
This book may be purchased from the publisher.
Please include $3.95 postage.
Try your bookstore first.

ACKNOWLEDGMENTS

During my long years of collecting and gathering military aircraft photographs, I've had the honor of meeting many very wonderful people. This seems to always be the case when aviation is the topic of conversation.

The success of these "projects" as I choose to call them, is totally and completely the result of these fine people. There were Groups that assisted, Manufacturers which assisted, AND veterans and enthusiasts who forwarded their much more than two cents worth, Then there is also the other historians, photographers, buffs, and affectionados. This work of love would never have come to be if not for their assistance and vigilance.

John M. Campbell

At this time I'd like to convey my personal thanks, and well done to these special people. 58th Bomb Wing Archives via Tom Britton, Chester Marshall of Global Twentieth fame; John Aldrich; and Mr. Bob Mann for his years of toil and sweat in gathering and creating an accurate listing of over 5,000 names and Serial nos. of B-29s and B-50s. Mr. Mann, along with the help of Tom Britton, really did a bang-up job. They still are gathering even more information as you read this. Mr. Tom Lubbesmeyer and the Boeing Aircraft Co. Archives in Seattle for the early production line photos and the detailed interior images; Dr. Hiroya Sugano, and the "Zero Fighters" admirers assn. Hickham AFB, Hawaii; and Leatrice Akagi, Chief of the Office of History for the information on Pearl Harbor. National Archives, Los Alamos Scientific Laboratories for information and assistance on The Manhattan Project. Robert Hunt Library, UASF Historical Research Center, and Dr. James Kitchens III, Wright-Patterson AFB and the Air Force Museum. The DAVA film library, the Oklahoma Air & Space Hall of Fame and Museum. The Glen Martin Museum. The Air & Space Museum/Smithsonian and Paul Garber facilities. Robert Mikesh, the Naval Aviation Museum in Pensacola, Fla.; Fred Johnsen, Cheryl Gumm, Dr. Young, and the Edwards AFB Flight Test Center. Brigadier Gen. Charles "Chuck" Yeager, Mr. John "Socks" Heyer, Gary James, Garry R. Pape, Steve Link, Jack Lambert, Arnold Fort, Wayne Watts, Wayne Walrond, the Bell Aircraft Company, Mr. Jim Root, Mr. Jack C. Moses, Mr. Mark Copeland, Russ Stoffer, Mr. Fred Johnsen. Ron Witt, Paul Swendrowski, the Kansas Aeronautical Historical Society and Boeing, Wichita. Mr. Robert Pickett, Tinker AFB/OCAMA Office of History, Dr. James Crowder PhD, and Dan M. Schill. Steve Birdsall, Dr. Donald Klinko, Hill AFB Office of History, Mr. Ron Willis and Mr. Thomas Carmichael, Mr. Ron McKay, Thomas William McGarry, Walter W. Beam, Richard M. Keenan, Al Lloyd, Jim Pattillo, Denny Pidhayny, Dr. Henry Zimmerman, Mr. "Mad" Mike Hill for his hours of assistance, Larry Davis, Nick Veronico, Mr. William Davis, Steve Pace, Mr. Bob Snodgrass and his collection from Amarillo Army Air Field, Kevin Herbert, Mr. Mitch Mayborne, Capt. Prentiss "Mick"" Burkett, James V. Crow, Herman Hetzel, Glenn Horton, Arden Accord, Mark Bacon, Marty Isham, E. VanHouten, Robert Esposito, H. W. Rued, Col. R. Uppstrom, Col. B Butcher, W. J. Balough, Sr., J. Hillard, W. Duncan, G. Michaels, Mr. Walter Scheffe, Pilot of Yokohama Yo Yo, Col. Barry Miller, Martin Caiden, Larry Steward USMC, Mark Curren, Tony "Two Guns" Stevenson, USMC, [illegible] Jacobs, Mark Elms, Terry Brewer, Cheryl Sweeney, Teresa Gieroba, H.G. Martin, CPL. Terry L. Thompson, USMC, Robt. Pickett, Mr. Raymond Loberg, Mark Turner, USN, Billy Thompson, Michael Haseltine, Darby Perrin, Tony Kastel, Randy Stromski, Garry Brum, Steve Bryan, and Tony Wiens, Richard McAbee, and "Butch' Maurey.

The Reverend Theodore Morgan, Randall Kenyon, John Szabo, Charles C. Worman, Wesley Henry, Don Finch, Stewart Howard, Lt. Col. Kenny Wilkerson, Tinker Flt. Test, Mr. Peter M. Bowers, Col. Mike Moffett, Vyron DeHass, Garland Leonard, Jay Reid, Fenton Morrison and the 73rd B/W Assn, T. Barnes, Lt. Col. R.Elam,497th B/G assn. A. Anderton, 79th B/W. Edward G. Longacre, Maj. Gen. Donald L. Marks, Maj. Woodrow P. Swancutt, Maj. Gen. Walter C. Sweeney, Will Rushing, Carla Livingston, Ralph Barrier, Yvonne Gordon, Maj. Gen. Roger S. Ramey, Cdr. 8th Air Force in 1949. Maj. James Gallagher, Joel Levine, Robin Pierce, Jon Maguire, Stanley Sommers, Glenn E. McClure, Wayne McClellan, Mr. Mike Merryman. Maj. S. D. Huff, Mike Conners of the Hobby Shop Crossroads Mall, OKC, named for "Operation Crossroads", Stan Piet, Mr. Paul Frederich, 19th B/W assn, Artist Steve Furgeson, Mr. Bob Vanderveen, Kee Bird, Mr. Allen Griffith for the Tu-4 info and images. Mr. Steve Wilson, Mr Richard Long, Kathy Long, and Mr. Dan Stroud. I'd also like to personally thank Rollie & LaDonna Fansler for their assistance with the computer glitches, "That always haunt a writer"; the Fisher family—Dolores, Terry, Michael, Donald, Linda, Ryan, and of course, Little Jesse; Cindy, Joshua, & Raina Brechbiel; and Pete & Nancy Schiffer, Bob Biondi, and the Editorial Staff at Schiffer Publishing, L.T.D., for their patience & attention to quality. I want to thank my Mother and Father, Ruth and F. D. Campbell, for their assistance, their love, and their understanding throughout all my projects. I would also like to thank all of the Men & women who helped to build, fly, and save the greatness of the B-29 Superfortress.

Bless Them All,

John M. Campbell

Capt. FAY D.CAMPBELL, U.S.ARMY AIR CORPS 14TH AIR FORCE CHINA, BURMA, INDIA, THEATRE OF OPERATIONS WORLD WAR II

"I heard about (Pearl Harbor) & I knew right then I had to go.
It was surprising how many people made that decision, the decision either to stay or to go"
Fay D. Campbell Dec.6,1995

Dedicated....

To the memory of those men who gave their lives....
whose brave acts and deeds have written the history....

CONTENTS

INTRODUCTION

The B-29 "Superfortress", one of the most revered heavy bombers of the Second World War, proved herself to be quite a worthy adversary. The men & women who built her had a fierce pride in what they had manufactured & built. Her pilots and crewmembers have an undying devotion to her and a solemn reverence for the missions they flew in her & her safe returns back to their home bases in the Pacific.

I will attempt at best to tell a little more of a personal account of what the men went through day by day—the hardships, the quieter moments, as well as the humor which was always present in these fine men.

I will dive headlong into the many roles the B-29s filled & filled well. The tasks the B-29 undertook, from tanker and cargo transport flying daily missions over the treacherous Himalayas, affectionately referred to in this journal as the "Hump", in the CBI. The bombing missions, the search and rescue missions, or "Dumbos" as they were referred to in that role. The supply drop missions to our POWs being held in Japan. The two Atom bomb missions. Many think only of "Enola Gay" and the Atom bomb dropped at Hiroshima, but the B-29 meant much more and did much more than that.

The B-29 was involved in experimental projects, and set many records of her own. It was the B-29 that air dropped the first rocket-powered aircraft to break the impenetrable "Sound Barrier", with Charles "Chuck" Yeager at the controls, now a Brig. General Retired from the United States Air Force. We will look at the B-29s' role in Strategic Air Command, and her brief but powerful role in the bombing of North Korea. New information will be revealed about the B-29s in the Soviets' hands, copied and re-manufactured into the TU-4, code named "Bull", and the Tu 126 "Moss", an AWACs conversion of the B-29 with Turpolev turboprop engines. The Communist Chinese even had the Russian variants in their aircraft inventory. Many were still in service in the late 1960s. I will report on the few still existing B-29s & the museum displays. I'll give you a brief look at the Operation Crossroads bombs of the Bikini Island tests, and a never before published look at the natural disaster at OC/AMA, Tinker AFB, Oklahoma, in 1947.

But whatever else you may find of value in this record, I hope it jogs fond memories and makes us all remember the many valiant men who flew, serviced, and admired this fine aircraft.

This book is to enhance not just an aircraft, but the many people who gave their toil, their sweat, their tears, and in many instances their blood to keep a free way of life and to oppose tyranny.

We owe these people for the very freedoms we now enjoy.

I had at the very beginning of this project, been told that "I was taking on an enormous task". This I do with great pleasure, Great Pride. Bless them All, "Tailwinds".

J.M. "Hooker" Campbell
Aviation Archivist, Oklahoma City, Ok, USA

Boeing

B-29

Superfortress

Chapter 1:
THE BIRTH OF A GIANT

Admiral Isoroku Yamamoto, the Commander in Chief of the Japanese Navy. Just prior to the invasion of Pearl Harbor, December 7,1941, stated to the Com manders of his Task Force still at anchor in Tokyo Bay, "I have traveled widely in America. I have seen the American's industrial might, and it is awesome." He further stated that,"the Americans are adversaries, worthy of you."

After his attack on Pearl Harbor, Yamamoto was again in conference with his Task Force Commanders in Tokyo Bay. While in the planning stages of the attack on Midway Island, and during the Japanese fleet's battle of the Coral Sea, he expressed his dismay and his anxiety about Midway, as well as the war when he stated that he was afraid that, "We [the Japanese] had awakened a sleeping Giant.", and, "These Americans with their tremendous resolve."

Just prior to World War II, studies by the engineering staff at Boeing Aircraft were in full swing. Their task was to improve on the earlier designed B-17 "Flying Fortress" and design a bomber which was much more than the legendary Flying Fortress. This bomber was to have tricycle landing gear, longer range, a larger bomb load, and duel load capacities. They also added a new dimension to aerial bombardment—the ability to fly much higher due to the pressurization of crews' compartments. This would enable the bomber to fly higher and farther than ever before. By May of 1940, Boeing had submitted their design proposal to the U.S. Army Air Corps. The design was accepted, and the Air Corps called the new design the XB-29. They placed an order for two prototypes in August and a third XB-29 to be used for static tests. In May of 1941, the Air Corps ordered 250 of the B-29 bombers to be constructed in Wichita, Kansas. Due to the attack on Pearl Harbor and America's Declaration of War against the Japanese the contract was raised to 500 B-29s. This was quite a big order for an as yet unproved bomber,and unprecedented for that day and time.

The other aircraft companies came up with their ideas and concepts, but only one aircraft would make its way onto the production lines. The B-32 Dominator, with only 125 built by Consolidated Aircraft, survived the competition. It was in place only as a back up plan, and, although several B-32s actually did see combat in the Pacific arena, these were assigned to the 5th Air Force.

Manned guns were dropped as an idea because of pressurization and the high altitudes at which the B-29s could fly. The B-29 was to be equipped with a remote fire control system. This system was to be proven much more than just effective.

On September 21, 1942, the First B-29 Superfortress taxied out, roared down the strip and gracefully rose into the sky at Boeing's Seattle Plant. Almost a full four months later, the 2nd XB-29 Prototype, with well known Test Pilot Eddie Allen, crashed. The XB-29 had an engine fire that could not be extinguished. Allen tried to return to the field and land the crippled bomber, but the XB-29 crashed into a building, causing the deaths of both Allen and his crew, as well as the personnel inside the building.

This necessitated the modification and retrofitting of new and improved equipment, which was done just as soon as the B-29s rolled off the assembly lines in Wichita, Kansas, and Renton, Washington.

This Mitsubishi A6M2, model 21, sits at rest on the flight deck of the Japanese Aircraft Carrier 'Akagi', the flagship of Vice-Admiral, Nagumo. 78 of these fighters would attack Oahu. Seen here at a quieter moment at rest in Tokyo Bay, a few days before the departure of the Invasion force. (Sugano)

The order,"Climb Mt. Nitaka", was the coded message to commence to launch aircraft. We see an A6M2 just leaving the flight deck of the Japanese Aircraft Carrier 'Soryu' early Sunday morning, December 7, 1941, codenamed-Zero. The Zeros were the Japanese Navy's best fighter aircraft; they could out-maneuver any of the aircraft based at Oahu. Armed with 2 wing- mounted 20mm cannons, and 2 7.7mm machine guns mounted in the engine cowling. The Zeros outgunned anything thrown up against them.Their primary role in this mission was to provide fighter protection for the one hundred and forty-three Nikajima Type 97,B5N2 model us (codenamed 'KATE') and the one hundred twenty-nine Aichi Type 99 dive bombers,D3A1 model IIs (code named 'Val'). (Campbell Archives)

One of 12 B-17's enroute from the mainland to Hawaii, unable to land at Hickham Field, which was currently under attack, made its way to a short strip at Bellows Field where she made a one wheel landing, ending up flat on the strip when the single gear collapsed.(L.Akagi)

B-17C, Serial No. 40-2074, which had arrived from Hamilton

Wreckage of a Japanese "Zero", shot down over Wahiawa outside Wheeler Field on December 7th. (L.Akagi)

The twisted wreckage of a Japanese "Zero" fighter lies crumpled in the Fort Kamehameha,Territory of Hawaii, a Japanese casualty of the December 7, 1941, attack on Pearl Harbor. (L. Akagi)

This close-up of a wrecked Japanese "Zero" cockpit shows the pilot's seat & control stick. (L.Akagi)

This "Zero" fighter was also shot down in Wahiawa near the civilian Conservation Corps camp on Oahu. Even though December 7th came as a total surprise to all but a very small few, the Japanese squadrons that attacked Pearl Harbor were not without losses of their own. (L.Akagi)

Consolidated's B-32 Dominator, "Direct From Tokyo", was assigned to the 312th Bomb Group of the 5th Army Air Forces, and was the only surviving contender in the race to build a Superbomber. (Accord)

Remote controlled guns were used on the B-29s, and early in war, training B-29s were in short supply. This TB-24L-FO, Ser. No. 44-49646, was fitted with the B-29 style remote turret and sight station as seen here at Kingman, Arizona, after her reclamation at war's end. This TB-24 and others like it assisted in training aerial gunners for B-29s till they were able to acquire the B-29s later in the war. (W.T. Larkins)

Many of the B-29s were sent to modification sites upon completion. These modifications consisted of engine, electrical, and structural modifications. Several B-29s saw combat in less than a month from their final dates of completion. (OCAMA, Tinker)

THE FLYING GUINEA PIG-41-002. The first prototype XB-29 was Boeing Aircraft's Flight Test Ship. As a flying testbed, the Guinea Pig worked long, hard hours, and was still flying in 1947. The test pilot was Elliot Marrill. This XB-29 never left the United States. (F. Johnsen)

210-, 42-24638 was used to train B-29 pilots and flight crewmen. (Snodgrass)

The Flying Guinea Pig stayed in Seattle until after World War II. Note the modified nacelle on her inboard engine. (F.Johnsen)

Boeing Aircraft Co. put on this show of power as they demonstrated, in flight, Boeing's contribution to the war effort in the field of aerial bombardment. (Boeing)

In many of Boeing's public relations efforts, Boeing and the War Department published inflight photos of some of America's airpower. Here we see a B-17G in the background with an early B-29 in her olive drab paint scheme. Note: Only the B-17 is fitted with guns at time of this photo. (OCAMA, Tinker)

Still in the O.D. paint, these two B-29s are departing for their foreign duty assignments. Taken on Oct.1, 1943, they are more than likely headed for the China, Burma, India theater. These B-29s are fully armed, as is visible with the cannon protruding out the tail. The tail skid on B-29s also marks the very early models. (Boeing)

The winter months in Wichita, Kansas, at the Boeing plant were mostly cold and blustery with snow. This B-29 is evidence of the moderate snowfall and colder weather they had to contend with. (OC-AMA, Tinker)

This view of the 3rd prototype XB-29, Serial no. 41-18335, gives us a rare view of the early three bladed props mounted to the four Wright R-3350-13 engines. During the test period this XB-29 crashed. The ensuing investigation of the crash led to changes in design and the moving up to the four bladed Hamilton Standard propellers. (Boeing Archives)

ABOVE: This is a complete view of the first prototype XB-29, Serial no. 41-002—the prototypes carried no armament, no turrets, and no tail gunners' compartment. It was, however, fitted with the teardrop shaped sighting blisters. Her wings were shorter at 141 feet 3 inches and 99 feet long. She went to Salina, Kansas, for flight tests because of the necessity for a longer runway. Boeing's N.D. Showalter was the Command Test Pilot of the first prototype, with Don Whitworth as the Test Engineer. The American insignia is early with no bars attached to the star and roundel. The tail skid is also of a much different design than that of the later Superfortress. (Boeing Archives)

OPPOSITE: XB-29, used for systems checks and the study of aerodynamics led to the overall improvement of the B-29 as a battle platform. This was the third and final prototype. This knight in shinning armor was destined to change the history of aerial warfare as we knew it. Seen over Mt. Ranier in western Washington State. (Boeing Archives)

On February 18, 1943, the second prototype XB-29, Serial no. 41-003, developed an engine fire while making a landing approach. The test pilot, veteran pilot, engineer, and designer Eddie Allen, crashed into the Frye Packing Co. in Seattle, Washington, seen here. The crash killed Allen and his 10 man crew, eleven of Boeing's elite test team. The crash impacted the 5th floor of the meat packing company. The crash killed nineteen people in the building and a fireman, as well as Alle' crew. The crash paved the way to many new modifications to the B-29 developmental program. The investigation discovered that a number of defective engines had been produced. This setback seemed to stall the B-29's production from advancing, but General H.H. Arnold simply said, "We are going to build it." (Boeing Archives)

During Autumn of 1943, deliveries of the B-29-BW were beginning to arrive at training units. The B-29 production lines were now getting fully underway. Here we see the Boeing Factory workers with their "JIBS" (assembly rigs) assembling the forward cockpit section of the B-29s, since the B-29 was built in compartmental stages. The Boeing team worked around the clock. Literally tons of steel and aluminum went through the Boeing Plants at Wichita, Kansas, and Renton, Washington. The workers were very proud of their work.(Boeing Archives)

The middle section of fuselage and mainspar with wing surface rolls down the B-29 rolling assembly line. Manufacturing resources were critical to B-29 production. This view of the assembly floor illustrates the considerable amount of space that was needed to roll out the big bombers at an astounding 100 B-29s a month during peak production years. The Wichita plant built more B-29s than any of the other three, thus earning Wichita the title, "Home of the B-29." (Boeing Archives)

The B-29s take shape in the final assembly stages, where cockpit sections are enjoined with main sections and the tail sections. But the work is far from over. They have to do landing gear drop checks, instrument checks, engine checks, rudder and flap, trim and electronic checks. When they roll off the line they are ready to engage a hostile enemy. (Boeing Archives)

This is a view of the XB-29 from a 3/4 rear position. There are no gun turrets or tail gunner's compartments on the XB-29s. This pre-completion photo shows her without all her engines even being mounted at the time of this photo. (Boeing Archives)

After all adjustments are made and all assemblies are checked the finished product is fine tuned, the engines get their run up time, and then they roll out for in-flight testing. These B-29s are in that stage of the journey. In a few short weeks they will be in places like Kharagpur, Chengtu, Guam, Saipan, Tinian, and most important of all, delivering a message from the United States that, "we will not tolerate aggression." (Boeing Archives)

During the early experimental phases of flight testing there was an idea to install and implement "hard points" for external bomb stores on the B-29s. This plan never went into practice because the payload of the B-29 was large enough to deliver a decisive blow with the available space allotted in the massive bomb bays. Serial no. 44-70060, a B-29-75-BW. (Boeing Archives)

This YB-29, Serial no. 41-36960, drones over the midwest countryside. The studies and information gathered from these flights greatly enhanced the future performance of the later production models that would evolve as the war progressed. The YB-29s were all built in Wichita, and were painted in the Olive Drab upper surface and light gull gray underside. (Boeing Archives)

On December 28, 1943, the first Renton built B-29A left the factory on a barge trip across the basin to the air strip. Her serial number was 42-93824. The Renton B-29s had a very different style about them. The wing structures were much different. The two piece center section was "bolted" together at Wichita and other factories, whereas the Renton built B-29As used a stub center section that extended a small distance beyond the fuselage. (Boeing Archives)

This exterior view of the "Tail Gunner's Compartment shows the massive bite of the B-29 if an assault from the rear was attempted. With twin .50 Cal. machine guns and a larger dose of 20 millimeter cannon, the effect of getting hit would equate to running into a brick wall. The radar directed 20 MM was lethal to enemy aircraft. (Boeing Archives)

"The Greenhouse" as it was refereed to by the Pilot, Co-pilot, & Bombardier, because of the heat generated by the sun's intensity when blistering through the Plexiglas. This B-29 is 42-93891, seen here on October 14, 1944. The sparse instrumentation is really bare bones in comparison to today's front line bombers, but the huge Plexiglas nose presented an almost perfect view for the Pilot & Co-pilot. (Boeing Archives)

It would appear by this photo that the Flight Engineer had more to do with instruments than the Pilot. The numerous throttles, instruments and gauges kept the F/E constantly occupied. (Boeing Archives)

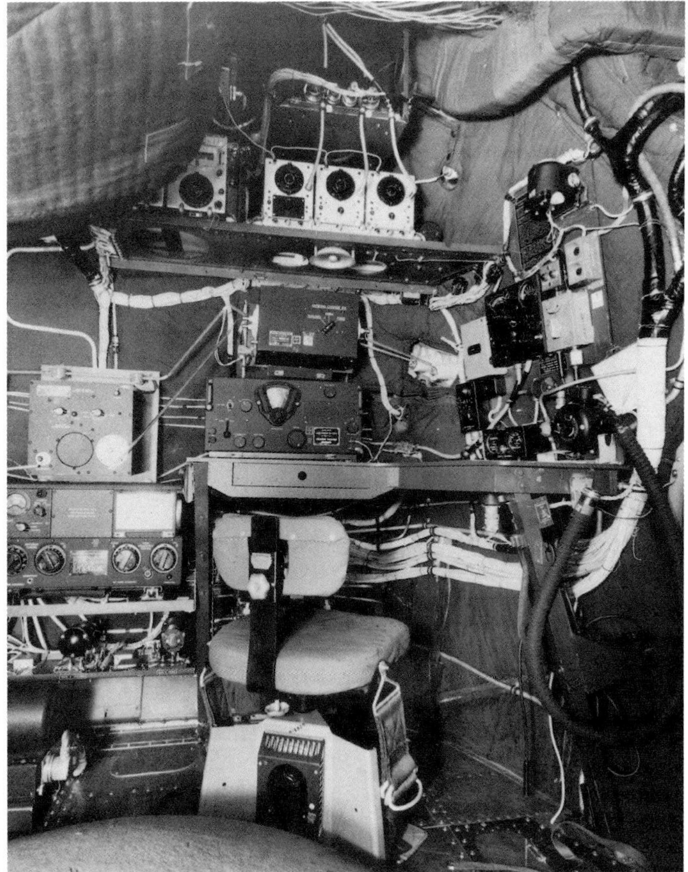

This is a view from behind the radio operator's position. Located on the right hand side of the fuselage and next to the F/E's station, the R/O would send and receive countless messages and signals. The Superfortress was built in such haste that the exposed wires were out in the open, and not behind a mat or panel of sorts. (Boeing Archives)

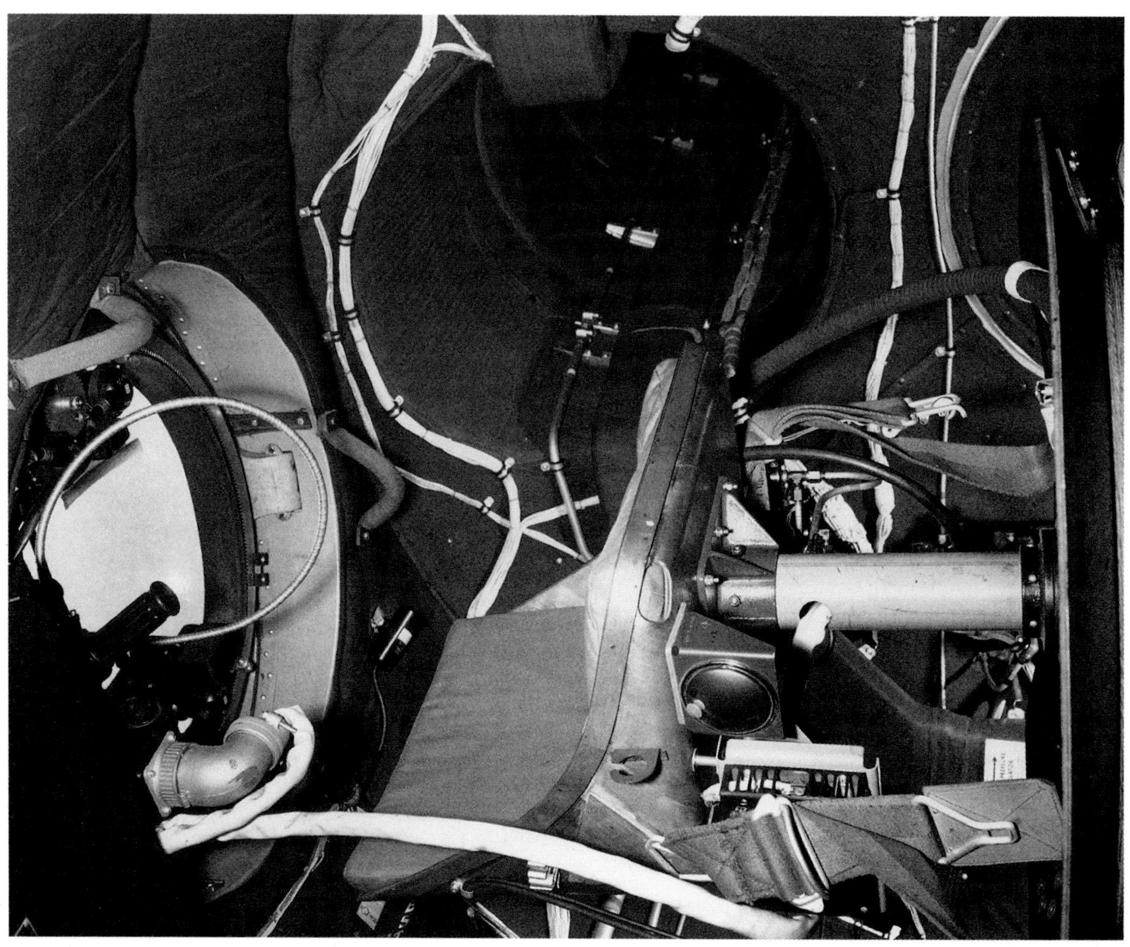

The Central Fire Control Gunner's position was located at one end of the tube. A little seat much like a bench seat is where the CFC Gunner would scan the horizon for enemy fighters. The "tube" traversed from one pressurized compartment to the next. (Boeing Archives)

SPIRIT OF LINCOLN-, 41-38954. Starting out as the very first YB-29, she was to become the one and only XB-39. Modified with four Allison inline engines, General Motors did the engine fitting. Feeling like this modification would be a viable one, tests were set and conducted in December of 1944. The overall performance was not great enough to facilitate any further conversions. (Boeing Archives)

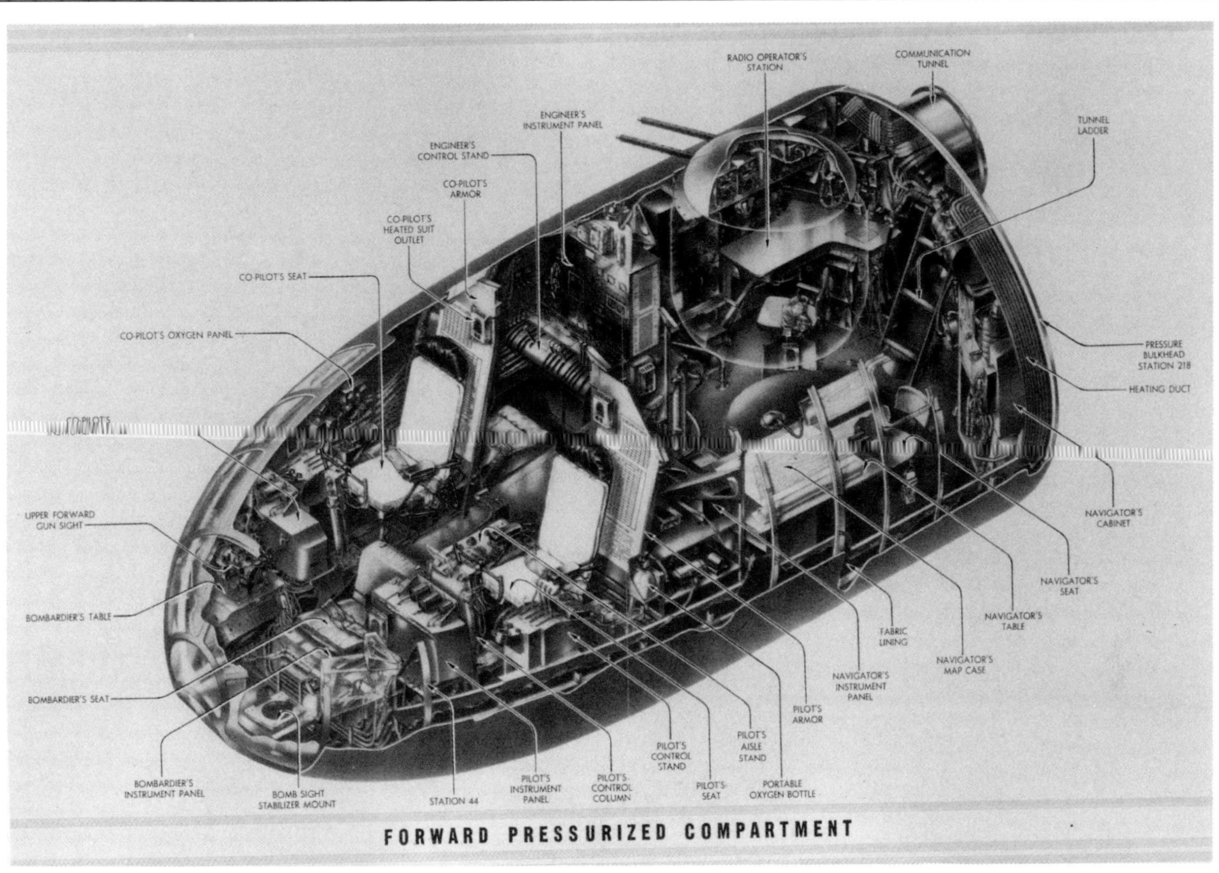

FORWARD PRESSURIZED COMPARTMENT

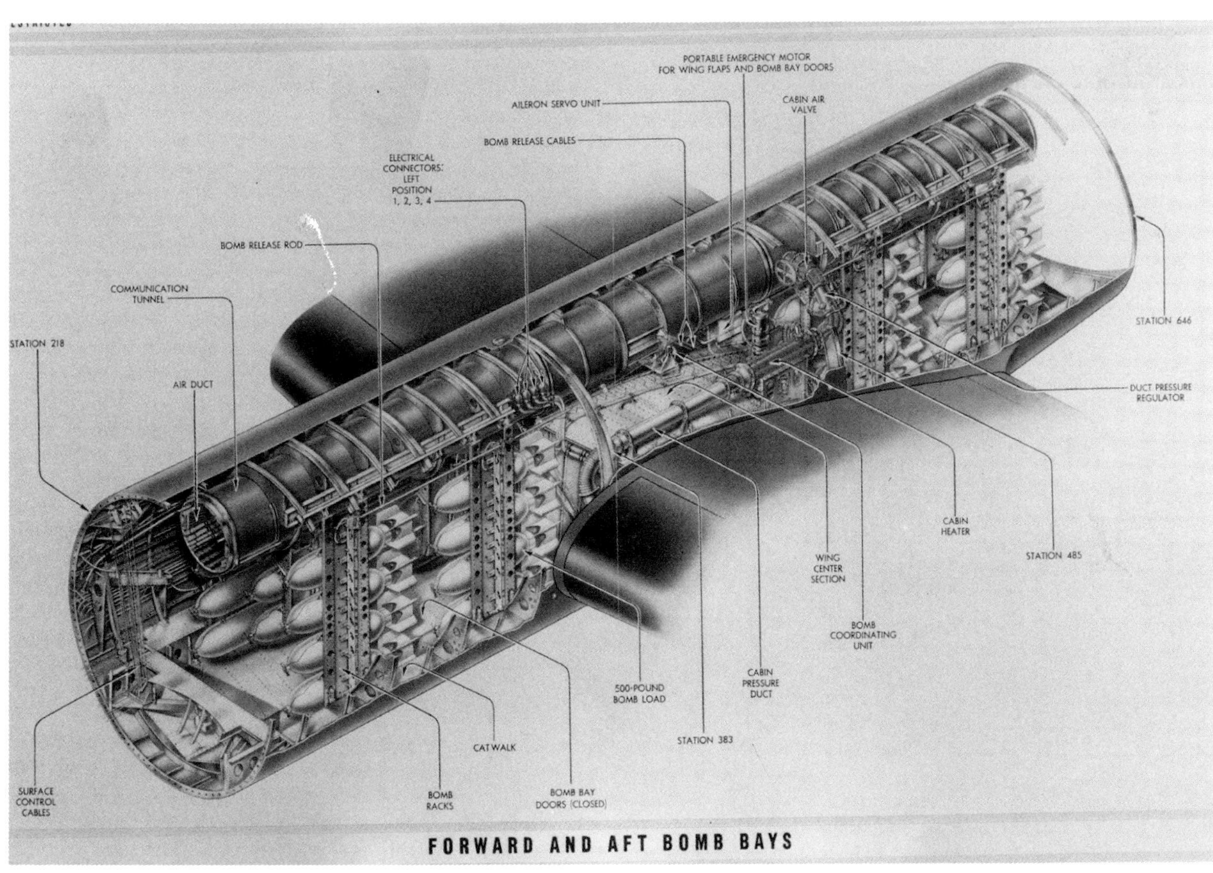

FORWARD AND AFT BOMB BAYS

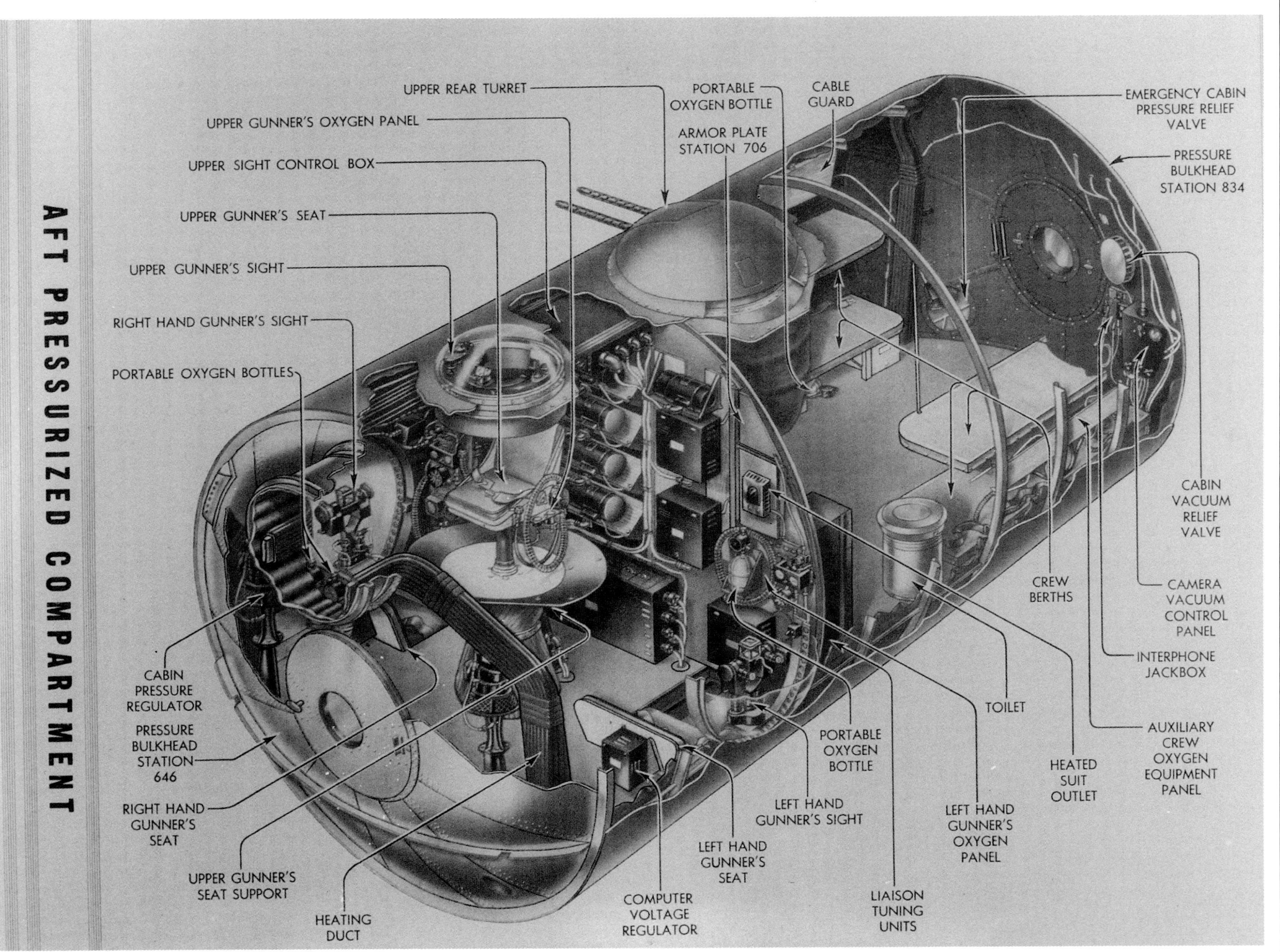

AFT PRESSURIZED COMPARTMENT

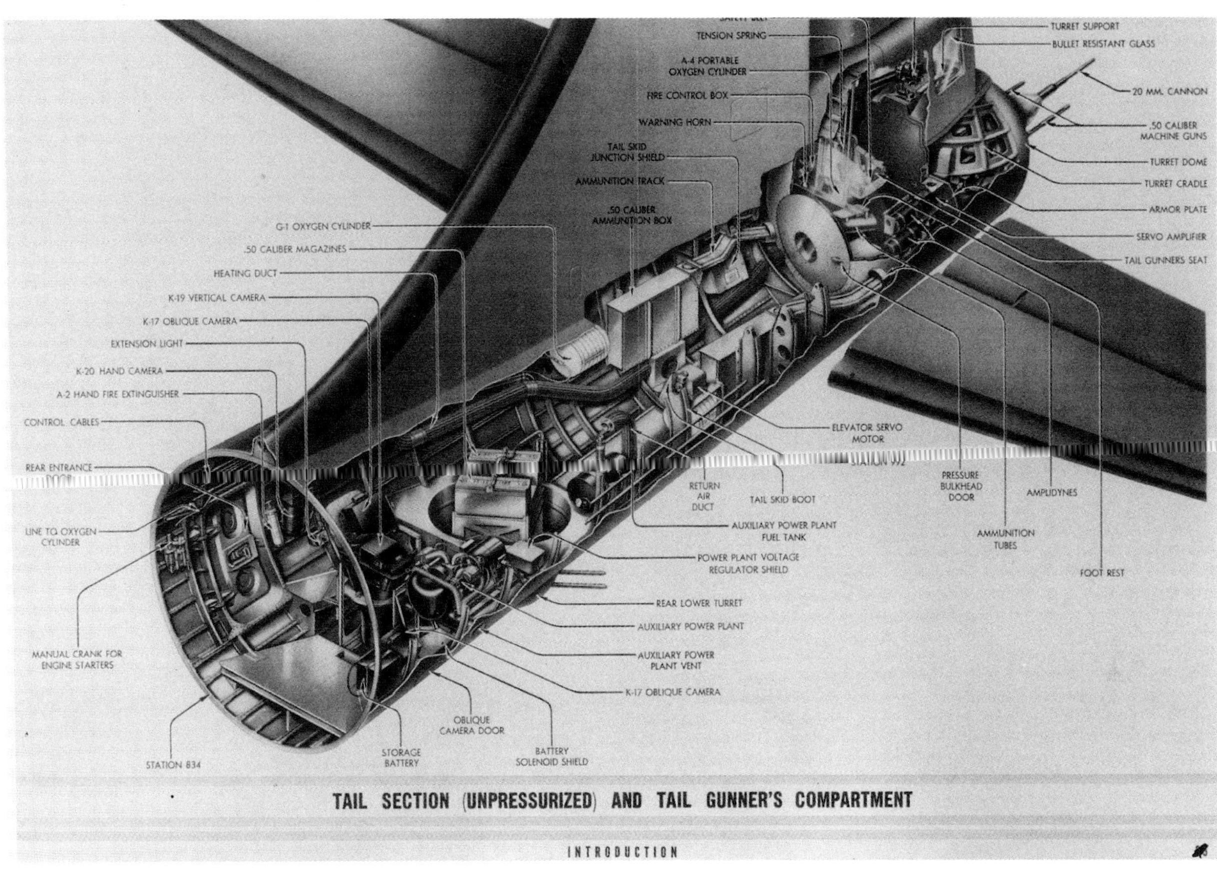

A typical Bomb Fuse with tag, screwed into the business end of the incendiaries and High Explosives. The little propeller spins and whines when the bomb drops, generating heat and static electricity so at impact the bomb is armed and detonates. (J. Heyer)

Bombardment Groups Assigned Tail Codes

BOMBARDMENT GROUP	LETTER
40th	C
444th	N
462nd	U
468th	S
497th	A
498th	T
499th	V
500th	Z
6th	R
9th	X
504th	E
505th	W
19th	M
29th	O
39th	P
330th	K
16th	B
331st	H
501st	Y
502nd	J

509th Composite Group
Had an arrow inside a circle pointing towards the front of the aircraft. As a security measure, "Enola Gay" had a circle with an R centered in the circle for the Hiroshima Mission.

Chapter 2:
THE "SUPERFORTRESS" ENTERS THE RING

The B-29 was tempermental and full of engineering bugs. But, the B-29s were new, and at that time in our aviation history the largest mass produced air craft ever built by the Allies. It was to become a back-breaking task to maintain the B-29s.

Grossing more than 60 tons when fully loaded, the Superfortress turned out to be a superb combat weapon. She could absorb a great deal of punishment and still be lethal to the enemy. Over, 3,000 men were shot down in B-29s over Japan, yet only a startling 1 percent was lost. Only 414 B-29s were shot down by fighters and anti-aircraft (Flak).It takes a lot to kill a 60 ton bomber. Enemy fighters had a very hard time attacking the Superfortress, but no aircraft can take a direct hit from Anti Aircraft Artillery. B-29 crews shot down 969 Japanese planes during World War II.

The two probably most famous B-29s were the "Enola Gay" and "Bock's Car". These two B-29s were to be the chosen B-29s to drop the first two Atomic Bombs. There were three aircraft companies that built the B-29 Superfortress. Bell Aircraft Co. of Marietta, Georgia, built 357 B-29s between February of 1944 and January of 1945. Boeing Aircraft Co. of Wichita, Kansas, built 1620 B-29s between September 1943 and October of 1945. Glen Martin Aircraft Co. of Omaha, Nebraska, built 536 B-29s between January 1944 and September 1945. The Boeing Aircraft Co. in Renton,Washington, exclusively built the B-29As. The major difference in the A Model B-29s was the way in which the wings were mounted to the airframe. 1,119 B-29As were built at Renton.

In building the B-29s, all the luxury for crews' compartments was dismissed. This was done in an effort to save weight. The B-29 could fly farther than any other aircraft in existence during the Second World War, as well as carry a heavier bomb load higher and farther.

The bombers in the Pacific had over 1,000 miles to fly to and from the targets in order to be able to hit Japan in its heartland. Better known for the role the B-29 played in the Atomic Bombings of Hiroshima and Nagasaki, the B-29s accomplished much, much more. The B-29, first and foremost, was not designed for the delivery of an Atomic Bomb. The B-29s had more technology than other 4-engined bombers. They had tri-cycle landing gear for better visibility when landing or taxiing, double wheels, and 4 retractable turrets. It was also the first "pressurized' aircraft of its type designed specifically for military applications. The B-29's upper turret was a remote controlled system directed by a central fire control gunner.

XB-29. The three XB-29s were identified by their 3-bladded propellers of 17 feet in diameter.There was no Armament present, and the earlier B-29s had a tail skid. 14 YB-29s were built in Wichita, featuring armament and the General Electric sighting system. The Early Production B-29s from Boeing, Wichita, were painted an olive drab over blue gray undersurface.(Boeing)

VITAL STATISTICS AND DIMENSIONS

Wing spa: 142 feet, 3 inches.

Wing area: 1736 square feet.

Lengt: 99 feet.

Height: 27 feet 9 inches. (vertical stabilizer)

Weight: Empty : 70,140 pounds.

Gross: 135,000 pounds, with a 12,000 pound bomb load.

Powerplant: 4- Wright R-3350-23 Cyclone, 18 cylinder radial engines.
8- General Electric, B-11 superchargers to give the Superfortress 2200 horsepower at take-off speed.

Propellers: 4- Hamilton Standard Hydromatics, 16 feet 3 inch diameter, constant speed governors and hydraulic pitch operation. Most all B-29s had this set-up, but some, however, were fitted with Curtiss Electric props which had reversible pitch as well as blade cooling cuffs.

Eng.Gear Ratio: 0.35, so at 2800 RPMs the props would turn at 980 RPMs.
Boeing later introduced the new R-3350-41, with baffles and oil crossover pipes for improved cooling on production blocks 50. Both Bell Aircraft and Martin Aircraft did this on Block 20. Boeing, Bell, and Martin started with the R-3350-57s by production's end.

Range: 3250 miles at 25,00 feet with fuel & 5,000 pound bomb load. Raised to 4100 miles with the advent of auxiliary fuel tanks in bomb bay.

Practical Operating Radius: 1600 miles rising to right at 1800 miles after engine modification and fuel improvements.

Maximum Ferry Distance: 5,600 miles, 6,000 miles after improvements.

Maximum Speed: 375 MPH at 25,000 feet. 450 MPH speeds have been reported while flying in the Jet Stream over Japan during 1944-1945.

Normal Cruising Speed: 200 to 250 miles per hour.

Fuel Load/Capacity: 8198 U.S. Gallons in the four wing tanks.
9548 U.S. Gallons after installment of extra tank in center section.
Boeing production Block-25 and Bell production Block-5.
Martin Aircraft had this onboard as standard equipment on all of their B-29s.
Under Operational Conditions, the Superfortress carried 6,988 U.S. Gallons of fuel, but only if semi-permanent fuel tanks had been removed from bomb bay area.

Climb Rate: Thirty-eight minutes to 25,000 feet with gross weight not exceeding 110,000 pounds.

Service Ceiling: 31,850 feet, altitude.

Bomb Capacity: 5,000 pounds of bombs over 1600 mile radius at high altitude.
12,000 pounds of bombs over a 1600 mile radius at medium altitude.
20,000 pounds of bombs maximum over short distances at low altitude.
High Explosives (H/E) and incendiary bombs were carried, either exclusively or mixed for effect depending on target & mission.

Armament: 10 .50 Cal. machine guns.
1- 20 MM cannon in tailsection.
Forward dorsal turret was increased to 4-.50 Cal. machine guns on Production Block-40 at the Boeing Aircraft Co. to increase forward protection against head-on ramming and assaults. Bell followed suit on their Block-10 B-29s.
All of the Martin built B-29s had 4-.50 Cal. machine guns in the dorsal turret.
The 20 MM cannon was deleted on Boeing Block 55, Bell's Production Block-25, and Martin's Block-25, B-29s.

Crew: The Superfortress had an eleven man crew.
The first 6 crew members were stationed in the forward pressurized cabin. The next 4 crewmen were stationed in the pressurized compartment, located mid fuselage, they were connected by a 34 inch diameter tube to the flight deck. The tail gunner was in his own separate pressurized compartment in the tail section. In certain specific B-29s there would be a crew of 13. The two extra crewmen would man the Electronic Countermeasure Equipped. (ECM). This equipment was two radio radar systems. These two crewman who operated the ECM equipment were called "RAVENS".

Radar Equipment: AN/APN-4 Loran (LOng RANge) constant beam navigational aid installed on earlier B-29s.
AN/APQ-9 systems were used during WWII. AN/APQ-13, a supersensitive radar navigational aid, mounted in a retractable radome, located between the two bomb bays, gave the Bombardier a clearer image of the ground, no matter what the overcast may be. This would greatly improve the results of high altitude bombardment of the Japanese Empire.
Almost all of the operational B-29s carried and dropped 'Chaff', sometimes referred to as 'Window', as in the European theater of operations. These thin foil strips cut exactly the same reflective wavelength as to give off the same return signal or 'blip' to enemy radars. This would have the effect of completely saturating, or whiteing out, their radar screens during the B-29s' inbound approach to the target area.

This YB-29 was assigned to the 444th B/G, 58th B/W, for crews training. It then went to the Boeing Aircraft Co./Seattle Washington's trade school. (Hill)

Since all of the B-29 crews took their training in the U.S. flying across the country, they often would pose for a crew photo, and were assigned a crew number, before their departure for their foreign duty assignments. In all, the crewmen seemed anxious to get into the action. (Beam)

When the different flights took to the air to cross the "pond" (Pacific Ocean), as it was called, it was a sight to behold. They flew in groups or gaggles of B-29s as opposed to alone, this being done to minimize the chance of losing an aircraft due to any faulty navigational equipment or errors in navigation. There were a few B-29s lost as it was to other mechanical problems. (Hetzel)

The factory workers in the United States, the designers, and the engineers took great pride in the B-29s that were built at their home factories. We see here a newly completed B-29 at the Bell Aircraft facility in Marietta, Georgia. The workers took a break from their assignments to pose for this image. They all seem very pleased with themselves as well, It should be (B.Snodgrass)

YB-29, Ser.No.41-36963, flew from Wichita to Miami. Took off under 'SECRET' orders and flew south over the the Atlantic ocean, where she then headed North to Gander, Neufoundland. Refueling there, she then took off and flew non-stop to Horsham, St.Faith, in England. Seen here just after her arrival at Horsham. (Campbell Archives)

Within about an hour of her arrival, she was spotted and photographed from the air by a Luftwaffe recon aircraft. She stayed in England for a very short time. Her mission there was to test out her new bomb radar over occupied France. This would set the stage for "PROJECT RUBY", a mission in the Summer of 1945, when a B-29 would eventually bomb the Submarine Pens at Farge, Germany, using an RAF 24,000 Big Tom Bomb. (Campbell Archives)

All of the 8th Air Force officers, as well as their enlisted subordinates, were anxious to get a closer look at the new bomber, fresh in from the U.S. It was the biggest they had ever seen. Horsham, St.Faith, was home of the 458TH Bomb Group, and they flew B-24J Liberators. (Campbell Archives)

When this YB-29 departed England she flew directly to the CBI, arriving at Kharagpur on April 6, 1944. She was the second B-29 aircraft to arrive. She carried the name "HOBO QUEEN", was assigned to the 462nd B/G, and was the only YB-29 to see combat. Hobo Queen, 41-36963, was used as a tanker to transport the much needed fuel over the "Hump" to keep the wheels moving against the Japanese Empire.(Campbell Archives)

B-29-35BW, Ser.No. 42-24537, assigned to D squadron 2 of the 500th Bomb Group. This was one of the earlier B-29s used for stateside training of aircrews. The Squadron was based in Kansas. (Hill)

An early production Model B-29 Serial no. 42-6885, B-29-5-BW. Many in-flight photos were taken for publicity, as well as for the purpose of keeping historical documentation. (Hill)

YB-29, Ser.no. 41-36958, the 3rd YB-29 built out of a total of only 13 aircraft built in this Model. (Boeing)

XB-29, Serial no. 41-18335, was the third and last of the XB-29 series built at the Boeing Seattle plant. The company produced 1,634 more B-29s at Wichita. Five factories built a total of 3,960 Superfortress bombers. (Campbell Archives)

In flight and high above the clouds, the third XB-29 goes through her flight test procedures. The Flying Guinea Pig, the 1st XB-29, Ser.no. 41-002 other XB-29 after the ill-fated crash of Senior Test Pilot: Eddie Allen in the 2nd XB-29, Serial No. 41-003. (Campbell Archives)

EDDIE ALLEN—named for Boeing Aircraft Company's Chief test Pilot: Eddie Allen, Ser. No. 42-24579, had severe battle damage and rendered unsafe. The wings were removed and the fuselage section as seen here, and were used for a ditching trainer for the crews. Assigned to the 40th Bomb Group, 45th Bomb Squadron. Surveyed on June 1945. (Stoffer)

ESSO EXPRESS—Serial No. 42-6242, had yellow rudder stripes, was assigned to the 468th B/G, 494th B/S. Was the 29th production line Superfortress to roll off the assembly line at Wichita, Kansas. On her arrival to the Group she was used as a tanker aircraft, given her name. Stripped of all her armament except the tail gunner's position, and armor plating and other equipment was also removed to make a lighter and cleaner aircraft. These converted B-29s were able to transport a considerable amount of fuel over the "Hump" to supply the awaiting fighter forces. (Ethell)

When the first of the B-29s started to arrive in the CBI, they were the center of attention. No one had seen an aircraft quite this big before, The camera man was making sure to record the event on film while members of Claire Chennault's "Flying Tigers", formerly the AVG, looked on. AVG stood for American Volunteer Group.(Campbell Archives)

With the large and stressful workload put on the B-29s, engine changes were very commonplace occurrences. A few B-29s flew their whole tour without an engine change, but that was more the exception rather than the rule. (Stoffer)

Before the B-29s could successfully operate off of the islands of Guam and Saipan, much work had to be done. The Naval Construction Battalions had to hard pack landing strips and lay in P.S.P. (Pierced Steel Planking) so the weight of the B-29s wouldn't tear up the airfields with their heavy loads. We see the Seabees hard at it laying in the decking for what was to become one of the Pacific's busiest airfields. (Campbell Archives)

Seabees seen here carrying interlocking strips of P.S.P. and forming what was to become the runway. The men labored with a passion to make the airfields ready for their new tenants. (Campbell Archives)

Bulldozers, graders, packers, and the engineers who designed, built, and readied the airfield were very busy indeed. They had a lot to do, and they did it fast and did it well. (Campbell Archives).

The Seabees had some other obstacles to overcome. In Guam in particular, there were still hostile Japanese die hards who took on the roll of sniper. After Iwo Jima and the flag raising they were more of a nuisance than a real threat merely because the Mud Marines kept a constant vigil so there were few men killed or wounded, War Correspondent Ernie Pyle died as a result of one of those lingering Japanese soldiers. The spoils of war seen here is an old Japanese tank remanent and reminder of the earlier battles fought on this tiny atoll. (Campbell Archives)

LASSIE COME HOME—42-24609, 498th B/G, 874th B/S, T square no.21. Aircraft Commander/Pilot: Wagner Dick. Was severely damaged on mission to Nagoya in such a way that she would never fly again. She was able to return to home field. (Ethell)

LITTLE JOE—42-24611, 498th B/G, 873rd B/S, A Square no.4. Shot down on April 29,1945, over Kyushu. (Ethell)

SUPINE SUE—42-24653, 500th B/G, 883rd B/S, Z Square no.42. First 500th B/G Superfortress to arrive on Saipan, October 31, 1944.

LIMBER RICHARD—44-70072, 9th B/G, 99th B/S, X circle no.55. Wichita built, flew 30 combat missions, 1 abort. Final: Mt.Home AFB, 12/23/53 to 07/18/54. Scrapped. The lower right side of image is B-29 JAKE'S JALOPY—44-69985, 9th B/G, 99th B/S, X circle no.53. Also Wichita built, she has 29 combat missions, 0 aborts. Final: McClellan AFB, scrapped 09/14/48. (J.Heyer)

BIG TIME OPERATOR—42-24791, 9th B/G, 1st B/S, X no.4. Aircraft Commander/Pilot:Capt.E.Shenefiel. Wichita built, flew 46 combat missions,2 aborts. Final: Robbins AFB, 04/28/46 to 10/31/50. Scrapped 12/06/50. Cockpit section with art is on display at Boeing's Seattle Museum. (Campbell)

DOTTIE'S DILEMMA—42-24796, 9th B/G, 5th B/S, X no.31 flew 34 combat missions, 5 aborts. Ran off runway on landing, was summarily scrapped. Started her career with the 9th B/G as no.16, Surveyed:07/06/45. (Campbell)

T.N.TEENY II-,44-69920, 9th B/G, 1st B/S, no.3. X circle.

"JACKPOT"—42-24797, 505th B/G, 484th B/S, K Aircraft Commander/Pilot: Lt.Warren. Lost on March 16, 1945, after a combined mission over Kobe and Nagoya. Out of 290 B-29s, the only loss was Jackpot. Getting named by her crew because it is said it is hard to `hit' the Jackpot. She had two engines shot out as they limped away from the target to an area about 250 miles off the coastline where she finally was forced to ditch.(Campbell Archives)

GOIN'JESSIE—42-24856, 9th B/G, 5th B/S, dropped the 2 millionth ton of bombs during World War II. Wichita built, flew 50 combat missions, 0 aborts. Final: (Unknown) (Campbell Archives)

THUMPER—42-63536, 504th B/G, E triangle. Artwork for the Walt Disney creation of Bambi. This is the second B-29 with this name in the Marianas. (via J.Heyer)

LUCKY LADY—42-34584, 9th B/G, 5th B/S, she had 10 trips over the 'Hump',13 combat bombing missions and 2 Japanese fighters to her credit. (via B.Davis)

FLYING STUD II—58th B/W, 444th B/G, 676th B/S diamond. This B-29 shot down 7 Japanese aircraft, flew 24 'Hump flights', and 16 bombing missions, 4 of which were into the Japanese Heartland 'Tokyo'. Also 1 photo recon mission and one looking glass flight denoted by the binoculars. (Campbell Archives)

VICTORY JEAN—331st B/G, 357th B/S, Triangle L no.51 seen here at rest on the island of Guam. (G.James)

THE STRAINED CRANE—16th B/G, Diamond B, this B-29 participated in many of the night incendiary missions over Japan. The rough weather and the elements have given considerable wear to this Superfortress. The natural metal finish of the B-29 is showing through the Gloss Black undersurface. The sand, wind, and salt air was a real challenge to the maintenance personnel who kept the B-29s in a state of airworthiness. (Campbell Archives)

In the Marianas, as in all the theaters of the war, many of the war weary aircraft made their final resting place the aircraft graveyard. Stripped of all useable parts and components, the carcass (as it is called) is hauled off to the dump site. A sad end for such proud machines. (Campbell Archives)

44-61647, assigned to the 19th B/G, shows a good view of the tail gunner's position and the tail. The gloss black undersurface is clearly defined and would indicate that this ship was used in the night bombing campaigns against Japan. (via J.Heyer)

This 19th B/G B-29 taxis out on another one of the missions against the Japanese Empire. (J.Heyer)

The landmark most used by Superfortress crews is of course Mt.Fuji, seen here in late July to early August because of the absence of snow. This sight was familiar to everyone who went on the bombing raids to Tokyo and the surrounding area. (B.Davis)

SAD TOMATO—42-65285, 9th B/G, 5th B/S, L no.22. Martin built, flew 40 combat missions, 6 aborts. Flew numerous 'Super-Dumbo' missions in the Search and rescue role. Final: Davis-Monthan,AFB, Arizona, 10/29/45. Scrapped: 05/10/54. (Campbell Archives)

This view revealing the clean lines of the backside of the Superfortress shows the turret in the top of the image as we look past the central fire control gunner's sighting blisters towards the control tower on North Field, Tinian, in 1945. (Campbell Archives)

A view out the port window at the two starboard engines and the flight line at North Field, Tinian. (B.Davis)

Going through last minute preparations and inspections, the crew is giving their B-29 the once over. The duce and a half truck is needed to transport flight crews and maintenance personnel out to the hardstands, which are a considerable distance away from the main quarters at North Field. (Campbell Archives)

This B-29 0f the 29th B/G, is retired for the day. The red engine inlet covers are in place and she is clearly at rest. Those black and white strips could be an indication that she is a Flight leader or pathfinder aircraft. These stripes are on the wings as well as mid-fuselage. (G.James)

SOME PUNKINS"6th B/G, 24th B/S,carries the group's painting of the bust of Pirate Jean Lafitte inside a triangle. L triangle 13. The cowlings are painted with red stripes as are the propeller hubs.(Campbell Archives)

T.N.TEENY II- 44-69920, 9th B/G, 1st B/S, X no.3. Shows the entire view of the Superfortress. assigned to the 313th B/W. As part of the 509th Composite Group she has red engine cowling stripes and the circle R on the tail. (Campbell Archives)

In mid 1945 the 9th B/G began painting the Group's insignia on the port right of the nose section. During WWII and Korea most crews had one form of artwork or another on the port side, though sometimes just a name or slogan. Putting the Group's insignia in this position, therefore, didn't interfere with the crew's renditions. (L.Davis)

44-68943, 73rd B/W, sits on her hardstand with her cargo encircled around her. All that is left to do is mount the fins on the bombs and load her up. In the background are other B-29s of the 73rd B/W on their hardstands, and farther back the flight line teems with more power to be brought to bear against the Empire of Japan. (Campbell Archives)

BOCKSCAR—44-27297, 509th Composite Group. On July 24,1945, she scored a direct hit on the Sumitoma Aluminum Plant, resulting in a ripple effect throughout the plant. The assigned Aircraft Commander/Pilot for which the B-29 is named is Capt.Fred Bock. On August 9,1945, this B-29, piloted, by Maj. Charles Sweeney, delivered the second of two Atomic Bombs to the Japanese city of Nagasaki. The device was named "Fat Man" and was much more powerful than the Hiroshima Bomb,"Little Boy". (via Barry Miller)

This SB-29 assigned to the 5th Rescue Squadron carries an A-3 Lifeboat. These boats were all metal and because of special built in air chambers, would return to an uprighted position if they happen to capsize. They are released over downed airmen until the PBY Catalina flying boats can make an effective water rescue. (B.Mikesh)

PBY, Catalina flying boat as seen here on Iwo, were the amphibious aircraft that would effect a water landing, pick up the downed crews from a potentially watery grave, and return them to safety at their home bases. (Stoffer)

SB-17G, The not so distant relative of the B-29, the rescue Fortress didn't have the range that the SB-29s had but were excellent for short hauls.They too were equipped to carry the A-3 rescue boats. (Campbell Archives)

ENOLA GAY—44-86292, sits in a state of disassembly at the Paul Garber, Silver Hill Facility in July of 1975. Lou Casey stands with guests of the Air Space Museum as they admire the aircraft that are taken to P.Garber for preservation and restoration. Enola gay is now restored and the subject of much controversy as to whether or not it was necessary for the U.S to use the Atom Bombs. (Campbell Archives)

A confident, yet pleasant Col. Paul Tibbets gives a wave goodbye as he prepares to embark on his historical mission. Not knowing what the end result will be, yet knowing the significance and importance of this mission. Enola Gay was the name of Col.Tibbets' mother, given to the B-29 the night of the mission, August 6th, 1945.

Col.Paul Tibbets standing next to Enola Gay on North Field, Tinian. This photo was taken on the afternoon before the mission and yet he seems to already know of the mission's success in advance. (OCAMA Tinker)

This is the housing of "Little Boy", the bomb dropped on Hiroshima. This of course is a facsimile, an empty and inert representation. It is on display at the Los Alamos Scientific Laboratory in New Mexico. Not far from Alamogordo, where the 1st Atom bomb was tested before taking the bomb to Tinian for delivery to the Japanese.(F.D.Campbell)

"FAT MAN"—the name given to the Plutonium bomb which was dropped on Nagasaki, Japan, on August 9, 1945, by the B-29 `BOCKSCAR' and Maj.Sweeney. This is also a display likeness to the actual bomb used, however, the two were exactly alike in size, weight, and appearance. Also on display at Los Alamos Scientific Laboratory, New Mexico. (F.D.Campbell)

FEE-NIX—this B-29 is at the U.S.Naval Weapons range at China Lake. The gloss black paint used to make the B-29 less visible to enemy searchlights has begun to fade and deteriorate. Nicknamed for the dream or belief that this B-29 might once rise and fly again. The China Lake facility is usually a last stop for older aircraft as they are used as ground targets for practice bombs and strafing maneuvers. This image was frozen in time in November of 1979. (via Barry Miller).

This side view of the entire B-29 Fee-Nix really shows the effect that the wear and weathering process has on derelict aircraft. This B-29 saw action in both WWII and Korea, judging by the markings which are nearly blurred into each other.This photo was also taken in November of 1979 at China Lake. (Barry Miller)

CITY OF PHILADELPHIA—assigned and or marked to the 330th B/G, 483rd B/S,sits today at the Pima Air Museum in Tucson, Arizona. (J.Heyer)

This B-29 is assigned to the 509 Composite Group, 58th Bomb Wing. This Superfortress was used as an electronic weather and monitor aircraft on Able Day during the Bikini Island Atomic Bomb tests. The crew is seen posing for the photographer in their May West flotation collars, all ready to go to make another entry for the record books. (Ethell)

B-29, Ser.no. 44-70016, seen at Tucson, Arizona. This Superfortress had formerly gone by the name Dopey, and had been assigned to the 1st Radar Calibration Squadron. (via Bill Davis)

This B-29 sits on static display at the entrance to OC/AMA, Tinker AFB, Oklahoma City, OK. She is the result of many man hours of effort and toil. The aircraft was recovered from the Aberdeen proving grounds in Maryland and is actually made of large sections of three B-29s. The weather and damage to the remains of the B-29s was so severe that the only surviving plexiglass was the cockpit and the tail gunner's position. She bears the insignia of the 57th Weather Recon. Squadron. (Campbell Archives)

THE CHAIN OF COMMAND FOR THE 20TH AIR FORCE IN WORLD WAR II

20TH AIR FORCE COMMANDERS

General Henry 'Hap' Arnold- April,1944 to July of 1945.
Major General Curtis E.LeMay- July,1945 to August 2, 1945.
LT.General Nathan F.Twining- after August 2,1945.

20TH BOMBER COMMAND, COMMANDERS

Brigadier General Kenneth B.Wolfe- Early 1944 till July 6,1944.
Brigadier General LaVerne G.Saunders- from July 6,1944.
Major General Curtis E.LeMay- from August 29,1944.
Brigadier General Roger M.Ramey- from January 20,1945.
Brigadier General Joseph Smith- between April 25,1945 and the 20th Bomber Command's deactivation on July 16, 1945.
The 20th Bomber Command was headquartered at Kharagpur, India, from March 28,1944 till June 17,1945. Transferring to Sakugawa, Okinawa, from July 7th till July 15,1945.
The 21st Bomber Command was activated March 1,1944. Based at Harmon Field,Guam from December 4,1944 till July 16,1945.

21ST BOMBER COMMAND, COMMANDERS

Brigadier General Haywood S. Hansell,Jr.- August 28,1944 until transfer of Command to
Major General Curtis E.LeMay- January 20,1945.

WING/GROUP COMMANDERS

58TH BOMBARDMENT WING COMMANDERS

Brigadier General LaVerne Saunders- March 5,1944 till November 15, 1945.
Col.Dwight O.Monteith- February 8,1945 till April 24, 1945.
Brigadier General Roger M.Ramey- April 24,1945 till wars end.
Call sign: LOYAL

58th Bomb Wings Group Commanders in squadron order.

40TH Bomb Group Commanders

Col.Leonard F.Harman till Aug.4,1944 Col.William H.Blanchard- till February 16,1945.
Col.Henry R.Sullivan- till February 27,1945.
Col.William K.Skaer- Final Commander.
Call sign:"ROBUST" later changed to "ACTOR".

444TH Bomb Group Commanders:

Col.Alva L.Harvey- till April 22, 1945.
Col.Henry R.Sullivan- till June 3,1945 Col. James C.Selser- Final Commander
Call Sign: "MASHNOTE' later changed to "OGRE".

462nd Bomb Group Commanders:

Col.Richard Charmichael- from August 26,1943 till his shoot down and capture on August 20,1944 Yawata mission.
Col.Alfred F.Kalberer- Final Commander
Call Sign: "WICKED".

468th BOMB GROUP

Col.Howard E.Engler- till August 3,1944.
Col.Ted S.Faulkner- till November 5,1944 when he was shot down over Singapore.
Col.James V.Edmundson- Final Commander.

73RD BOMBARDMENT WING COMMANDER:

Brig.General Emmett O'Donnell,Jr. till wars end.
Call Sign: "HUSKY"

497th Bomb Group Commanders:

Col.Stuart P.Wright- till February 26,1945.
Col. Arnold Johnson- Final Commander.
Call Sign: "HAPPY" then "SHYSTER".

498th Bomb Group Commanders:

Col.Wiley Ganey- till August 10,1945.
Col.Donald Saunders- Final Commander:
Call Sign: "MASCOT' then " WAXWING".

499th Bomb Group Commanders:

Col.Samuel R.Harris- till March 17,1945.
Col. Morris J.Lee- till August 13,1945.
Lt.Col.Walter E.Chambers- Final Commander.
Call Sign: "SANDY" then "NORDIC".

500th Bomb Group Commanders:

Col.Richard T.King- till shot down over Tokyo,December 3,1944. Col.John E.Dougherty- Final Commander.
Call Sign: "PLUTO" then "WISDOM"

313TH BOMBARDMENT WING COMMANDERS

Brig.General John H. Davies
Call Sign: "GOLDBUG".

6th Bomb Group Commander:

Col.Kenneth H.Gibson- Sole Commander.
Call Sign: "DAREDEVIL" later changed to "CUCKOO'.

9th Bomb Group Commanders:
Col.Donald W.Eisenhart- till March 6,1945.
Col.Henry C.Huglin- Final Commander.
Call Sign: "DOMINO' later changed to "CROSSTOWN".

504th Bomb Group Commanders:
Col.James T.Connally- till February 6,1945.
Col.Glen W.Martin- Final Commander.
Call Sign: "ALBATROSS" then "GULFBIRD".

505th Bomb Group Commanders:
Col.Robert A.Ping- till July 1,1945.
Col.Charles M.Eisenhart- Final Commander.
Call Sign: "SKEEZIK" then "SKYBLUE".

509th COMPOSITE GROUP COMMANDER
Col.Paul W.Tibbets,Jr. Sole Commander.
Call Sign: "DIMPLES".

314TH BOMBARDMENT WING COMMANDERS
Brig.General Thomas S.Power- till July 23,1945.
Col. Carl R.Storrie- Final Commander.

19th Bomb Group Commander;
Col. John A.Roberts,Jr. Sole Commander.
Call Sign: "KINGBIRD' then "CURIOUS".

29th Bomb Group Commanders:
Col.Carl R.Storrie- till July 23,1945.
Col.Robert L.Mason- Final Commander.
Call Sign: "DRACULA" then " TOBY".

39th Bomb Group Commanders:
Col.John G.Fowler- till March 16,1945 Col.George W.Mundy- till August16,1945.
Col.James E.Roberts- Final Commander.
Call Sign: "BLACKJACK" then "MISER".

330th Bomb Group Commanders:
Col.Elbert D.Reynolds- till August 12.1945.
Col.Douglas C.Polhamus- Final Commander.
Voice Code: "BALDEAGLE" changed to "MIZPAH".

315TH BOMBARDMENT GROUP COMMANDERS:
Brig.General Frank A.Armstrong,Jr.- Sole Commander.

16th Bomb Group Commanders:
Col.Samuel C.Gurney- till July 11,1944.
Lt. Andre' F.Castellotti- Final Commander.
Call Sign: "BLUEPLATE" changed to "ABIE".

331st Bomb Group Commander:
Col.James N.Peyton- Sole Commander.
Call Sign: "BAYWOOD" changed to "SLICKER'.

501st Bomb Group Commander:
Col.Boyd Hubbard- Sole Commander.
Call Sign: "PATHWAY" changed to "BAILIFF".

502nd Bomb Groupm Commander:
Col. Kenneth O. Sanborn- Sole Commander.
Call Sign: "STOPWATCH' changed to "TEMPER".

1ST PHOTO RECONNAISSANCE SQUADRON COMMANDERS:
Maj. Harry B/Allen- till May 1945.
Capt.George B.Alfke,Jr.- till July 9,1945.
Capt. Daniel H.Forbes- Final Commander

3RD PHOTO RECONNAISSANCE SQUADRON COMMANDERS:
Lt.Col.Patrick McCarthy- till June 21,1945.
Maj.Robert Hutton- Final Commander
Call Sign: " HELLHOG"

TAGALONG—44-61651, 40th B/G, 44th B/S, Triangle S, sits next to a B-24J Reclaimed: 10/03/53. (J.Heyer)

The Flight Engineer's station inside the B-29 was a vast array of instrumentation. Tho F/E, as the crews referred to him, had a great deal of responsibility in transferring fuel displacement and aircraft overall performance. (B.Davis)

HEAVENLY BODY—42-63510, 498th B/G, 874th B/S, T square, no.38. This B-29 was so badly shot up on the April 1, 1945, mission to bomb the Tokyo Aircraft Industrial Engine Plant, mission no.357, that on return from this sortie she was sent up to Guam and forever lost to the 498th Bomb Group. She had been originally assigned to the 313th B/W, 505th Bomb Group. On her mission of April 1, 1945, 121 B-29s participated in the mission, and 115 bombed the primary. 115 tons of bombs were dropped in one hour and forty two minutes. The formation bombed from between 6,000 and 7,960 feet altitude. One Japanese aircraft was shot down and one probable. 6 B-29s were lost. (via John 'Socs' Heyer)

LUCKY IRISH—42-63432, 498th B/G, 874th B/S, T square, no.28. Aircraft Commander/Pilot: Lt.William Kelly, This B-29 was forced to ditch on return from the December 3, 1944, mission to bomb the Aircraft Engine Plant at Tokyo. 86 B-29s participated in this mission (no.11). 60 B-29s bombed the primary target, and 141 tons of bombs were dropped in approximately one hour and twenty seven minutes. No enemy aircraft were shot down on this mission, and Lucky Irish was the only aircraft lost this day. The formation bombed from between 16,000, and 33,200 feet. The little green 'Shamrocks' were used as mission designators on this B-29.(via 'Mad'Mike Hill)

TANAKA TERMITE—42-24749, 498th B/G, 874th B/S, T square,no.29. flew 60 combat missions before being returned to the U.S. as war weary in August of 1945. Seen here pictured just before her 4th bombing mission. ('Mad' Mike Hill)

THE GREAT ARTISTE—44-27354, 509th Composite Group, Aircraft Commander/Pilot: Maj.Charles 'Chuck' Sweeney. This B-29, loaded with blast gauges and other special equipment, was assigned as the instrument ship on the 1st Atomic Bomb mission to Hiroshima. She recorded critical data on the effects of the actual bomb's detonation.

Chapter 3:
B-29
THE SUPERFORTRESS ENTERS THE WAR
THE 58TH BOMBARDMENT WING

On the 12th of October 1944, the 58th Bomb Wing had been disbanded in India and its Bomb Groups put under operational control of XX Bomber Com mand. Just three months later, the 58th Bomb Wing was to be reactivated at Hilje, India, on February 8, 1945, shortly thereafter regained Command of the original 4 Groups assigned to the 58th Bomb Wing. These Groups were the 40th B/G, the 444TH Bomb Group, and the 462nd and 468th Bomb Groups. The 40th Bomb Group's Squadrons—the 25th, 44th, 45th and 395th Bomb Squadrons—were sent to Chakulai, India, from April 11, 1944 to April of 1945. The 40th Bomb Group and her squadrons were relocated/transferred to West Field, Tinian, till November of 1945, when they returned to the United States at war's end. They were then assigned to March Field in California.

The "Hump"—the mountain range of the Himalayas. Missions would be airlifted to airfields containing fuel, supplies, personnel and other goods to forward airfields bringing the war closer to Japan's heartland.

The 40th Bomb Group was awarded 3 distinguished Unit Citations: Yawata, Japan, 20 August 1944; Japan, 5-14 May 1945; and Japan, 24 July 1945. During World War II the 40th Bomb Group conducted anti-submarine patrols and combat in the CBI, as well as in the Western Pacific.

THE STARS AND STRIPES

Super-Forts Bomb Japan

Yanks Peril Nazi Lines to Cherbourg

House Told Tokyo Hit; Believe Planes Struck From China

THE STARS AND STRIPES

War on Tojo's Doorsteps

Pilotless German Planes Now Are Bombing Britain

Yank Threat To Key Port Is Mounting

'Retaliation' Has Begun, Berlin Cries

THE STARS AND STRIPES

Robot Toll 2,752; London Worst Hit; Yanks Quit La Haye; Rundstedt Ousted

Reds Smash Near 3 Key Rail Towns

Yanked From Japs

Von Kluge Takes Over In France

Buzz-Bomb Facts Issued By Churchill

Saipan Victory Near—Nimitz

Japs Using Gas, Yank Confirms

Headline News, *Stars and Stripes*, printed in New York, London, Paris and circulated through the enitre world to military servicemen everywhere. Announcing the Superfortresses were starting their bombing campaigns against Japan.

The 444th Bomb Group and her squadrons were first assigned to Charra, India, on April 11, 1944, and then on July 1, 1944, moved up to Dudhkundi, India. They stayed at Dudhjundi till April of 1945 when they too were sent to West Field, Tinian. The squadrons assigned to the 444th Bomb Group were the 676th, 677th, 678th, and the 679th Bomb Squadrons. They saw combat in the CBI and Western Pacific.

The 468th Bomb Group was based at Kharagpur, India, from April 13, 1944, to May 4, 1945. On May 7, 1945, the 468th Bomb Group was sent to West Field, Tinian. Kharagpur, India, had been the Headquarters for the XX Bomber Command. Squadrons assigned to the 468th Bomb Group were the 792nd, 793rd, 794th, and 795th Bomb Squadrons. At war's end they were sent to Ft. Worth AAF (now Carswell AFB) on December 1, 1945.

The pre-existing runways in China had been used primarily for B-24 Liberators, and had to be lengthened from 6,000 feet to 7,200 plus feet and to 200 feet in width. The Chinese people—mostly farmers—provided most of the labor. Some 200,000 people were to assist in the effort.

The B-29 Operations were strictly under the Command of General Henry 'Hap' Arnold. General Curtis E. LeMay would arrive in the CBI on August 29, 1944, and assume Command. A superb leader, he would replace the 4 ship diamond bombing formation with the 12 ship defensive box formation.

After each mission or raid, an intelligence summary would be posted to Bomber Command. An average Intelligence summary would read as follows.

INTELLIGENCE SUMMARY

Mission Date:	24 November 1944
Target:	Aircraft and Industrial Plants, Tokyo Area.
Time Over Target:	12:30 Hours.
Enemy Opposition:	Moderate
AAA-Flak:	Meager to Moderate
Enemy Aircraft Destroyed in the Air:	7
Our A/C lost on the Mission:	2
Results of Bombing:	Totally Successful

In the CBI, the 58th Bombardment Wing had each Group & Squadron's B-29s paint coded for ease in identification.

40th Bomb Group-	4 horizontal stripes on tail wingtips.
444th Bomb Group-	3 vertical rudder stripes
462nd Bomb Group-	had a belly band painted just aft of the National Insignia on the fuselage.
468th Bomb Group-	2 diagonal stripes on the rudder.

The individual squadrons were identified by way of colors on these Stripes.

Red-	676th B/S
Blue-	793rd B/S
Yellow-	45th B/S
Green-	794TH B/S

AIRCRAFT OF THE 58TH BOMB WING

ABLE FOX, The, 42-24466, 40th B/G, 395th B/S. Abandoned over China, 12/19/44. 4 black stripes.

THE AGITATOR-, 444th B/G, 678th B/S Diamond

AGITATOR II-, 42-24899, 444th B.G, 678th B/S. Diamond. Reclaimed: 05/10/54.

AIRBORNE-, 42-65268, 444th B/G, flew 37 combat missions, Reclaimed: Pyote, TX, 09/11/50.

AMERICAN BEAUTY-, 42-24703, 468th B/G, 792nd B/S, 2-White Rudder Stripes.Surveyed:06/05/45.

ANDY'S DANDY-, 42-65208, 468th B/G, 794th B/S, 2-Yellow rudder stripes. Returned to the U.S. as war weary February 23, 1945. Reclaimed: Tinker AFB, OCAMA, 05/15/47.

ASSID TEST II-, 42-65336, 462nd B/G, 769th B/S, Solid Rudder.

BACHELOR QUARTERS-, 42-24507, 444th B/G, 678th B/S, Diamond. Flew 32 combat missions, 23 "Hump" flights, and had 3 confirmed aerial victories. Reclaimed: Chanute 04/25/49.

AMERICAN BEAUTY III-,44-87661, 468th B/G, 792nd B/S, Triangle I. During WWII her name was changed to 'Ugly', and then changed again to 'Koza Kid' after her assignment to the 98th B/G in the Korean War.

ANGEL IN DISGUISE-,

ANN'S RAIDERS-,

ARSON INC,-, 444th B/G,678th B/S, Diamond

ASSID TEST-, 462nd B/G, 769th B/S, Solid Rudder.

BAD PENNY-, 42-65274, Transferred to RAF on 05/27/50.

B-SWEET-, 42-63425, 40th B/G, 395th B/S, 4-Black stripes, Abandoned over the "Hump" on 08/19/44 on return from Yawata.

B-SWEET II-, 42-63498, 40th B/G, 25th B/S, 4 Red Stripes Class 26 Kirtland 12/31/45.

B-SWEET III-, 42-24522, 40th B/G, 25th B/S,4 Red Stripes. On Tokyo mission dropped bombs and on return back to Tinian ran out of fuel. The crew opted to bail out rather than risk a night ditching. The Pilot who bailed out watched his B-29 go into a long descending turn to the right, calculating that the B-29's path would arrive at his projected position at the same time. The Superfortress ended up passing just under Aircraft Commander/Pilot: Otto Kerstner circling again for another try. At about 3/4 of the way into the turn the plane crashed into the sea at a 10 degree angle. The crew was spotted by a PBY who radi oed their position to a rescue boat. 05/24/45.

BELLE RINGER-, 42-63464, 468th B/G, 794th B/S, 2-Yellow Rudder Stripes. Aircraft was assigned as part of the advanced echelon to the 313th Bomb Wing on Tinian. The Shooting Star was on all of the 468th's B-29s. She flew 23 combat missions and 5 "Hump" flights. Seen here on War Bonds Drive at Amarillo Army Airfield in 1945. Reclaimed:09/ 11/50.

BATTLIN'BEAUTY-, 42-63457, 462nd B/G, 762nd B/S, Solid Rudder 'T. Final: Unknown.

BATTLIN'BEAUTY-, 42-24457, 40th B/G, 25th B/S, 4-Red Stripes, MIA over Bangkok,12/14/44.

THE BEACHCOMBER-,

BELLA BORTION-, 42-63355, 468th B/G, 793rd B/S, 2-Blue Rudder Stripes,(Bell) Aircraft Commander/Pilot: Maj. Douglas Hatfield. Had close call when a 'Zeke' tried to ram her and hit the propeller on the no. 1 engine while on a mission to bomb Mudken, Manchuria, December 7, 1944. No.3355.

BENGAL LANCER-, 42-6348, 40th B/G, 44th B/S, 4-Blue Rudder Stripes. Reclaimed: Pyote AB, TX, 12/21/49.

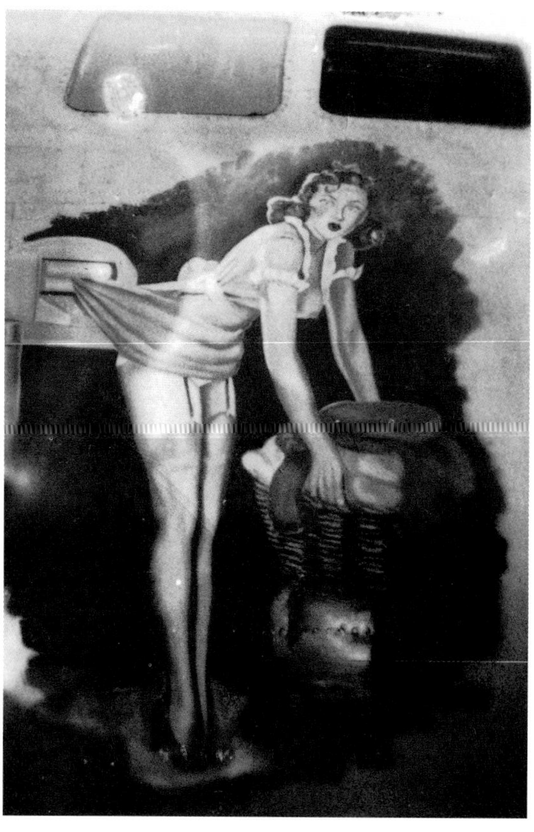

BELLE RINGER-, viewed from right side.

BETTER'N'NUTIN-, 42-24538, 444th B/G, 676th B/S. Diamond. Class 01Z Lowry AFB, 07/31/46.

BIG POISON-, 42-6353, 444th B/G, 677th B/S, Diamond 30. Aircraft Commander/Pilot: Col. Winton 'Wimpy' Close. Arrived in India, April 13, 1944. Flew both the June missions and several dozen "Hump" flights. Reclaimed: Pyote AB, TX, 12/31/49.

BIG POISON 2ND DOSE-, 42-65270-, 444th B/G, 678th B/S, Diamond, lost over Osaka 06/01/45.

BENGAL LANCER-, 42-24487, 468th B/G, 793rd B/ S, 2-Blue Rudder Stripes, Aircraft Commander/ Pilot: Maj. James Pattillo. A/C was sent from the CBI to the 9th Bomb Group ahead of the main force enroute to the Marianas. The name 'Bengal Lancer' commemorates the China Burma India actions and the coming of Maj. General Curtis E. LeMay to the Marianas from Command of the XXth Bomber Command to assume Command of the XXIst Bomber Command. This aircraft made the flight in February 1945. Aircraft No.487, a B-29-30-BW, with increased fuel capacity. Reclaimed: Pyote Field, TX, 05/02/49. (Kent Roberts)

CELESTIAL QUEEN-, 44-87660, 40th B/G, 44th B/S. No. 49.

CHAT'NOOGA CHOO CHOO-, 42-24471, 468th B/G, 892nd B/S, 2-White Rudder stripes. Flew 3 photo missions in November of 1944, including 1 over Singapore. The mission markings denote bombing missions, "Hump" flights, and photo recon missions. Reclaimed: Keesler AFB, 08/24/49.

COCK SURE-, 462nd b/G.

CONVINCER-, 44-61521, 468th B/G, 793rd B/S, Triangle I, Reclaimed: 05/10/54.

DARK EYES-, 42-63555, 40th B/G, 45th B/S, 4-Yellow Stripes. Reclaimed: 09/11/50.

THE CHALLENGER-, 42-6284, 468th B/G, 794th B/S, 2-Yellow rudder stripes, Final: Unknown. Had 23 "Hump" flights, and 13 combat missions.

CHICAGO SAL-, 44-61562, 468th B/G, 792nd B/S, 2-White Rudder Stripes, B-29A.

CRAIG COMET-, 42-63445, 468th B/G, 794th B/S, 2-Yellow Rudder Stripes, Aircraft Commander/Pilot: Estey crashed on runway at Tinian after mission #1 to Tokyo. Repaired and went missing in action on 05/24/45.

DEACON'S DISCIPLES I-, 42-24492, 40th B/G, 25th B/S, abandoned past Iwo from Japan 05/14/45.

DELIVER THE GOODS-,

DEUCES WILD-, 42-6222, 40th B/G, 45th B/S,4-Yellow Stripes, Surveyed:09/11/44. crashed at B-4 due to lack of fuel.

DING HOW-, 42-6313, 40th B/G, 45th B/S,4-Yellow stripes, Reclaimed: Pyote Air Base TX, 12/31/49.

DEACON'S DISCIPLES-,42-24492, 444th B/G,

DEVILISH SNOOKS-, 42-63527, 40th B/G, 44th B/S,4-Red Stripes. Reclaimed: Tinker OCAMA 09/11/50.

DRAGGIN'LADY-, 42-63505, 40th B/G, 25th B/S, 2-Blue Rudder Stripes, Class 26 Sheppard, 05/17/54.

DING HAO-, 42-6358, 468th B/G, 794th B/S, 2-Yellow Rudder Stripes, assumed lost over target November 21,1944, mission No.17. The B-29 had 11 combat missions, 9 transport missions. Aircraft Commander/Pilot: Hennin. Mickish was in command of B-29 when lost. The mission was Omura, as it was to be discovered the Superfortress had been interred at the Vladivostok Naval Air Base in Siberia.

DRAGON BEHIND-, 44-86247, 444th B/G, 676th B/S, Diamond.

DRAGON LADY -, 42-65277, 444th B/G, 676th B/S, The femme fatale is from the cartoon strip of Milton Caniff, 'Terry & the Pirates'.

DREAM BOAT-, 44- , 444th B/G, Diamond.

DUCHESS-, 444th B/G, Diamond.

DUMBO-, 444th B/G, Diamond

EARTHQUAKE MCGOON-, 444th B/G, Diamond.

EDDIE ALLEN II-, 44-70151, 40th B/G, 45th B/S, Triangle S No.47.Salvaged:12/23/51.

EIGHT BALL CHARLIE-, 42-65328, 40th B/G, 45th B/S, 4-Yellow Stripes, Reclaimed: Davis Monthan on 07/14/54.

EILEEN-, 42-6323, 444th B/G, 678th B/S, Diamond. Off inventory 06/26/44.

DRAGON LADY-, 44-69663, 468th B/G, 793rd B/S. 2-Blue rudder stripes.

DREAM GIRL-, 42-63480, 462nd B/G, Solid rudder. B-29-21-BA, (Bell)

EASY'S ACES-,

EDDIE ALLEN-, 42-6242, 40th B/G, 45th B/S, 4-Yellow Stripes. This B-29 was paid for by the employees of Boeing Aircraft Co. in Wichita with bond purchases during the 5th war loan. The 'EDDIE ALLEN' ended up on Tinian, having bombed targets in 7 countries. On the 25th of May 1944 mission to Tokyo this B-29 was so badly damaged that it went to salvage. His service was far from over. Removing the wings, the Eddie Allen was used for a ditching trainer. Named in honor of 'Test Pilot Eddie Allen", a thin, balding 43 year old who had been the first individual to span the distance between designer, engineer, and Test Pilot. Allen was considered to be the highest authority on stability and control of Heavy aircraft. Allen was killed in the crash of the second prototype during a flight test on December 28, 1942. The B-29 is credited with 10 missions over the "Hump" and at least 23 combat missions.

ESSO EXPRESS-, 42-6242, 468th B/G, 494th B/S, 2 Yellow Rudder Stripes, she was the 29th production Superfortress to roll off of Wichita's line. On arrival at her group assignment she was given her new name. Used as a Tanker, she was stripped of all of her armament except for tail gunner's position, all armor plating, and other equipment was also removed to make a lighter, cleaner aircraft. These converted B-29s were able to transport a considerable amount of precious fuel over the "Hump" to supply the awaiting bomber force.

FADED-, 40th B/G.

FAITHFUL FAYE-, 444th B/G Diamond.

FEATHER MERCHANT-, 42-6308, 40th B/G, 45th B/S, 4-Yellow Rudder Stripes. Abandoned over Laohokow on return from Yawata mission, 08/20/44.

FAST COMPANY-, 42-63495, 468th B/G, 792nd B/S, 2-White Rudder Stripes, Final: Unknown (B. Davis)

FLAK MAGNET-, 44-61634, 40th B/G, 44th B/S, Triangle S No.25. Transferred to RAF 05/10/50.

THE FLEDGELING-, 462nd B/G, Solid Rudder.

FLYIN'HOME-, 42-24909, 468th B/G, 793rd B/S, 2-Blue Rudder Stripes, Reclaimed: 09/22/53.

FLYING JACKASS-, 42-24580, 444th B/G, 678th B/S, Diamond.

FLYING STUD-, 42-6320, 444th B/G, Diamond. Crashed returning from Yawata, 08/21/44. B-29 had caught fire, crew bailed out 75 miles from home.

FIRE BELLE-, 44-61653, 444th B/G, 677th B/S, Triangle N No.22. Reclaimed: 05/10/54. (J. Heyer)

FLAK MAID-, 44-70129, 444th B/G, Triangle N. 15 combat missions. B-29A.(Campbell)

FLYING STUD II-, 444th B/G, Diamond, 7 Japanese flags,25 hump flights,16 bomb missions,1 photo mission and 1 observation flight. (J. Heyer)

FUBAR-, 444th B/G, 676th B/S early Wichita production model B-29.

FU-KEMAL-, 444th B/G, 676th B/S, Diamond.

The GEAR BOX-, 42-24704, 468th B/G, 793rd B/S. On January 2, 1945, B-29 struck target at the Rama VI Bridge at Bangkok, Thailand, for the 2nd time. The target was only slightly damaged, proving that bridge busting from 18,000 feet is somewhat difficult.

GENIE-, 42-63455, 40th B/G, 25th B/S.4-Red Stripes, flew 18 combat missions, 2 transport missions.

GENIE II-, 44-61812, 40th B/G, 25th B/S, Triangle S, No.9,Reclaimed:09.22/53.

GEORGIA PEACH-, 42-63356, 468th B/G,793rd B/S,2-Blue Stripes, was 10th Bell, B-29 built. Aircraft Commander/Pilot: Maj. John Miller. This Cobb County, Georgia, boy saved the honor of Georgia when he named his B-29. The "Peach" participated in the Yawata mission.

FU-KEMAL-TU-, 42-6352, 444th B/G, 676th B/S, Diamond 21, Reclaimed: Pyote AB, TX. 3/21/49.

GALLOPIN'GOOSE-, 42-6390, 468th B/G, 794th B/S,2-Yellow Rudder Stripes. Rammed at Mudken by Japanese 'Nick' fighter 12/07/44. Rammed the tail section and sheared most of it off. Only one parachute was spotted as she plummeted straight down.

GENERAL "HAP" ARNOLD SPECIAL-, 42-6365, 468th B/G, 794th B/S,2-Yellow Rudder Stripes. Interred Vladivostock Naval Air Base, Siberia. Aircraft Commander/Pilot: Weston H. Price. This B-29 was forced down by fighter of the USSR, giving the Russians 2 complete B-29s.The Soviets were able to duplicate the B-29, their version being called the TU-4. Code Named `Bull'. From 1945 to 1960 the Russians produced a fair amount of copies which served in the "Dalnaya Aviatsiya" (Soviet Stratecic Air Command). The Russians also sent a number of TU-4s to their Allies, the Communist Chinese. It was later discovered that the General H "Hap" Arnold Special had been `escorted' into Vladivostok Naval Air Station. The crew was interred until their release by way of Iran on February 2, 1945. Until just recently no word ever came of just what happened to this B-29. Last seen on November 16, 1944, on Mission 16 to bomb Omura. (Campbell Archives)

GLOBE GIRDLE MYRTLE-, 462nd B/G, Solid Rudder. (G. James)

GERTRUDE C-, 42-6334, 468th B/G, 794th B/S, 2-Yellow rudder stripes. On August 20, 1944, she was rammed by a "Nick" fighter piloted by Sgt. Shigeo Nobe of the 4th Sentai (squadron), Kamakazi. Making a straight in attack, the "Nick" hit the port wing just outside the No.1 engine. Gertrude C disintegrated. Parts of G.C. hit another B-29, "Calamity Sue". Yawata mission.

GLOBAL GLAMOUR-, 44-70139, 40th B/G, 44th B/S, Triangle S, 17.

GONE WITH THE WIND-, 42-6331, 40th B/G, 25th B/S, 4-Red Stripes, accidentally shot down by RAF Beaufighter on December 20, 1944.

GRAND SLAM-, 40th B/G, 45th B/S. seen here on Isley field after setting down a little too hard and suffering landing gear collapse. (W.Watts)

HEAVENLY BODY-, 42-6281, 40th B/G, L. was hit by fighters near Nagasaki on October 16, 1944.The target had been Okayama. The B-29 was shot up pretty bad with two crewmen wounded. Pilot tried to reach a friendly field in China but couldn't make it. All crew members bailed out and survived except one. (J. Heyer)

HAP'S CHARACTERS-, 42-63424, 468th B/G, 792nd B/S, 2-White rudder stripes. Aircraft Commander/Pilot: Capt. Good. The Vice-Commander of the Squadron, Col. Edmundson, had referred to Good's crew as a bunch of "Characters" hence forth the name, "Hap's Characters". All crew members survived the missions except one, Daryl Owens, who had flown with Capt. Watson and was lost in a crash on take-off from West Field, Tinian. This B-29 had between 35 and 38 combat missions. When this crew was in Kharagpur, they found 3 baby Himilayan Sloth bear cubs. One died and another was given to a local family. The last cub was kept as a mascot and was named "Gertie". Her eyes were not yet opened and she weighed only about 1 1/2 pounds. One of Gertie's favorite pastimes was to get into someone's room and turn it into a disaster. Coca Cola was her favorite beverage, until someone introduced her to beer. She quickly developed a taste for beer, and the more she drank the more entertaining she became. At war's end on the return flight to the U.S. she had a little too much beer and got loose from her restraints. She completely demolished the inside rear area where the "Eagle" Radar equipment was mounted, ripping up everything in sight to try to find more beer. She was given to the San Francisco Zoo on her arrival in the states where she lived until about 1965.

GOOD HUMPIN'-, 42-6268, 468th B/G, 794th B/S, Diamond. Flew 78 "Hump" flights from India to China.

GRAND OLD MAN, 468th B/G, 333-. This B-29 was flown into theater of operations by Brigadier General Saunders. Also the first B-29 to reach the forward bases in China. 43 round trip "Hump" flights when the B-29 first arrived. In her first month, flew three consecutive "Hump" flights in four days, thus completing one half of the squadron's total gas delivery requirement.

GRAVEL GERTIE-, 42-63500, 468th B/G, 792nd B/S, 2-White Rudder Stripes, B-29 crashed on take- off enroute to bomb Takamatsu on 07/03/45.

GREEN JOB-, 40th B/G, 45th B/S, This B-29 was stripped down and converted into a fuel tanker.

GUNGA DIN-, 42-24504, 468th B/G, 792nd B/S, 2-White Rudder Stripes. this B-29 crashed on take-off enroute to bomb Omura on 10/25/44. Entire crew was killed.

THE GUSHER-, 42-6356, 468th B/G, 792nd B/S,2-White rudder stripes. This B-29 was converted into a tanker to haul fuel to the 468s awaiting bomber force. B-29 tankers would consume 3 gallons of aviation fuel for every gallon delivered.

HELLBIRDS-, 462nd B/G, 768th B/S. L2. This B-29 overshot runway on Iwo like so many others had. Yhis was one of the last crack-ups on Iwo prior to war's end. (M. Hill)

HELLBIRDS WITH MALICE TOWARDS SOME-, 462nd B/G, 770th B/S. This logo was used on aircraft of the 462nd Group.

HELLON WINGS-, 444th B/G, Diamond. 26 missions,5 "Hump" trips. (Campbell)

HI-STEPPER-, 44-65275, 468th B/G, 794th B/S, 2 Yellow rudder stripes, Reclaimed: McClellan AFB, 07/15/54.

HIGH AND MIGHTY-, 44- 444th B/G, 677th B/S, name taken from the Hollywood production of the same name, starring John Wayne.

HAP'S HOPE-, 42-6240, 40th B/G, 395th B/S,4- Black stripes. Went missing in action on 07/30/44 over the "Hump". Target was Anshan, Taku.

HARRY MILLER-, 42-24740, 40th B/G, 45th B/S,4-Yellow stripes. Salvaged on 06/07/45.

HAULINAS-, 444th B/G, Diamond.

HELL N GONE-, 462nd B/G. L.

HELL'S BELLS-,

HER MAJESTY-, 444th B/G, Diamond. No. K-269.

HERE'S HOPEN-, 444th B/G, Diamond.

HERO HEATER-, 44-61702, 468th B/G, 793rd B/S, Triangle I, Reclaimed: 09/28/54.

HIMALAYA HUSSY-, 42-6319, 40th B/G, 44th B/S, 4-Blue stripes. Reclaimed: Pyote AB, TX, 12/21/49.

HOBO QUEEN-, 41-36963, 462nd B/G. This YB-29 tanker, flown by Capt. Miles Thomas, established a record of over 4,000 gallons of gasoline delivered to China. 6 bomb bay tanks, and 60 5-gallon cans stored in the tail, her crew of 7, and a ton of cargo weighed about 137,000 pounds. The only YB-29 in the CBI, she had gone to England earlier in the war and had flown as a stager in preparation for the upcoming mission to bomb German submarine pens with an RAF Big Tom bomb. (Campbell Archives)

HOLLY HAWK-, 58th B/W.

HO HUM Lets Do It Again-, 44-70123, 462nd B/G, 768th B/S. 17 combat missions.

HOMBICRISMUS-, 58th B/W. decked with holly and depicting 58 hump flights.

HOODLUM-HOUSE II-, 42-24475, 462nd B/G, 796th B/S, Solid Red rudder. Survived the Omura mission of October 25, 1944.Reclaimed: Kelly AFB, 05/02/45.

HOLLYWOOD COMMANDO-, 444th B/G, Diamond.

HONEYWELL HOMER-, 42-24738, 40th B/G, 44th B/S, 4-yellow stripes. No.37. Reclaimed: Davis Monthan, 05/10/54.

THE HOUND OF HEAVEN-, 462nd B/G.

HULL'S ANGEL-, 42-63362, 462nd B/G. named for her pilot. Aircraft Commander/ Pilot: Capt. Carl Hull, 7 combat missions, 9 "Hump" flights. Solid rudder. Reclaimed:

HUMP HAPPY JR.-, 42-6310, 40th B/G, 25th B/S,4-Red stripes, Reclaimed: Pyote:12/21/49.

HUMP HAPPY MAMMY-, 42-6241, 40th B/G, 44th B/S,4-Blue stripes. Reclaimed: Pyote AB, 12/21/49.

HUMP HAPPY PAPPY-, 42-6254, 40th B/G, 45th B/S,4-Yel low stripes. Reclaimed: Pyote AB, TX, 12/21/49.

HOREZONTAL DREAM-, 444th B/G, 678th B/S, Diamond. 5 Hump missions, 3 ships sunk, 27 bombing missions, and 2 enemy aircraft downed. (Walrond)

"humpin honey"-. 42-24648, 462nd B/G, 769th B/S. This earlier view shows "Honey" still in the CBI, prior to rotating to North Field Tinian. Her No. K-28 served as the B-29's call/battle number. (M. Hill)

HUMP"N HONEY-, 42-24648, 462nd B/G. B-29-41-BW. (T. Charmichael)

HUN-DA-DEE-, 44-61546, 444th B/G,678th B/S, Triangle N No.28 flew more than 20 missions at war's end. (Hill)

IRON GEORGE-, 44-27640, 444th B/G, 678th B/S, Triangle N, flew 11 combat missions. (M. Hill)

JANIE-, 44-86438, 58th B/W went to Korean war

JOKERS WILD II-, 42-24897, 444th B/G, 677th B/S, Diamond. Reclaimed: 05/10/54. (Campbell)

INCHCLIFFE CASTLE-, 444th B/G, 678th B/S, Triangle N.

JACK'S HACK-, 44-61566, 468th B/G, 794th B/S, Triangle I, Reclaimed:

JO-, 42-65337, 444th B/G, 677th B/S, Diamond.no.29. On May 24, 1945, a casualty of the Tokyo mission, JO was sideswiped by another B-29 over the target. She made it back to Iwo with no brakes and miraculously no injuries to the crew. Part of the tail section of the other B-29 was lodged in her engine. Jo crashed and was cannibalized for parts. Originally named and christened "ELANOR" after the 1st Lady, an inscribed certificate from the 570 sheet metal workers at Martin Aircraft Co., Omaha, were to inscribe, "She is our special pride, for we built her and shaped her many parts. We watched her progress, we thrilled when she took to the air. She's yours now fellows! When her good crew packs the punch to those Sons of the setting sun, we will get an even bigger thrill". Good Luck...and May God Bless You."

JOHNNY REBEL-, 44-61674, 468th B/G, 794th B/S, Triangle I. Reclaimed: 03/28/54. 3-149

JOLLY ROGER-, 42-63415, 468th B/G, 793rd B/S, 2- Blue rudder stripes. Reclaimed: 06/27/46. (M. Hill)

JOY-OUS VENTURE-, 44-61821, 444th B/G, Triangle N. Reclaimed: 07/14/54. (Hill)

KAGU TSUCHI-, 40th B/G. 4-rudder stripes, "Scourge of the Fire God". (W. Watts)

JOURNEY FOR MARGARET-, 444th B/G, Diamond.

THE JUKE BOX-, 42-63353, 469th B/G, 792nd B/S, 2-White rudder stripes. Reclaimed: 12/12/49.

KATIE-, 42-6298, 40th B/G, 25th B/S,4-Red stripes. On return from mission blew a tire on landing and ground looped on 03/19/45.

KICKAPOO LOU-, 42-24678, 468th B/G, 792nd B/S. Failed to return from mission no. 41, Singapore, shot down by Flak. on March 2, 1945. 2-White rudder stripes. Aircraft Commander/Pilot: Ed Miller. 10 combat missions.

KICKAPOO II-, 42-6232, 468th B/G, 792nd B/S, 2- Yellow rudder stripes. Converted to tanker on June 30, 1944. Transferred to 792nd on Oct.20,1944. Returned to U.S. as war weary on November 25, 1944. Aircraft Commander/Pilot: Maj. Nye.

KRITZER BLITZER-, 42-63542, 40th B/G, 44th B/S, 4-Blue stripes. Reclaimed: Tinker OCAMA, 09/11/50.

LADY-, 444th B/G.

KING SIZE-, 42-6347, 462nd B/G,769th B/S, Solid yellow rudder. "Life" magazine photographer Bernard Hoffman flew aboard this B-29 on the June 15, 1944, mission to Yawata. This particular mission was not a hot fight. 16 Japanese fighters had been spotted, but only 3 fired on the formation, and nothing was hit. The Flak was heavy but not very accurate, only did slight damage to six B-29s.The next morning all were back on the ground in time for potatoes and eggs for breakfast. King Size was one of the 47 B-29s that completed the first "Superfortress" mission to bomb Japan on June 15, 1944. (Hill)

LADY BE GOOD-, 42-65227, 468th B/G, 792nd B/S, 2- White rudder stripes. Aircraft Commander/Pilot: Lt. Ed Shafer flew this B-29 into India on November 20, 1944. 12 combat missions, 5 "Hump flights". (Campbell Archives)

LADY BE GOOD-, 42-65227, 468th B/G, 792nd B/S, 2- White rudder stripes. This view shows a close-up of her scoreboard. 30 bomb missions, 5 "Hump trips" and one enemy aircraft shot down. (Campbell Archives)

LADY BE GOOD-, 42-65227, 468th B/G, 792nd B/S, 2- White rudder stripes. Shows entire port-side view of the Lady with bomb bays open and ready to load. Based at Khargpur, India, Chengtu, China, and North Field, Tinian. Reclaimed. (Campbell Archives)

LADY CHOUTEAU-, 44-87674, 468th B/G, 793rd B/S, Triangle I.

LADY FRANCES-, 44-61640, 444th B/G. Diamond. (Campbell Archives)

LADY HAMILTON-, 42-6274, 468th B/G, 794th B/S,2- Yellow rudder stripes. Shot down over Anshan 07/29/44.

LASSIE TOO-, 42-63460, 468th B/G, 793rd B/S,2- Blue rudder stripes. Final: Unknown. Both Aircraft Commanders Meints and Capt. Bores flew this aircraft. (Campbell Archives)

LADY IN WAITING-, 44-84068, 444th B/G, 677th B/S. Triangle N. Also went by the name "Shaft Absorber" earlier in this B-29's career. Under each crewman's position. (Campbell Archives)

LADY JANE-, 468th B/G.

LADY LUCK-, 444th B/G. 678th B/S.

LARGE CHARGE-, 444th B/G, 676th B/S, Triangle N.

LASSIE-, 42-63356, 468th B/G, 793rd B/S,2- Blue rudder stripes. Aircraft Commander/Pilot: Capt.. Meints, returned to U.S. as war weary in 1944. Reclaimed: 12/21/49.

LAST RESORT-, 42-63394, 40th B/G,44th B/S,4-Blue stripes. Salvaged: 01/14/45. Aircraft Commander/Pilot: Major Donald Roberts. After being raked by Japanese Fighters, this B-29 escaped and made an extra short emergency landing on a little air field at Laohokao, China. They patched her up with parts from another B-29 that had crashed nearby. Repaired in under a day, the Chinese fueled her up and she returned to her base. She was also riddled by shrapnel on January 14, 1945, when a bomb loading accident destroyed another B-29, Serial no. 42-24582.

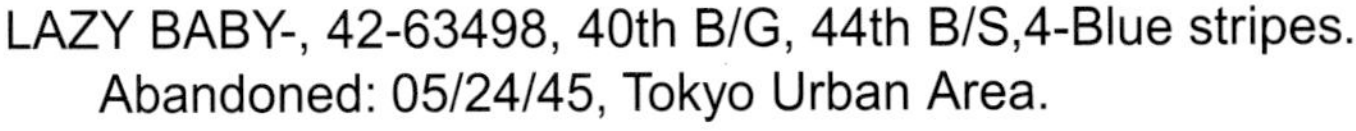

LAZY BABY-, 42-63498, 40th B/G, 44th B/S,4-Blue stripes. Abandoned: 05/24/45, Tokyo Urban Area.

THE LEMON-, 42-63462, 40th B/G, 44th B/S, 4-Blue stripes. Surveyed:05/03/45

LETHAL LADY-, 42-6370, 468th B/G, 793rd B/S, 2- Blue rudder stripes. Aircraft Commander/Pilot: Ted Faulkner. Crashed into Bay of Bengal on October 16, 1944. No trace was ever found. B-29 was on mission to Singapore.

LI'L HERBERT-, 58th B/W.

LADY MARGE-, 444th B/G, 676th B/S. Diamond.

LASSY TOO!
Times A Wastin!-, 42-93894, 462nd B/G, 768th B/S. Solid rudder. L. (Campbell Archives)

LIMBER DUGAN-, 42-6320, 468th B/G, 792nd B/S,2- White rudder stripes. Shot down over Yawata, June 15,1944.

LIMBER DUGAN II-, 42-65315, 468th B/G, 792nd B/S,2- White rudder stripes. Reclaimed: Davis Monthan, 05/10/54.

LITTLE CLAMBERT-, 42-24582, 40-the B/G, 44th B/S, 4-Blue stripes. Destroyed in bomb explosion and resulting fire at B-4, 01/14/45.

LITTLE GEM-, 42-24596, Reclaimed:09/09/53.

LITTLE MIKE-, 42-63422, 444th B/G, 677th B/S, Diamond. Excess: 11/30/45.

LAZY JANE-, 468th B/G, 2-Rudder stripes.

LI'L YUTZ-, 42-24892, 468th B/G, 794th B/S,2- Yellow rudder stripes. Reclaimed: 11/17/53.

LIBERTY BELLE-, 462nd B/G. Solid rudder.10 bomb missions. (Campbell Archives)

LITTLE ORGAN ANNIE-, 42-24893, 468th B/G, 794th B/S, 2 Yellow rudder stripes. B-29A. Reclaimed: 11/12/53.

LONG JOHN SILVER-, 42-63502, 462nd B/G, 769th B/S, solid Yellow rudder. Reclaimed: Lowery AFB, 07/31/46.

LUCKY LADY-, 42-65272, 468th B/G, 793rd B/S, 2- Blue rudder stripes. Reclaimed: Davis-Monthan,08/16/54. (Campbell)

LUCKY LADY-, 42-65272, 468th B/G, 793rd B/S, 2- Blue rudder stripes. right side artwork. (Campbell Archives)

LUCKY 13-, 444th B/G, 676th B/S. Seen here at Davis Monthan AFB, Arizona. This overview shows how the B-29s sent to DMARC were sealed up in a cocoon. This B-29 is being taken out of her preservative shell. (Campbell Archives)

LUCKY 13-, 444th B/G, 676th B/S. This close-up view of the "mothballed" Superfortress show how thick the preservative seal of spraylate is. The squadron insignia and bomb missions have been uncovered. The aircraft data card is seen, uncovered on the very tip of Lucky 13's nose section. (Campbell Archives)

MALE CALL-, 42-63537, 444th B/G, 676th B/S, Diamond 13, Aircraft Commander/ Pilot: Capt. James Williams. B-29 hit by "Flak" over Singapore, 5 crewmembers were injured. Later shot down over Tokyo Urban Area 05/25/45. (Campbell)

MALE CALL-, 42-63537, 444th B/G, 676th B/S. Same aircraft with a little different artwork. Art was changed on her arrival at North field, Tinian, just prior to her getting shot down. (Campbell)

MAIDEN USA-, 444th B/G. Diamond.

LUCKY SEVEN-, 42-6407, 468th B/G, 794th B/S. 2-Yellow rudder stripes. Reclaimed: Pyote AB, TX, 12/21/49.

MAD DOG-, 444th B/G, Diamond.

MALFUNCTION JUNCTION-, 42-6241, 40th B/G, 44th B/S, 4-Blue stripes. Reclaimed: Pyote AB, TX, 12/21/49.

MAN-O-WAR-, 462nd B/G. Solid rudder

MARIANNA BELLE-, 44-70015, 40th B/G, 44th B/S, Triangle S. Salvaged: 06/02/52.

MARIETTA BELLE-, 42-63396, 40th B/G, 25th B/S, 4-Red stripes. Crashed on 06/19/45, on mission to bomb Toyohashi Urban Area.

MARIETTA MISFIT-, 42-63363, 40th B/G, 395th B/S, 4- Black stripes. abandoned: 12/07/44.

MARY ANN-, 42-24494, 468th B/G, 792nd B/S, 2- White rudder stripes. Crashed on return from Formosa on 01/14/45.

MAMMY YOKUM-, 42-63536, 468th B/G, 792nd B/S, 2- White rudder stripes. MIA over Tokyo on 05/25/45. From cartoon strip Li'l Abner.(Kent Roberts)

THE MARY K-, 42-24525, 468th B/G, 793rd B/S, 2- Blue rudder stripes. Reclaimed: Keesler AFB, 02/02/50. Seen here at Open House in 1945 at Amarillo Army Air Field. 9 "Hump Flights", 33 combat bombing missions. (Bob Snodgrass)

MIS-CHIEF-MAKER-, 42-24896, 462nd B/G, 769th B/S. Solid yellow rudder. Reclaimed: 09/22/53. Her little quote says "I've had it before, and want some more, come and get it, Who's next." (J. Heyer USMC)

MARY'S LIL'LAMBS-, 42-63332, 444th B/G, 678th B/S.

MILLION DOLLAR BABY II-, 42-63532, 468th B/G, 793rd B/S, 2- Blue rudder stripes. This B-29 was part of the advanced echelon sent to the 313th Bomb Wing on Tinian. Each Group of the 58th B/W sent their 4 most experienced crews. Final: Unknown. (J. Heyer)

MISS LACE-, 44-87658. 468th B/G, 792nd B/S, Triangle I. Transferred to 462nd B/G. (B. Davis)

MILLION DOLLAR BABY- 42-6397, 468th B/G, 793rd B/S,2-Blue rudder stripes. Reclaimed: Davis-Monthan, 06/27/49.

MISS DONNA LEE-, 42-24915, 40th B/G, 45th B/S, 4-Yellow stripes. Reclaimed: 09/11/50.

MISS JUDY-, 44-61555, 462nd B/G, 770th B/S,No.53. Triangle U. B-29 is one of Col. Alfred Kalberer's Hellbirds.

MISS MINETTE-, 42-6272, 468th B/G, 794th B/S, 2-Yellow rudder stripes. Reclaimed: 12/21/49.

MISS PEGGY-, 44-69977, 468th B/G, 793rd B/S, Triangle I.

MISS SANDY-, 44-87659, 468th B/G, 793rd B/S.

MISS PACIFIC-, 468th B/G, 793rd B/S.2-Blue rudder stripes. Notice the patch work lettering. (Campbell)

MISS SHORTY-, 42-65272, 468th B/G, 793rd B/S.2- Blue rudder stripes. Reclaimed: Davis-Monthan, 08/16/54. (K. Roberts)

MISS LEAD-, 42-24734, 468th B/G, 793rd B/S,2- Yellow rudder stripes. Crashed on Tinian on 08/06/45,on return from mission to Saga urban area.

MISS N.C. 42-63376, 444th B/G, Diamond. Reclaimed:06/30/46. Recalled to action to serve with S.A.C. during Korean War. (Watts)

MISS YOU-, 44-70100, 40th B/G, 44th B/S,No.44. Triangle S. (Campbell)

THE MISSOURI BELLE-, 42-63557, 444th B/G, 678th B/S. 1 "Hump" flight, 27 combat missions. Also shows the straight line application of the black anti-glare undersurface. (Harold Goldsworthy)

MISSOURI QUEEN-, 42-6359, 462nd B/G.
Aircraft Commander/Pilot: Capt. Stanley Brown. On the return trip home from the August 10, 1944, mission to Nagasaki, B-29 became lost after suffering mechanical problems. Almost dry on fuel, she set down at Hwaning. The next morning, while in repairs, Japanese fighters strafed her, damaging the engines. Mechanics were flown in and patched her up, and 12 days later she was flown to Chiung Lai with a crew of four. She was later Surveyed: 12/21/44.

MONSOON-, 42-6294, 40th B/G, 25th B/S, 4-Red stripes. Reclaimed: Pyote AB, TX, 12/21/49.

MONSOON II-, 42-24846, 40th B/G, 25th B/S,4-Red stripes. Reclaimed: 09/11/50.

MONSOON MINNIE-, 42-6295, 40th B/G, 45th B/S, 4-Yellow stripes. Reclaimed: 12/21/49.

MOONSHINE MINNY-, 40th B/G, 45th B/S, 4-stripes.

MY BUDDY-, 42-65279, 468th B/G, 794th B/S,2- Yellow rudder stripes. Reclaimed: Davis- Monthan AFB, 07/14/54.

MY GAL SAL-, 44-69660, 468th B/G, 749th B/S, 2- Yellow rudder stripes.

MYSTERIOUS MYSTRESS-, 42-6312, 462nd B/G, 771st B/S, Solid Blue rudder. Reclaimed: Pyote AB, TX, 05/02/49.

NIPPON NIPPER-, 42-6289, 40th B/G, 44th B/S,4-Blue stripes. Burned on the ground 07/08/44.

MONSOON GOON-, 42-93828, 468th B/G,794th B/S, 2- Yellow rudder stripes. flew 18 combat missions, 4 into the Japanese heartland, and 24 "Hump" flights. Reclaimed: Pyote AB, TX, 11/20/48.

MUSN'TOUCH IT-, 44-61548, 40th B/G, 44th B/S, Triangle S No.24. (Campbell)

NAUGHTY NANCY-, 42-63496, 444th B/G, 677th B/S, lost missing in action on 06/01/45, over Osaka. Diamond 50. (M. Hill)

NIPPON NIPPER II-, 42-24503, 40th B/G, 44th B/S, 4-Blue stripes, Reclaimed: Amarillo AAF, 06/30/46.

NIPPON NIPPER II-, 42-63503, 40th B/G, 44th B/S, 4-Blue stripes. Final: Unknown

NIPPON NIPPER III-, 42-24729, 40th B/G, 44th B/S, 4-Blue stripes, Reclaimed: Davis-Monthan, 05/10/54.

OLD AQUANTANCE-, 58th B/W.

THE OLD CAMPAIGNER-, 42-6272, 468th B/G, 794th B/G,2-Yellow rudder stripes. Reclaimed: 12/21/49.

OLD CHARRA 444th B/G, 678th B/S, Triangle N.

OLD CRACKER KEG-, 42-6276, 40th B/G, 395th B/S, 4-Black stripes. abandoned over the "Hump" on 12/19/44 mission no.22 to bomb Omura.

OLD MAN MOSE-, 462nd B/G. Solid rudder.

NIGHT MARE-, 42-6311, 468th B/G, 792nd B/S, 2-White rudder stripes, Reclaimed: Davis- Monthan, 06/27/49. 13 missions. (M. Hill)

OLD-BITCH-U-AIRY BESS-, 42-6273, 462nd B/G. 769th B/S, Solid Yellow rudder. Aircraft Commander/Pilot K.D. Thompson "Bess" was painted by tailgunner "Big Red" Arents. Whether it was Bess herself or the enemy, she would certainly have her own contributions to the Obituary Column. Thompson made a dead stick landing and ran out of fuel while taxing to hardstand. B-29 was returning from the Palmburg mission 11 August 1944. Reclaimed: Pyote AB, TX, 12/21/49. (B. Davis)

OUR GAL-, 42-24484, 468th B/G, 2-rudder stripes, Reclaimed: Davis-Monthan,06/27/49.

OURS-, 42-6285, 462nd B/G, 769th B/S, Solid yellow rudder. Reclaimed: Pyote AB,Tx. 12/21/49.

PATIENCE REWARD-, 44-70131, 444th B/G, 679th B/S, Diamond. 21 combat missions, with one into the heartland Tokyo. (Campbell Archives, OKC)

O'REILLY'S DAUGHTER-, 42-6264, 468th B/G, 792nd B/S, 2- White rudder stripes. Aircraft Commander/Pilot: Col. James Edmundson. On return from the Yawata mission had only 1600 gallons of fuel remaining on June 15, 1944. Later, on August 21, 1944, mission to Yawata, Aircraft Commander/Pilot: Col. William Savoie went down. Messages arriving nearly a week later reported that the B-29 had been found on the Northeastern coast of China. Col. Savoie and 3 crewmen made it back to India in late November. They had bailed out over occupied China. The other crewmembers had bailed out over the Yellow Sea & were never heard from again. She had 7 combat missions and 5 transport missions.

O'REILLYS DAUGHTER I-, 44-61703, 468th B/G, 792nd B/S, Triangle I. Reclaimed:09/08/54.

OLE GAS EATER-, 42-24798, 40th B/G, 45th B/S, 4- Yellow stripes. Reclaimed: 12/31/45.

OUIJA BIRD-, 40th B/G, 4-stripes.

OUR GAL-, 44-61932, 462nd B/G, 769th B/S. 3-350

THE OUTLAW-, 42-24685, 40th B/G, 44th B/S, 4-Blue stripes. Crash landed on Tinian on 08/07/45 on return from Fukayama Urban Area bombing mission.

THE OUTLAW-, 44-69668, 40th B/G, 45th B/S, 4- Yellow stripes.

PACIFIC PRINCESS-, 44-61813, 444th B/G, Triangle N. Reclaimed: Johnson AB, Japan, 12/19/50.

PAMPERED LADY-, 42-6306, 40th B/G, 395th B/S, 4- Black stripes. Reclaimed: Pyote AB, TX, 12/21/49.

PAPA TOM'S CABIN-, 44-87668, 468th B/G, 792nd B/S, Triangle I.

PARTY GIRL-, 42-6389, 468th B/G, 792nd B/S.2- White rudder stripes. On return from the December 7, 1944, mission to bomb the Manchuria Aircraft Manufacturing Co. at Mudken. Party Girl crashed into side of mountain killing the entire crew. 7 total aircraft were lost on this mission.

PATCHES-, 44-70085, 40th B/G, 45th B/S, Triangle S No.41.

PIONEER- 42-6208, 468th B/G, 793rd B/S, 2-Blue rudder stripes, Reclaimed: Pyote AB, TX, 12/21/49.

PIONEER II-, 42-24737, 468th B/G, 793rd B/S,-2Blue rudder stripes, Reclaimed: Pyote AB, TX, 09/23/53.

PEPPER-, 42-6217, 468th B/G, 792nd B/S,2-White rudder stripes. Reclaimed Pyote AB, TX, 12/21/49. Returned to the U.S. as war weary, December 25, 1944. 10 combat missions, 6 transport missions, and one photo recon mission. Aircraft Commander/Pilot: Major Christy. (Kent Roberts)

POWER PLAY-, 42-24442- 468th B/G, 793rd B/S,2-Blue rudder stripes. Bombed the Sasebo Naval Base and Yawata Steel works, as well as Nagasaki and Omura, all on the island of Kyushu. (Watts)

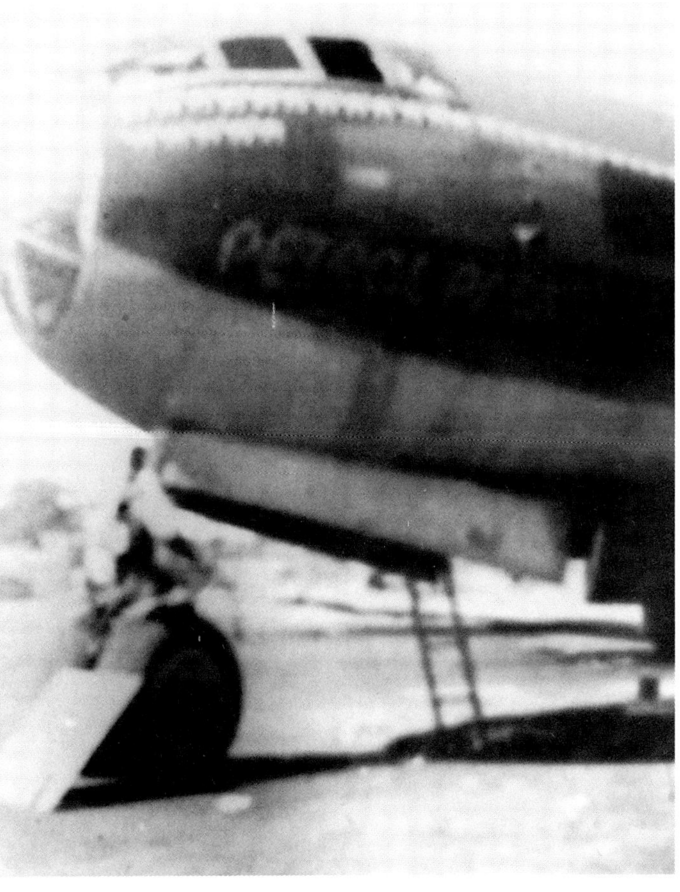

PETROL PACKIN'MAMA-, 42-6219, 462nd B/G, Solid rudder and OD paint scheme. was a tanker conversion to help fulfill the constantly growing need for aviation fuel. Class OIZ Roswell NM. 05/31/46. (J. "Socks" Heyer USMC)

PHONEY EXPRESS-, 42-24801, 462nd B/G, 769th B/S, Solid rudder. North Field Tinian, 1945. (Campbell Archives)

POSTVILLE EXPRESS-, 42-6279, 468th B/G, 794th B/S, 2- White rudder stripes. was hit in the right wing by the remains of a "Nick" fighter that had just rammed the B-29 ahead of her in formation. The Express was able to return to base and get repaired. Aircraft Commander/Pilot: Maj. Humphery. Returned to U.S. as war weary December 30, 1944. 13 combat missions, 3 transport missions. Was the last Superfortress to bomb Japan, 06/15/45. Reclaimed: Pyote AB, TX, 12/21/49.

PIONEER III-, 42-63534, 468th B/G 793rd B/S,2-Blue rudder stripes. Reclaimed Pyote AB, TX, 09/11/50.

CITY OF PITTSBURG-, 42-24895, 468th B/G, 792nd B/S.2 White rudder stripes. Kharagpur, India. Aircraft Commander/Pilot: Lt.Jackson. Reclaimed: 09/11/50.

PRETTY BABY-, 42-63396, 40th B/G, 25th B/S, 4-Red rudder stripes. Crashed on 06/19/45, on return from the Toyohashi raid.

PRINCESS EILEEN III-, 444th B/G, 678th B/S, Diamond.

PRINCESS EILEEN-, 42-24462, 444th B/G, 678th B/S, Diamond. She flew 20 combat missions, 30 "Hump" flights, sank 2 Japanese ships and was credited with shooting down 3 Japanese fighters. Reclaimed: Amarillo AAF, 06/30/46. (James)

PRINCESS EILEEN II-, 444th B/G, 678th B/S, Diamond. Had 31 "Hump flights", 27 combat missions, 3 enemy aircraft shot down. (Campbell Archives, OKC)

RAIDEN MAIDEN II-, 42-65276, 468th B/G, 793rd B/S, 4- Blue rudder stripes. Reclaimed: 12/21/49. (M. Hill)

PRINCESS EILEEN IV-, 42-65327, 444th B/G, 678th B/S, Diamond B-29 left Luliang, China, on March 20, 1945, as part of the advanced echelon of the 58th B/W sent ahead to West Field, Tinian. Aircraft Commander/ Pilot: Capt. John Siler. Lost on May 25, 1945, mission to Tokyo while flying as a pathfinder over the Ginza District. Shot down after 32 combat missions. Capt. Siler's wife was named "Eileen". Capt. Siler's B-29 had been featured in Bond Drives, Comic Strips, News reel footage, and there had even been recruiting posters honoring the Princess Eileen.

QUEENIE-, 42-93831, 40th B/G, 45th B/S, 4-Yellow stripes. Abandoned over Rangoon 12/14/44.

RAIDEN'MAIDEN-, 42-6265, 468th B/G, 793rd B/S, 2- Blue rudder stripes. Reclaimed: Davis-Monthan, 06/27/49.

RAMBLIN'RECK-, 40th B/G.

RAMBLIN'WRECK-, 42-24471, 468th B/G,792nd B/S, 2- White rudder stripes. Reclaimed: Keesler AFB,08/24/49.

RAMP TRAMP- 42-6256, 462nd B/G, 771st B/S, Solid Blue rudder. Interred at Vladivostok on 07/29/44.

RANKLESS WRECK-, 42-63420, 40th B/G, 25th B/S,4-Red rudder stripes. On mission to Kobe June 5, 1945, this B-29 was jumped by a "George" class Japanese fighter. The left outboard engine was hit with a 20MM round and quit immediately. The other 20MM round hit the dead center of the bomb bay. The crew was later to discover that they had 148 holes in the bomb bay area. She limped her way back to Iwo with another B-29 flying protective escort. Reclaimed: 05/24/49.

RAMP TRAMP II-, 42-24904, 462nd B/G, 769th B/S, Solid Blue rudder. Reclaimed: 11/07/50. (M. Hill)

READY BETTY-, 42-24879, 468th B/G, 792md B/S, 2- White rudder stripes. Aircraft Commander/Pilot: Bill Garland. Reclaimed: 09/15/54. (Campbell)

RUSH ORDER-, 42-63393, 462nd B/G, 768th B/S, Solid red rudder. B-29-10-BA. Bell aircraft built. this B-29 was one of the first B-29s with the new 4-gunned top turrets. She got her name because she flew her first combat bombing mission just 15 days after rolling off the production line at Bell's Marietta Georgia plant. Reclaimed: 03/20/46. (Campbell Archives, OKC)

READY TEDDY-, 42-63561, 468th B/G,792nd B/S, 2- White rudder stripes. Shot down by "Flak" over Yawata on August 20, 1944. She went down with all crew members aboard.

REEEL ROUGH-, 444th B/G, 678th B/S. Diamond. ROBERT J.WILSON-, 42-24714, 468th B/G, 794th B/S, 2- Yellow rudder stripes. Final: Unk.

ROGER THE LODGER-, 42-6243, 468th B/G, 792nd B/S, 2- White rudder stripes. This B-29 crash landed at Hwaning China on 08/10/44 on return from mission to Sasebo Naval Base. The crew was rescued.

ROUND ROBIN ROSIE-, 444th B/G, Diamond.

RUSHIN'ROTASHUN-, 42-63417, 468th B/G, 792nd B/S.2- White rudder stripes. She was part of the 58th B/W's advanced echelon to be sent to the 313th B/W on Tinian. Reclaimed: 05/10/49.

SAN ANTONIO ROSE-, 42-24587, 40th B/G, 44th B/S, 4 Blue rudder stripes. Class 01Z Amarillo AAF. 06/30/46.

SATAN'S ANGEL- 42-65202, 444th B/G, 678th B/S, Diamond. This B-29 was the first all-Omaha built Martin B-29A. Crashed in a mid-air collision with another B-29 on 03/25/45 over the Bay of Bengal. (John "Socks" Heyer)

SCRAPPER-, 462nd B/G, 769th B/S.

SENTEMENTAL JOURNEY-, 444th B/G, 678th B/S, Triangle 'N'

SHAG'N HOME-, 42-93859, 40th B/G, 45th B/S, 4- Yellow rudder stripes. Reclaimed:

SHANGHAI LIL-, 42-6277, 444th B/G, 676th B/S, Diamond. Crashed into sea on 09/07/44 returning from Anshan, Manchuria, raid.

SHOOT YOU'RE FADED-, 42-63407, 40th B/G, 45th B/S, 4-Yellow rudder stripes. Reclaimed: 05/15/47.

SATAN'S SISTER-, 42-63453, 444th B/G, 678th B/S, B-29A-21-BA. Reclaimed:

SHANGHAI LIL RIDES AGAIN-, 42-24723, 444th B/G, 676th B/S, Diamond. Abandoned over Iwo, on return from mission to bomb the Tokyo Urban Area. Crew had to bail out due to severe "Flak" damage. Bailing out over the water, all but one of the crewmen was found. Flew 19 combat missions, 8 "Hump" trips as a tanker, 3 photo recon missions, and 8 mining missions. (M. Hill)

SENTEMENTAL JOURNEY-, 44-61634, 40th B/G, 44th B/S. Transferred to RAF, 05/10/50.

THE SHRIKE-, 462nd B/G, 769th B/S, 16 combat missions, 25 "Hump" trips. (J. Heyer)

SHAFT ABSORBER-, 44-84068, 444th B/G, 686th B/S, Triangle N, Reclaimed 08/17/49. Aircraft Commander/Pilot: Jim Marie. (Campbell)

SISTER SUE-, 42-6342, 40th B/G, 395th B/S, 4- Black rudder stripes. Abandoned on 10/16/44, on mission to bomb Formosa. (M. Hill)

SKY QUEEN-, 44-69698, 40th B/G, 44th B/S, Triangle S, No.42.(Campbell)

SKY BLUES-, 444th B/G, 676th B/S, Diamond. (Campbell Archives)

SLEEPY TIME GAL-, 42-24620, 40th B/G,44th B/S, 4- Blue rudder stripes. Reclaimed: Pyote AB, TX, 09/11/50. No.21.

SKY SCRAPPER-, 462nd B/G, 769th B/S. note: the nose wheel dust cover and plain shark's teeth and eye motif. 29 missions. (M. Hill)

SLOW FREIGHT-, 42- , 444th B/G, 678th B/S. (W. Walrond)

SMOKEY STOVER-, 42-6269, 4Oth B/G, 45th B/S, 4- Yellow rudder stripes. Reclaimed: Pyote AB, TX, 12/21.49. (J. Heyer)

SNUFFY-, 42-24873, 444th B/G, 676th B/S, Diamond. Reclaimed:05/10/54. "Them Shif'Less Skonks". 4 "Hump" flights, 7 combat missions. 1 mining mission and 4 Japanese fighters destroyed. CBI.

THE SPEARHEAD-, 44-69975, 468th B/G, 792nd B/S, part of the advanced echelon sent by the 58th B/W to the 313th B/W at Tinian, was at one time named Man-o-War. Later transferred to U.S.Army 05/23/46 (right side view).

SIR TROFREPUS-, 42-6237, 40th B/G, 25th B/S, 4- Red rudder stripes. Shot down at Nanking 0n 11/11/44.

SKIPPY-, 42-__177, 444th B/G, 678th B/S, Diamond.

SKY CHIEF-, 444th B/G, 676th B/S, Diamond.

SMILIN'JACK-, 42-24888, 40th B/G, 25th B/S, 4- Red rudder stripes. Reclaimed: 09/23/53.

SNAFUPER BOMBER-, 42-6275, 40th B/G, 45th B/S, 4- Yellow rudder stripes. Abandoned on return from the November 21, 1944, mission to bomb Omura, no.17.

SNOOKY'S BRATS-, 42-93877, 468th B/G, 792nd B/S, 2- White rudder stripes. Reclaimed:

THE SPEARHEAD-, 44-69975 This view depicts the image of the flag raising at Iwo Jima. This conception was prior to the monument being erected at Arlington National Cemetery. (R. Stoffer)

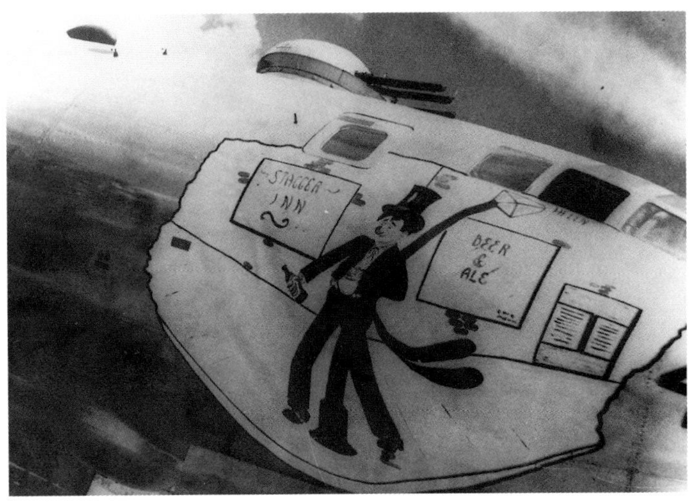

STAGGER INN, BEER & ALE-, 40th B/G Bell built A model, with 4-gunned upper turret. (W. Watts)

STARDUSTER-, 42-6305, 462nd B/G, 796th B/S, Solid yellow rudder. On August 20, 1944, had insufficient power to take-off and had to raise landing gear and belly in. Surveyed: 10/01/44. (W. Walrond)

SUPER MOUSE-, 42-24524, 444th B/G, 676th B/S, Diamond, no.17. B-29-36-BW. Has 22 "Hump" flights, 22 combat missions, 4 missions to the Japanese heartland "Tokyo", Lost over Osaka on 06/01/45. (Campbell Archives)

SUPERSTITIOUS ALOYSIOUS-, 42-65233, 40th B/G, 25th B/S, 4- Red rudder stripes. Reclaimed:

SURE THING-, 42-63557, 444th B/G, 679th B/S, Triangle N. Final: Unknown. (Campbell)

THIS IS IT-, 42-6321, 444th B/G, Diamond. Crashed on return from the 11/21/44 Omura raid. (G. James)

THUNDERBIRD-, 42-63454, 462nd B/G, 770th B/S, Solid Red rudder, no. X 3. Reclaimed: 09/11/50.Davis Montham AFB.(Heyer)

STOCKETT'S ROCKET-, 42-6261, 40th B/G, 45th B/S, 4-Yellow rudder stripes. Crashed on "Hump" trip 06/14/44 returning from Yawata mission.

SWEET MARILYN-, 444th B/G, Diamond.

SWEET THING-, 444th B/G, 678th B/S, Triangle 'N'.

TABOOMA II-, 42-63374, 40th B/G,25th B/S, 4-Red Stripes. Class 01Z 05/31/46.

TABOOMA III-, 42-65233, 40th B/G, 25th B/S, 4- Red rudder stripes. Reclaimed:

TABOOMA IV-, 44-69906, 40th B/G, 25th B/S, 4- Red rudder stripes. Triangle S, no.46.

TAGALONG-, 44-61651, 40th B/G, 44th B/S. Triangle S. Reclaimed: 10/03/53.

TAKE OFF OR BUST-, 58th B/W.

TALLY HO-, 444th B/G, 676th B/G, triangle N.

TARFU-, 42-24456, 462nd B/G, Solid rudder. Reclaimed: Davis-Monthan, 06/27/49.

TOKYO TROLLY-, 58th B/W.

TOTIN TO TOKYO-, 42-6454, 468th B/G, 793rd BS, 2-Blue rudder stripes. Reclaimed: Davis-Monthan, 06/27/49.

TYPHOON McGOON III-, 42-6303, 444th B/G, 678th B/S, 4-Black rudder stripes. Reclaimed: Davis-Monthan, 06/27/49.

TORRID TOBY-, 462nd B/G. (M. Hill)

TOTIN TO TOKYO II-, 42-63530, 468th B/G, 793rd B/S, 2-Blue rudder stripes. 7 combat missions, 1 "Hump flight'. (M. Hill)

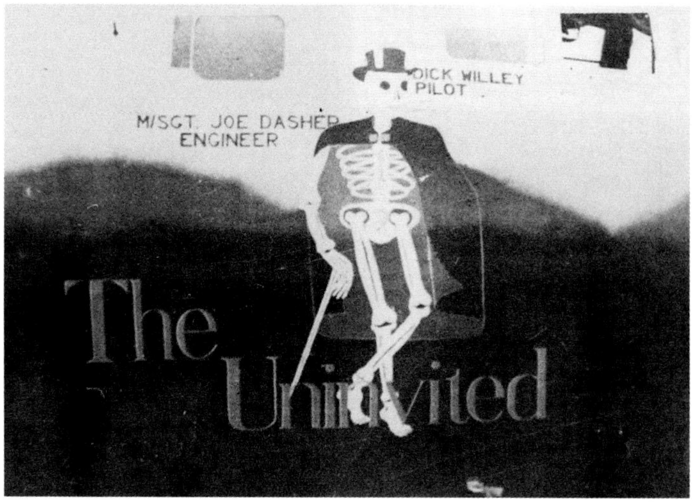

THE UNINVITED-, 42-6409, 468th B/G, 794th B/S. 2-Yellow rudder stripes. Reclaimed: Pyote AB, TX, 12/21/49. (M. Hill)

U.S.—??-, 444th B/G, 678th B/S, Diamond.

THE UNINVITED II-, 42-24719, 468th B/G, 794th B/S, 2-Yellow rudder stripes.

UNCONDITIONAL SURRENDER-, 444th B/G, 678th B/S, Triangle, N. 3-

URGIN VIRGIN-, 444th B/G, 676th B/S. Diamond.

VALKYRIE QUEEN-, 42-63356, 498th B/G, 793rd B/S,2-Blue rudder stripes, Reclaimed: Pyote AB,Tx. 12/21/49.

VIRGINIA TECH-, 44-61529, 40th B/G, Triangle S, no.29. Salvaged: 04/08/51.

WEIRITE-, 468th B/G, 794th B/S.

WEMPY'S BLITZBURGER-, 42-6290, 40th B/G, 44th B/S, 4-Blue rudder stripes. Hit by 444Th aircraft at Lianshan. 11/23/44.

WHAM BAM-, 42- 334, 468th B/G, 794th B/S.

WHAT HAPPENED-, 42-93829, 40th B/G, 4-stripes, Interred in Russia from Yawata mission 08/21/44.

UNDECIDED-, 44-24580, 444th B/G, 676th B/S, (Wichita) 4 enemy fighters shot down, 18 combat missions, 22 "Hump" flights. (Campbell)

UNCONDITIONAL SURRENDER-, 444th B/G, 678th B/S, Triangle, N. 3-443

URGIN VIRGIN II-, 444th B/G, 676th B/S, 4-Hump" trips, 1 photo recon mission, 7 combat missions. (M. Hill)

UNTOUCHABLE-, 42-24506, 462nd b/g, 768th B/S, Solid red rudder, 1 P. Crashed on a test flight in the CBI on 12/02/45. (Hill)

U.S.S.COMFORT'S REVENGE-,44-61556, 40th B/G, 45th B/S. Triangle S, no.39. (M. Hill)

UP N' COMIN'-, 44-8767-, 444th B/G, Diamond. 9 missions. (Campbell)

VICTORY GIRL-, 42-24731, 444th B/G, 678th B/G, Diamond 65. 37 combat missions, 8 "Hump" trips (Campbell)

WHAT HAPPENED ?-, 42-24829, 40th B/G, 395th B/S, Abandoned over China, 08/20/44.

WICHITA WITCH-, 42-24752, 40th B/G, 44th B/S, 4-Blue rudder stripes, Reclaimed: Lowery 07/31/46.(W. Walrond)

WINDY CITY-, 42-6253, 468th B/G, 794th B/S, 2-Yellow rudder stripes. Surveyed: 10/11/44.

WINGED VICTORY-, 58th B/W.

WINGED VICTORY II-, 42-63538, 40th B/G, 44th B/S, 4-Blue rudder stripes. MIA over Tokyo, 05/25/45.

WINNIE-, 444th B/G. Diamond.

YELLOW ROSE OF TEXAS-, 42-24621, 40th B/G, 44th B/S, 4-Blue rudder stripes. Reclaimed: Pyote AB,Tx.12/21/49.

YUCATAN KIDS-, 44-61587, 40th B/G, 44th B/S, Triangle S, No.26. Reclaimed: 06/23/54.

WICHITA WITCH-, 42-24442, 468th B/G, 793rd B/S, 2-Blue rudder stripes, class 01Z at Amarillo 06/30/46. (M. Hill)

WILD HAIR-, 42-24505, 462nd B/G, 769th B/S, Solid yellow rudder, shot down at Mudken, Manchuria, 12/22/44. (Watts)

WINDY CITY II-, 42-24486, 468th B/G, 794th B/S, 8"Hump" flights, 21 bomb missions. 2-Yellow rudder stripes, class 01Z Keesler, 02/10/48. (S. Wilson)

WINNIE II-, 444th B/G, Diamond. North Field, Tinian. flew 25 missions (Campbell)

LITTLE GEN-, 42-24596, 497th B/G, 869th B/S, A No.1, seen here with the civilian personnel at the Amarillo Army Air Field. She flew 40 combat missions and shot down 3 Japanese aircraft. The 73rd Bomb Wing's Barb and ball insignia has replaced the Female Art Form that once had adorned this B-29. (via B. Snodgrass)

This line-up of four B-29s, seen here at Amarillo Army Air Field on May 24, 1945, shows some of the war weary veterans after they returned from battle in the China, Burma, India theater of operations. The early tail markings reveal that these B-29s were from the 58th Bomb Wing. They are being used here to train B-29 flight crews.
The turrets have been removed so their training mission would appear to be more pilots' training and navigational training in the primary stages. The second B-29 in the line-up is "SAN ANTONIO ROSE', Ser.no.42-24587, of the 44th B/G, 44th B/S, assigned to Class 01Z at Amarillo on 06/30/46. She has 4 Blue rudder stripes and Blue tips. The B-29 in the foreground is Serial no.42-63403, Diamomnd, no.39, ia a B-29-15-BA, the second Bell built model 15. (via B. Snodgrass)

ANNIE-, 42-26224, seen here at Amarrillo Army Air Field in late 1945. One of the B-29s used as a training hack, she still carries her armament minus the guns in the rear turret. In this view she is undergoing engine repairs. (via B. Snodgrass)

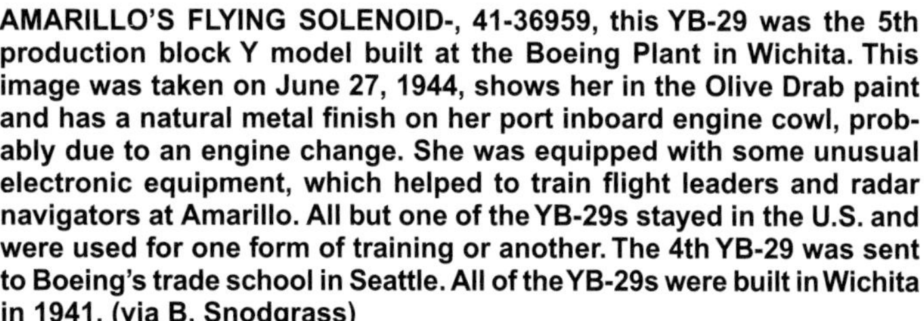

AMARILLO'S FLYING SOLENOID-, 41-36959, this YB-29 was the 5th production block Y model built at the Boeing Plant in Wichita. This image was taken on June 27, 1944, shows her in the Olive Drab paint and has a natural metal finish on her port inboard engine cowl, probably due to an engine change. She was equipped with some unusual electronic equipment, which helped to train flight leaders and radar navigators at Amarillo. All but one of the YB-29s stayed in the U.S. and were used for one form of training or another. The 4th YB-29 was sent to Boeing's trade school in Seattle. All of the YB-29s were built in Wichita in 1941. (via B. Snodgrass)

KLONDIKE KUTEY-, 42-24612, #12. Assigned to the 236th B/U, operating out of Alaska, their main role there was more of a test role. Weather endurance, and Arctic Climate studies, she saw duty at the Amarillo Army Airfield, but was reclaimed at Tinker where she was involved with a collision with a B-17G while taxing. She was sent to Pyote Air Base on 09/11/50. (via B. Snodgrass)

B-29-15-BA, 42-63403, diamond, no.39. seen here being serviced and fueled at Amarillo Army Air Field on May 24, 1945. It is believed that this B-29 flew with the 58th Bomb Wing in Kharagpur. In 1944 she was retired as war weary and sent to the states. She was then assigned to Class O1Z at the B-29 flight training school at Amarillo. The majority of B-29s at AAAF came from the 58th or 73rd Bombardment Wings. (via B. Snodgrass)

B-29s of the 468TH Bomb Group release their bombs over a Japanese supply depot at Rangoon. The bombs being dropped are 500 pound general purpose bombs, HE High Explosives.

To "police" Formosa, General Curtis E. LeMay sent the 40TH Bomb Group of the 58th Bomb Wing. They bombed targets, such as Japanese ships in Takao Harbor, sent here Oct.16, 1944.

Bomb Squadrons of the 58th Bomb Wing were all disbanded in September and October of 1944. They were then sent to join up with the other Groups on Tinian, mostly to the 313TH bomb Wing, while those showing signs of too much wear were returned to the States.

During missions over the China Sea, an occasional opportunity would arise to release a salvo over shipping transports, Because they were slower, they made then prime targets in these bombings.

This view of the tail and tail gunner's position shows how easy the Group and squadron marking would be to identify in flight at high altitude. The crew is seen here proudly posing with their Superfortress. 42-24879, "Ready Betty". of the 468th B/G, 792nd Bomb Squadron. (Snodgrass)

This view of B-29, serial no. 42-65276, "Raiden Maiden II" of the 468TH bomb Group, 793rd Bomb Squadron seen here with her bomb vertically rowed up, seeing that the tail guns are missing would indicate that they are probably being serviced. This shot was taken at Kharagpur in June of 1944.

This B-29, of the 444th B/G, drones towards her target. The Triangle N indicates this photo was taken in 1945 after their arrival at Tinian, Saipan. Assigned to the 678th Bomb Squadron, the clean lines of the Superfortress are clearly visible. The APQ-13, Radar, radome can clearly be seen on the middle section of the fuselage.

This view of the B-29 just taking off reveals an unusually close view of the radar dome for the APQ-13 radar. This dome is the turret-shaped style as opposed to the teardrop in the previous photo. This style radome was retractable.

These three B-29s of the 40th Bomb Group, 395th Bomb Squadron are just releasing their payloads over a target somewhere in Japan. This photo was taken in late June or early July of 1945. They are in a v formation, dropping high explosives as opposed to incendiaries on this mission. The incendiaries were specifically used when bombing urban areas because of the many fires and mass destruction that could be generated.

This squadron of B-29s enroute to their target is from before May of 1945. The Diamonds on the tails with numbers centered illustrate the earlier months of the bombing campaign against Japan. Assigned to the 444th Bomb Group, and due to the high numbers inside the Diamonds, would indicate that these are from the 678TH Bomb Squadron. The B-29 in OD paint is probably the oldest B-29 pictured here.

The broken cloud cover in the Western Pacific was almost always present. Broken visibility is most generally the rule, rather than the exception. This flight of Superforts from the 58th B/W is on their way to yet another pounding for the Empire of Japan.

These B-29s of the 444th B/G, are headed home after their day's work. They belong to the 678th B/S. The appearance of the aircraft would seem that they met very little resistance this time. This photo was taken in late July to Early August of 1945.

B-29s of the 58th Bomb Wing, 444th Bomb Group, 677th B/S, fly past a familiar sight by now, Mt. Fujiyama. In July of 1945, Clear sky and visibility unlimited. (Campbell)

The "American Beauty" drones onward towards her next target, Nagoya. The Group has not yet changed over to the Triangle tail markings at the time of this photo. Taken in late 1944 or very early 1945.

The nose art seen here on "Fast Company" is a little more modest than most. Later in the war the Wing Commanders got a little more strict on the nudity, due to more and more news media attention to the missions of the 20th Air Force.

B-29 returning from her mission. The crews were always anxious to get home for a nice warm meal and some sleep, especially after a long haul. This Superfortress is from the 678th B/S, 444th Bomb Group.

Sitting on her hardstand awaiting her crew. Soon they will be loading the bombs you see in the foreground with another delivery for Tojo. This 676th Bomb Squadron B-29 is Ready for action.

B-29s of the 40th B/G in tight formation, headed out on one of the last bombing missions of the war. Unknown to the crews, the war would be at an end in just a few short weeks.

The ground crews with assistance from flight crew personnel are making the final preparations for a P.O.W. supply drop. All of the Groups, as well as all squadrons, participated in this much needed operation. The food, medical supplies, and clothes were essential for the survival of the internees until the liberating forces could arrive and assist further.

The "Conga Line" is forming. After take-off the mission will be to drop supplies to the POWs, both American and our allies. These "Mercy Flights" would assist the men until final liberation would come to be realized.

The crew is at rest, as is this B-29, seen here in China. The rather crude implement in the foreground is a cement, or stone, roller used to hardpack the landing strips for the B-29s. It is probably a 20 man power roller !

A crewchief inspects the damage to his lady. This B-29 had lost her nose gear on landing, resulting in the severe damage to the undersurface of the Superfortress and to the port inboard engine nacelle.

This is another view of a target in Manchuria. Bridges were destroyed, and supply lines were cut off. The B-29s put a strangle hold on the Japanese ground forces.

When a B-29 was damaged beyond economic repair she was used for spare parts or cannibalized. This B-29 has suffered the fate of many like her. Missions were notoriously hard on many of the bombers, but when they became war weary and were at risk to even fly back to the U.S. they still fulfilled a useful purpose, sad as it may seem to see a great airplane end up this way.

The mechanics and ground crews kept the Giants flying, checking oil, magnetos, fittings, and fuel lines. Whenever the need and demand called for, the men were there and did their jobs well. The team spirit and combined effort of all personnel won the war.

This painting depicts the true feelings of the Chinese towards their American visitors and Allies during World War II. Many of these type of images were used to promote the purchases of war bonds.

Chapter 4:
B-29
73rd BOMBARDMENT WING
-A TORCH TO THE ENEMY

In the very same month that the 58th Bomb Wing was taking shape, the 73rd Bomb Wing (Very Heavy) was activated at Smokey Hill Army Air Field, Kansas. On November 20, 1943, it became the second B-29 Superfortress Wing. Her four Groups were activated on the same day: the 497th Bomb Group, the 498th Group, the 499th Group, and the 500th Bomb Groups (Very Heavy).

February and March saw the first arrivals of their B-29s. In April the Groups of the 73rd Bomb Wing started taking over the airfields that were vacated when the 58th Bomb Wing departed for India. Originally it was planned for the 73rd to join the 58th Bomb Wing in the CBI, but it was decided to send this new wing to the Marianas.

On the 12th of October 1944, the first 73rd Bomb Wing B-29 touched down at Isley Field, Saipan. This B-29 was named JOLTIN JOSIE, of the 498th Bomb Group. The 497th Bomb Group had three Squadrons; the 869th Bomb Squadron, the 870th Bomb Squadron, and the 871st Bomb Squadron. All three squadrons were assigned to Isley Field, Saipan. The 73rd Bomb Wing and all squadrons received the Distinguished Unit Citation twice, for actions against the Japanese, 27 January 1945, and again for the bombing missions over Japan from July 26, 1945, to August 2, 1945. At war's end the 73rd Bomb Wing returned to MacDill Field, Florida, with all three squadrons.

The 498th Bomb Group also had three squadrons; the 873rd Bomb Squadron, the 874th Bomb Squadron, and the 875th Bomb Squadron. These three squadrons were also assigned to Isley Field, Saipan. All three squadrons received two Distinguished Unit Citations for actions against the Japanese. The 873rd and 874th squadrons received the Air Force's Outstanding Unit Award. The 499th Bomb Group and her three squadrons—the 877th Bomb Squadron, the 878th Bomb Squadron, and the 879th Bomb Squadron—were also based at Isley Field, Saipan. All three squadrons of the 499th Bomb Group received the Distinguished Unit Citation for their role in bombing Nagoya, Japan, 23 January 1945 and Japan again from 22 April to 28 April 1945.

The 500th Bomb Group had three squadrons, like her sister groups; the 881st Bomb Squadron, the 882nd Bomb Squadron, and the 883rd Bomb Squadron. Based at Isley Field, Saipan, they too were awarded the Distinguished Unit Citation for their participation in the bombing of Nagoya, Japan, January 23, 1945, and the bombing campaign from 15 June 1945 to 20 June 1945, hitting the Japanese in their heartland, Tokyo.

At war's end the entire Group would return to March Field, California. Inside a six month period, 2,251 B-29s landed on Iwo Jima. The missions were rough, and the countless hours of flying could really wear a person down quick. While on missions to bomb the Japanese Empire, headwinds would often reach velocities exceeding 200 miles per hour. This put even more strain on the planes, the Pilots, and the crews.

Superfortresses of the 73rd Bombardment Wing

ABROAD WITH ELEVEN YANKS-, 44-70083, 499th B/G, 877th B/S, V, no.8. MIA over Osaka, 06/21/45. (Hill)

AMERICAN BEAUTY-, 42-24686, 500th B/G, 882nd B/S, Z, square, no.25. Ditched on 12/27/44, returning from mission over Tokyo. (J. Heyer)

ADAM'S EVE-, 42-24600, 500th B/G, 883rd B/S, Z square, no.47. Ditched on return from Tokyo mission, 04/07/45. (J. Heyer)

AMERICAN MAID-, 42-24593, 497th B/G, 869th B/S, A square, no.7. Reclaimed: Tinker, OCAMA. Aircraft Commander/Pilot: Lt. J.D. Bartlett. Among other missions she took part in the 1st attack January 3, 1945, against Nagoya and earned her niche in the hall of fame. Heavily attacked over the target, American Maid took hits in the tail and left sighting blister, which caused the blister to blow out. Her tail gunner had a finger shot away, but completed the mission without further incident.

ANTOINETTE-, 42-24751, 498th B/G, 875th B/S, T, square no.48. Lost in combat over Tokyo, May 23rd 1945. (G. James)

ANCIENT MARINER-, 44-70113, 500th B/G, 883rd B/S, Z, no.58. (M. Hill)

THE ANCIENT MARINER-, 42-65296, 500th B/G, 883rd B/S, Z, square, no.53. Reclaimed: Davis-Monthan, 05/10/54. This B-29 had a reputation for being the oldest, most decrepit B-29 on the flightline.

ANN DEE-, 42-65249, 500th B/G, 881st B/S, Z, square no.3. Reclaimed: Tinker, OCAMA. 09/11/50.

ANTOINETTE-, 44-70135, 498th B/G, 875th B/S, T,48.

ARKANSAS TRAVELER-, 42-65331, 498th B/G, 873rd B/S, T, square, no.17. Reclaimed Hill, AFB. 11/17/53.

BAD BREW II-, 42-63539, 497th B/G, 869th B/S, A square, no.6. Reclaimed: Pyote AB, TX, 09/11/50.

BALL OF FIRE-, 73rd B/W.

BARBARA ANN-, 42-24652, 500th B/G, 883rd B/S, Z square no.42. Reclaimed : Amarillo AAF, 06/24/50.

BATAAN AVENGER-, 44-69753, 499th B/G, 878th B/S, V square. Built and named by the employees at Boeing Wichita as a tribute to the many whose lives were lost on the Bataan death march. She flew on the first Tokyo B-29 raid, November 24, 1944. The Avenger flew a total of 30 combat missions. Salvaged: 09/06/49.

BATTLIN'BETTY-, 42-24606, 498th B/G, 875th B/S, T square, no.41. Salvaged: 01/06/45.

BATTLIN' BETTY II- 42-24760, 498th B/G, 875th B/S, T square, no.41. Ditched on return from the 02/10/45 mission to Ota.

BELL RUTH-, 42-24680, 500th B/G, 881st B/S, Z square, no.7. Final: Unknown.

BEAUBOMBER II-, 42-63442, 499th B/G, 879th B/S, V square, no.47. Flew a Super-Dumbo search and rescue mission, setting a record of 18 hours in flight. (Hill)

BAD BREW-, 42-24594, 497th B/G, 869th B/S, A square, no.6. Aircraft Commander/Pilot: John Brewster. Art was applied by Lin Decker. Just after take-off, enroute to bomb Nogoya, B-29 was forced to abort mission due to problems. When "Bad Brew" unloaded her bomb load over the water, she had less than 300 feet of altitude. The resulting explosions from the bombs caused the B-29 to crash into the sea on January 23, 1945. (Campbell Archives)

THE BARRONESS-, 42-24675, 500th B/G, 883rd B/S, Z square, no.41. Reclaimed: Spokaine 10/26/46. (Hill)

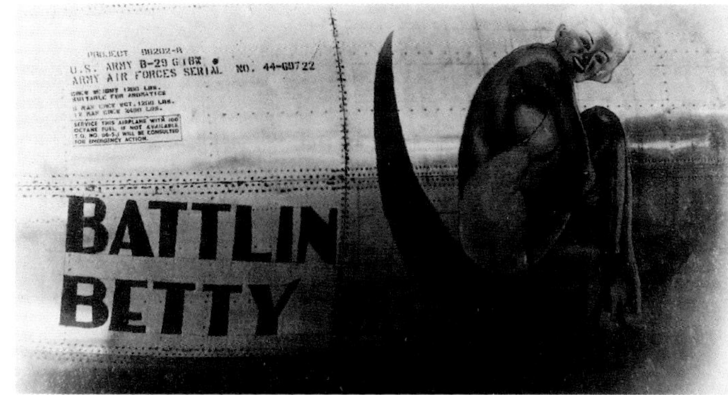

BATTLIN'BETTY III-, 44-69772, 498th B/G, 875th B/S, T square, no.41/48. (J. Heyer)

BEDROOM EYES-, 42-24610, 498th B/G, 874th B/S, T square, no.22. Flew a record 61 combat missions from Saipan during the war. She survived the war and returned to the U.S. Reclaimed: (Campbell Archives)

BEN'S RAIDERS-, 44-69725, 500th B/G, 883rd B/S, Z square, no.43.

BETTY BEE-, 499th B/G, 878th B/S, V square, no.37. Aircraft Commander/Pilot: A. Ray Brashear. Was first B-29 over Kobe on June 5,1945. Did not receive any damage, but took 15 to 20 fighter attacks on way into target area. On return flight home took a hit in the right horizontal stabilizer, tearing it off. The B-29 made it back to Saipan, landing safely. She had 16 combat missions, and shot down 3 enemy fighters.

BLACK BART'S REVENGE-, 44-69706, 498th B/G, 875th B/S, T square, no.53.

BOOZE HOUND-, 44-69746, 500th B/G, Z square.

BLACK MAGIC-, 42-24672, 500th B/G, 881st B/S, Z square, no.4. (J. Heyer)

THE BIG STICK-, 42-24661, 499th B/G, 877th B/S, V square, no.44. flew 44 combat missions. Reclaimed: Pyote AB, TX, 08/20/50. (W. Walrond)

BUCKIN' BRONC-, 44-70136, 500th B/G, 882nd B/S, Z, no.28. Shot down by Russians 08/29/45. (Hill)

CORAL QUEEN-, 42-24615, 497th B/G, 869th B/S, A square no.8. Aircraft Commander/Pilot; Capt. Pershing Yon. The pin-up was painted by Bud Sprenger, a Marine assigned to the 3rd Battalion, 10th Marines. In the states he had been a sign painter. For his efforts and talent he earned about $175.00 and some whiskey for each job. Coral Queen ditched 35 miles short of Iwo on April 8, 1945. Only 3 crewmen survived. They had just bombed Kanoya, a base being suspected of housing the Kamikaze suicide squadrons. (J. Heyer)

CONSTANT NYMPH-, 42-63487, 500th B/G, 882nd B/S, Z square, no.30. The pin-up was the same on both sides of this B-29. Reclaimed: 01/05/30. 1 photo mission, 4 bombing missions at time of photo. (Hill)

DAUNTLESS DOTTY-, 42-24592, 797th B/G, 876th B/S, A square, no 1. flew 26 missions, and shot down four Japanese fighters. Crashed on take-off from Kwajalein on 06/06/45. (Campbell Archives)

BUCKIN'BRONCO-, 42-63436, 500th B/G 882nd B/S, Z square. Reclaimed: 05/10/49.

THE CANNUCK-, 42-24668, 500th B/G, 882nd B/S, Z square. Aircraft Commander/Pilot: Col. Jack Dougherty. Led the Group to bomb Tokyo Urban area March 9, 1945. Cannuck is a slang for Canadian.

COMMAND PERFORMANCE-, 499th B/G, V square.

CY-, 499th B/G, V square.

DANNY MITE-, 44-69777, 498th B/G, 874th B/S,T square,no.28. Went down over Tokyo after loosing two engines on May 24, 1945. The crew was captured by the Japanese and sent to the Omori POW camp till wars end.

DINA MIGHT-, 498th Bomb Group. She was credited with sighting the Japanese man of war "Yamato" in the Inland Sea, and alerting the U.S. Navy to her position. The Japanese Battlewagon was later pounded with aerial torpedoes and bombs until she exploded and sank.

DOLLY ANN-, 500th B/G. Z square.

R/S view of Constant Nymph

DESTINY'S TOTS-, 42-65293, 497th B/G, 869th B/S, A square, no.6. Reclaimed Hill AFB, 11/17/53. This air crew used diapers to indicate bomb missions. (Lloyd)

DEVIL'S DARLIN-, 42-24629, 498th B/G, 873rd B/S, T square no.9. Ditched on 02/04/45 returning from mission over Kobe Urban area. (Campbell Archives)

DEVIL'S DELIGHT-, 42-24652, 500th B/G, 882nd B/S, Z square no.21. Hit several times by "Flak" over Nagoya, January 27, 1945, on their 9th mission. Several crewmen were injured, and the oxygen system was almost gone but they managed to get her home. 26 combat missions. Reclaimed: Amarillo AAF, 06/24/46. (Campbell Archives)

DEVIL'S DELIGHT- 42-24652, 500th B/G, 882nd B/S, Z square no.21. Later in the war the 73rd B/W went to the winged barb as a Group insignia—this is same aircraft as previously mentioned. (Snodgrass)

DIXIE DARLIN'-, 42-63413, 497th B/G, 878th B/S, A square no.45. Ditched on 12/13/44, on return from Nagoya, after collision with A square 44 of the same squadron. (Campbell Archives)

DRAGGIN LADY-, 42-24604, 497th B/G, 870th B/S, A square, no.24. MIA due to weather strike, 04/13/45. (Hill)

THE DRAGON LADY-, 42-63425, 497th B/G, 871st B/S, A square no.41. Reclaimed: 11/01/48. (T. Carmichael)

THE EAGER BEAVER III-, 42-24750, 498th B/G, 873rd B/S, T square. (Hill)

FEVER FROM THE SOUTH-, 42-63497, 500th B/G,882nd B/S, Z square no.32, flew 50 combat missions. The image here is early in the war, before changing to the winged barb artwork. Reclaimed: Amarillo AAF,05/23/45.

FAY-, 42-65210, 498th B/G, 874th B/S, T square, no.26. was reported as missing in action over Nagoya on 03/24/45. This B-29 had led this mission, no.34 target no. 193. (the Mitsubishi Aircraft Engine Plant). Fay was the only B-29 lost on this mission. 7 other B-29s were damaged. 213.23 tons of bombs were dropped on this mission. She was Martin's 14th B-29 to be completed with tail cannon and 4-gunned upper turret. Artwork was applied by Corporal Guillermo Hernandez, a mechanic. (T. Carmichael)

FEVER FROM THE SOUTH-, 42-63497, seen after changing her artwork to the standardized winged barb, less vulgar than the Group's image. The crew seems in good spirits. (Snodgrass)

THE DRAGON LADY-, 44-69777, 498th B/G, 873rd B/S, T square, 46.

DREAM GIRL-, 42-24673, 499th B/G, 879th B/S, V square 43. Reclaimed:

DUKE OF ALBUQUERQUE-, 44-69829, 500th B/G, 881st B/S, Z square 8.

FANCY DETAIL-, 42-24696, 500th B/G, 882nd B/S, Z square 50, made numerous photo and bombing missions over Japan.

FAST COMPANY-, 42-63[illegible], 499th B/G, 877th B/S, V square, no.12. Reclaimed: 10/30/46 (Hill)

FAY II-, 498th B/G, 874th B/S, T square. On April 1, 1945, she took off for a night mission to bomb the Musashino Aircraft Engine Plant, mission no.37. Target no.357 was located in the Tokyo Urban area. FAY II was never heard from again.

FILTHY FAY-, 498th B/G, 874th B/S.

FILTHY FAY II-, 42-9399-,498th B/G, 874th B/S, T square no.26. reported missing on 04/02/45 mission to bomb the Musashino Aircraft Engine Plant, target no.357. She was on her first mission.

FILTHY FAY III-, 44-69852, 498th B/G, 874th B/S, T square no.26. On mission to bomb the Tokyo Urban area May 25, 1945, Fay III was lost and never heard from again. She was the only B-29 lost on this mission—number 73.

FLAGSHIP 500TH-, 44-61669, 500th B/G, 883rd B/S, Z No.49.

FLYING FOOL-, 42-84698, 499th B/G, 878th B/S, V square no.8. B-29 had an engine fire over Agrihan Island, enroute to bomb Miyazaki Airfield, mission no.59, on 04/27/45.

GEISHA GERTIE-, 42-24763, 498th B/G, 873rd B/S, T square, no.34. Had to ditch on the return trip from the January 14, 1945, mission to bomb the Mitsubishi Aircraft Factory at Nagoya, mission No. 19. Gertie was the only B-29 lost on this mission. 11 Japanese fighters were shot down by B-29s participating in this raid.

GONNA MAK'ER-, 42-65231, 497th B/G, 871st B/S, A square no.51. On mission number 47, April 18, 1945, to bomb Tachiari Airfield in Kyushu, she was rammed by a Japanese fighter. The stricken bomber slowly rolled over, went into a dive, and crashed.

FICKLE FINGER-, 42-63426, 497th B/G, 871st B/S, A square, no.49 was reported missing on 12/22/44 mission to bomb Nagoya, "The city that would not die". (J. Heyer)

FORBIDDEN FRUIT-, 42-24607, 499th B/G, 878th B/S, T square, No.50. completed 65 missions, Reclaimed: Shephard AFB,09/15/49. (Campbell)

FRISCO NANNY-, 42-93889, 500th B/G, 882nd B/S, Z square no.34. Reclaimed; Davis-Monthan AFB. (J. Heyer)

GOLDEN STATE EXPPRESS-, 73rd B/W A/C No. 3, 37 combat missions. (M. Hill)

HAM'S EGGS-, 42-24670, 499th B/G, 879th B/S, V square no.45. Final: unknown.

HASTA LUEGO-, 42-24647, 499th B/G, 878th B/S, V square, no.22. On return from mission no. 19, target 194, The Mitsubishi Aircraft Plant at Nagoya, January 14, 1945, the B-29 was forced to ditch 150 miles North of Saipan.

THE GHASTLY GOOSE-, 42-63541, 497th B/G, A square. On mission no. 22, January 27, 1945, after being attacked by Japanese fighters over Tokyo and the Urban Dock area. Aircraft Commander/Pilot: Capt. Dale Peterson's Goose, having been badly shot up and losing gas from her punctured tanks, prepared for a ditching at sea. She was given cover by a Jumbo II who observed the "Goose" make a perfect ditching into the sea of Japan. The crew, however, was never rescued because of a severe storm that lasted nearly a week.

GRAVEL GERTIE-, 42-65221, 500th B/G, 882nd B/S, Z square no.29. She flew a total of 49 combat missions. The 73rd Bomb Wing used a barb and ball with the B-29's name inscribed in the barb as a unit designator. Crashed on take-off 08/06/45, enroute to bomb the Nishinomiya urban area. (M. Hill)

HAULINAS-, 42-24461, 499th B/G, 878th B/S, V square. 11 combat missions. (Campbell)

HALEY'S COMET-, 42-24616, 497th B/G, 870th B/S, A square, no.22. On mission no.22, January 27, 1945, Tokyo and the Urban Dock area was their target. The last mission that the wing would take on alone. Not a single B-29 bombed the primary. 62 B-29s made their way through an estimated 900 fighter attacks. The 73rd Bomb Wing claimed 60 Japanese fighters destroyed, though the actual figure was somewhat lower. Twenty-four year old Capt. Teruhiko Kobayashi, Commanding the 244 Sentai, would become the Japanese highest scoring Superfortress killer with 10 confirmed B-29s to his credit. Haley's Comet was to be his 6th victory. The Comet had suffered damage from both fighter attack and "Flak". Flames were streaming into the bomb bay, and the B-29 shuddered and started to lose airspeed. Aircraft Commander/Pilot: Lt. Walter McDonnell tried to manage to control the ship, but was last seen banking into a cloud bank for cover protection. At war's end the Radar Operator and Tail Gunner were released from a POW camp, the only survivors of `Haley's Comet'. (Campbell Archives)

HELL'S BELLE-, 42-24680, 500th B/G, 881st B/S, Z square no.37. Final: unknown.

HELL'S ELLE-, 500th B/G.

HELL'S BELLS-, 499th B/G, V square. destroyed on ground 11/27/44.

HOMER'S ROAMERS-, 42-24794, 498th B/G, 873rd B/S, T square no.3. Reclaimed: 05/19/50.

HONSHU HAWK-, 42-64444, 498th B/G, 875th B/S, T square 45. Reclaimed: Pyote AB, TX, 09/11/50.

HONSHU HURRICANE-, 499th B/G, 875th B/S, T square 51.

HOUSTON HONEY-, 42-63475, 498th B/G, 875th B/S, T square 51. Final: unknown.

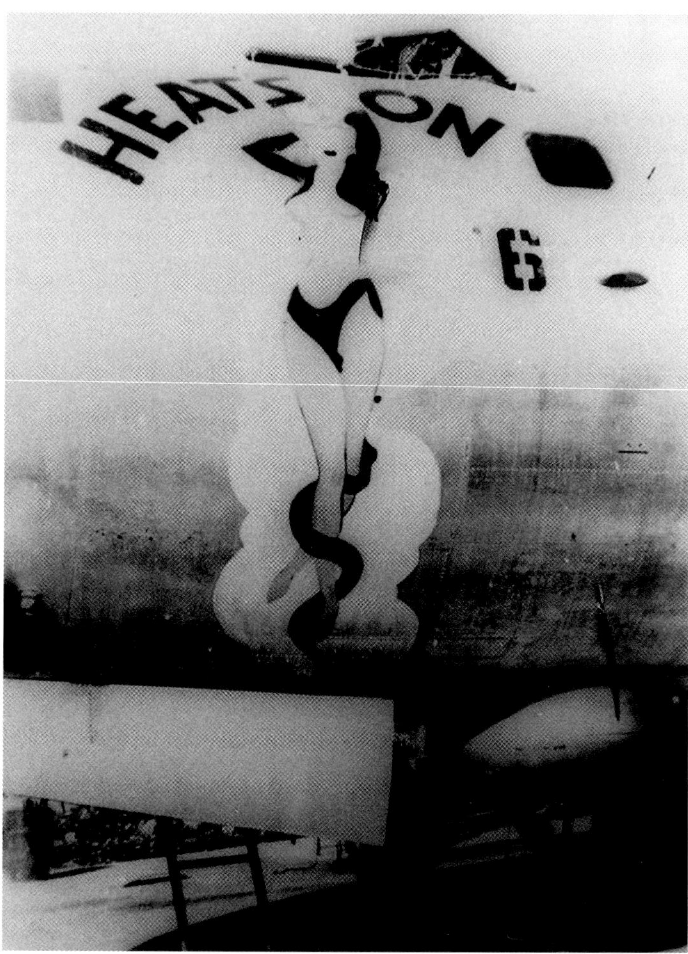

THE HEAT'S ON-, 42-24605, 498th B/G, 875th B/S, T square, no.2. Aircraft Commander/Pilot: Lt. Wayne Dameron, participated in mission over Tokyo, December 27, 1944, to bomb target no.357, the Musashino Aircraft Plant. She was met with heavy fighter opposition, and, crippled by fighter attack, she was forced to ditch. Except for four men, the entire crew was lost when the fuel transfer system failed. (Hill)

(RIGHT) HONEY-, 42-24669, 499th B/G, 879th B/S, T square no.42. Reclaimed: Tinker AFB, OCAMA, 09/11/50. (Hill)

HEAVENLY BODY-, 42-63510, 498th B/G, 874th B/S, T square, 38. was so badly shot up on April 1, 1945, on mission no.357 that she was sent up to Guam and lost to the Group. She had been originally assigned to the 505th B/G 313th B/W. Reclaimed: Davis-Monthan. (J. Heyer)

HOG WILD-, 42-63436, 500th B/G, 882nd B/S, Z No.28. She was the last B-29 to be shot down during World War II. She was shot down on August 29, 1945, while on a supply mission—a victim of Soviet Fighters. The B-29 was forced to land. The crew was safely returned, along with some of the equipment, flight instruments, gun sights, bomb sight, radar, etc., but not the aircraft itself. (Campbell Archives)

INSPIRATION-, 42-83440, 499th b/G, 877th B/S, V square, no.10. B-29 lost on test hop when engine caught fire 06/04/45.

JOKER'S WILD-, 42-24626, 497th B/G, 871st B/S, A square,no.42. B-29A. Aircraft Commander/Pilot: Maj. Clarence Fowler. The artist at work, Bud Springer, a U.S. Marine assigned to duty on Saipan. Most all of the bombers of World War II were adorned with lavish pin-ups, political slogans, slurs against the Axis aggressors, etc. This unique form of art gave personality to the individual aircraft and their crews. Its been stated more than once that the art had a positive effect on the morale of the service men, as well as making the aircraft easier to identify. A Royal Flush over the Japanese Empire, this B-29 was reported missing in action over Nagoya, Japan, on 01/03/45.

IRISH LASSIE-, 42-65246, 497th B/G, 871st B/S, A square,no.52. Aircraft Commander/ Pilot: Lloyd Avery. On January 27, 1945 mission to bomb the Urban Dock Area of Tokyo, Avery's B-29 was rammed in quick succession by two Japanese fighters. The first fighter impacted with the left wing behind the no.1 engine, shearing off about 8 feet of aileron and ripping into a fuel tank, causing fuel to flush out. Amazingly, the engine continued to run. The crew had 4 Japanese fighters to their credit. Another Japanese fighter—a "Jack" fighter—rammed into the tail section, tearing away the whole left side of the tail. "Lassie" struggled back to Isley Field, Saipan, where she landed. Her landing gear held up, but the nose gear folded up into the nose of the B-29, then broke in half. The tail gunner was wedged into the tail gunner's compartment so tightly it took an hour to get him free from the wreckage. The entire crew was lucky this time, and they all survived. 01/27/45. (Hill)

JUG HAID II-, 42-24650, 499th B/G, 877th B/S, V square, no.2. was reported missing and assumed shot down on 04/07/45. The Jug had been on a bombing mission over Tokyo. (Campbell Archives)

JOLTIN'JOSIE,-, 42-24614, 498th B/G, 873rd B/S, T The Pacific Pioneer square, no.5. "Josie" was the first B-29 to arrive at Saipan on October 12,1944. Piloted by Brig. General Haywood S. "Possum" Hansell, already a veteran of the B-29 program, he was largely responsible for perfecting the attacks to be made against mainland Japan. He also flew on the first mission. Joltin'Josie and her crew were lost on April 1, 1945, after having a fire and explosion just after take-off. She crashed into Magacienne Bay and exploded on impact. The note painted on the nose landing gear door reads, "Clean Your Feet". Capt. Wilson Currier was the Pilot. (Hill)

JUGHAID III-, 499th B/G, 877th B/S, V square 2. 46 combat missions,3 Japanese fighters destroyed. (Campbell)

HUMP'S HONEY-, 42-24648, 497th B/G, 871st B/S, A square, no. 48. Reclaimed: Pyote AB, TX, 09/11/50.

IRON SHILLALAH-, 42-63519, 497th B/G, A square suffered severe damage and was forced to ditch on return from the 04/18/45 bombing mission over Tachiari.

JUMBO II-, 42-24855, 497th B/G, 871st B/S, A (King of the Show) square, no.55. flew 18 combat missions and shot down 11 Japanese fighters. Reclaimed: 05/10/54. (Hill)

JUMBO-, 42-63418, 497TH B/G, 871st B/S, A King of the Show square,50. Ditched on 01/03/45 on return from mission to bomb the Dock area of Nagoya. 150 tons of bombs were dropped this mission, and 14 Japanese fighters were shot down by the combined force of 97 B-29s. (Hill)

THE JANICE E. 42-93947, 500th B/G, 883rd B/S, Z square, no.55. Reclaimed: 07/14/54.

JE REVIENS-, 44-70101, 500th B/G, 881st B/S, Z NO.16.

KANSAS FARMER-, 498th B/G

THE JUMPIN STUD-, 42-63414, 497th B/G, 871st B/S, A square,no.49. Ditched on 07/02/45 on return from Kumamato Urban area raid. 1113 Tons of bombs were dropped and 4 enemy fighters shot down by the combined strike force. (T. Carmichael)

LADY EVE-, 42-65211, 498th B/G, 875th B/S, T square, no.48.B-29 suffered heavy battle damage over the Urban area of South Tokyo on mission no.72, May 23, 1945, a night incendiary strike. The crew bailed out over Iwo, and the crewless B-29 headed out to sea. The next day a Dumbo found Lady Eve about 90 miles from Iwo where she had ditched herself perfectly, without any crew. (Campbell Archives)

LADY EVE II-, 42-24663, 498th B/G, 875th B/S, T square, no.43. Reclaimed: Pyote AB, TX, 09/11/50. (Hill)

LADY MARY ANNA-, 42-24625, 498th B/G, 874th B/S, T square, no.24. returned to states as war weary on 07/12/45. Reclaimed: Tinker AFB 09/11/50. (Campbell)

LADY MARY ANNA-, 42-24625, 498th B/G, 874th B/S, T square, no.24. seen here after her artwork was changed over to the ball and barb design of the 73rd Bomb Wing. This stateside photo was taken at an open house at Tinker Air Force Base in the late 40s. 17 combat missions. (Campbell Archives)

LADY MARY ANNA-, 42-24625, 498th B/G, 874th B/S. T square,no.24. This photo shows the Lady undergoing an engine change on Saipan. (Hill)

LASSIE COME HOME-, 42-24609 498th B/G, 874th B/S, T square, no.21. Aircraft Commander/Pilot: Wagner Dick. On January 14, 1945, mission to bomb the Mitsubishi Aircraft Factory at Naogya. With one engine backfiring over the target, another set fire by fighter attack,and the radio and oxygen systems shot out, she was still able to limp home. She was so badly damaged she'd never fly again. The artwork had been applied by Corporal Guillermo Hernandez. The B-29 was named for the Squadron Commander, Maj. Edward Lass. Salvaged: 03/21/45.

LITTLE BUTCH-, 42-94014, 498th B/G, 873rd B/S, Z square, no.5. Reclaimed: Pyote AB, TX, 09/11/50.

LASSIE II-, 42-24769, 499th B/G, 878th B/S, V square no.27. B-29 was shot down on the January 27, 1945, mission to bomb the Tokyo Urban area. (Carmichael)

KAYO KID-, 44-69987, 498th B/G, 873rd B/S, T no.14.

LEADING LADY-, 500th B/G, Z square.

LI'L ABNER-, 44-69657, 500th B/G, 882nd B/S, Z square, no.36. art is from cartoon strip character.

LI'L LASSIE-, 42-24693, 499th B/G, 878th B/S, V square, no.27. Was one of three B-29s lost on the December 7, 1944, bombing raid over the Tokyo Urban area.

LITTLE FELLOW-, 44-61782, 500th B/G, 881st B/S, Z no.9. Reclaimed:09/09/53.

LITTLE JO-, 44-69932, 498th B/G, 873rd B/S, T square, no.49.

LITTLE GEM-, 42-24596, 497th B/G, 869th B/S, A square 4. Aircraft Commander/Pilot: Capt. O'Neal Archer. On December 3, 1944, bombed through heavy cloud cover on mission number 10. The target was again number 357, the Musashino Aircraft plant, Tokyo. They received the best bombing results at that time over Tokyo. These raids were for the most part incendiary bombing. The art was painted by Corporal Bud Springer.

LITTLE GEM-, 42-24596, 497th B/G, 869th B/S, A square,4. This picture was taken after return to the states. The artwork has been replaced by the barb and ball, Group insignia. Flew 40 combat missions and has 3 Japanese aircraft victories to her credit. (Snodgrass)

LITTLE J0-, 42-24611, 498th B/G, 873rd B/S, T square no.49. "Jo" was shot down April 29, 1945, on mission no. 63, the Miyazaki Airfield at Kyushu. The crew bailed out just after passing the Japanese coastline. Eleven parachutes were seen, but only six crewmen were picked up. Aircraft Commander/Pilot: Fisher. (Ethell)

LUCKY IRISH-, 42-63492, 498th B/G, 874th B/S, T square, no.28. Aircraft Commander/Pilot: Lt. Willaim Kelley. The 497th (color print) had an unusual substitute for mission markers. Lucky Irish used Shamrocks, Starduster used Stars, Thumper used little rabbits riding a bomb, and Destiny's Tots used diapers. This B-29 crashed on 06/07/45 on return from Osaka. (Hill)

LONG DISTANCE-, 42-24544, 498th B/G, 875th B/S, T square, no. 48. On December 3, 1944, mission #10 (target no.357), the Musashino Aircraft Plant, Tokyo, this B-29 was rammed by a Japanese "Tony" class fighter, which cartwheeled and collided with another B-29 following close behind. Aircraft Commander/Pilot: Lt. Donald Dufford flew the damaged Superfortress home safely. It was first thought that the rammings were damaged Japanese fighters, but it was later discovered that the "Taiatari" (body crashing) attacks at this time were not considered suicidal, as their pilots survived these attacks and repeated the ramming tactics. These units of the Japanese Air defense arm were the 10TH, 11TH, and 12TH Shinten Seinten (Heaven Shaking-Air Superiority Unit). Reclaimed: Keesler 05/31/50.(J. Heyer)

LUCKY 'LEVEN'-, 42-24695, 498th B/G, 873rd B/S, T (color print) square, no.6. Aircraft Commander/Pilot: Lt. Barton Yount. Crew named her after a close call, "good choice.." She flew 60 combat missions and survived the war. Lt. Yount flew the first Tokyo mission, November 24, 1944, and her 60th mission on August 14, 1945, the day before the war ended. Reclaimed: Chanute Field, 05/10/49. (Campbell)

LUCKY LYNN-, 42-24591, 497th B/G, 869th B/S, A square, no.3. Aircraft Commander/Pilot: Len Cox. B-29 was named for Cox's daughter, born just before Cox's crew departed the U.S. Artwork done by Lin Decker. This B-29 had to ditch on return from the 01/14/45 mission to Nagoya. The "Lucky Horshoe" should have been turned up instead of down, so that the "Luck" wouldn't spill out. (T. Carmichael)

LUCKY IRISH-, 42-63432, 498th B/G, 874th B/S, T square, no.28. Ditched on 12/03/44 on return from a mission to bomb Tokyo.

LUCKY SEVEN-, 44-61734, 498th B/G, 873rd B/S, T no.6. 6 bomb missions and 7 transport missions, returned to U.S. as war weary On January 11, 1945. Reclaimed: 02/03/54.

LUCKY STRIKES-, 42-94030, 498th B/G, 873rd B/S, T square,no.10. Reclaimed:08/19/54. Named for a popular brand of cigarettes.

MAIDEN'S PRAYER-, 44-61678, 498th B/G, 874th B/S, T no.28. Salvaged: 07/25/51.

MARY ANN-, 42-24550, 499th B/G, 878th B/S, V square,no.27. 10 enemy fighters shot down Final: Unknown.

MARY ANNE-, 42-24693, 499th B/G, 878th B/S, V square, no.27. Final Unknown—off USAF inventory 12/07/44 and assumed lost.

THE MARILYN GAY-, 44-70113, 500th B/G, 883rd B/S, Z no.58.

MACNAMARA'S BAND-, 498th B/G, T square.

MIGHTY FINE-, 44-61655, 498th B/G, 873rd B/S, T no.7. Reclaimed: 05/10/54.

MIGHTY THOR-, 499th B/G, 879th B/S, V square, no. 57. Final: Unknown

MARIANNA RAM-, 44-69732, 497th B/G, 873rd B/S, A square, no.7. Small goats were used to represent her completed bombing missions.(Watts)

MISS HAP-, 42-24774, 497th B/G, A square,no.22. was reported missing and presumed lost on 07/04/45 mission to bomb the Kochi Urban Area. (via M. Bacon)

MISS BEHAVIN-, 42-24655, 497th B/G, 871st B/S, A square, no.46. 01/09/45, rammed by Japanese fighter over Tokyo while bombing the Musashino Aircraft Plant. Two "Tony" class fighters rammed the Superfortress. The Japanese Pilots were Lt. Sukeyuki Tange and Lt. Shoichi Takayama of the 244th Sentai. Lt. Tange was killed, but Takayama survived. Miss Behavin disappeared into the clouds. (via T. Carmichael)

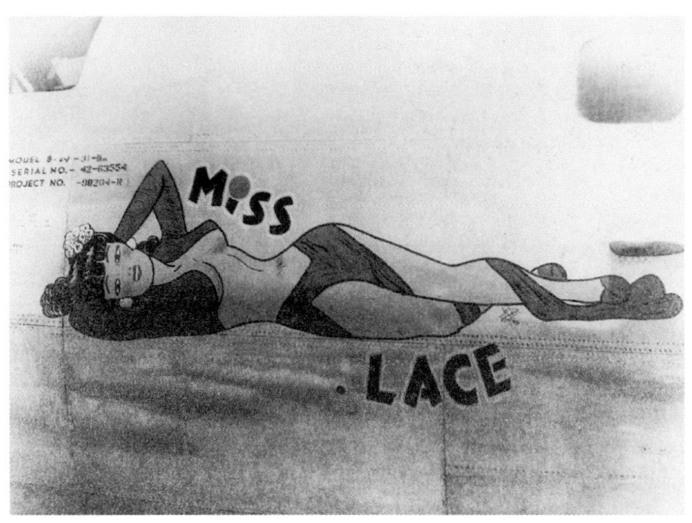

MISS LACE-, 42-63554, 498th B/G, 874th B/S, T square,no.25. Flew 49 combat missions without an abort. The artist's character is from Milton Caniff's cartoon strip, "Terry and the Pirates." (via G. James)

MISS-LEADING-LADY-, 73rd B/W. (W. Walrond)

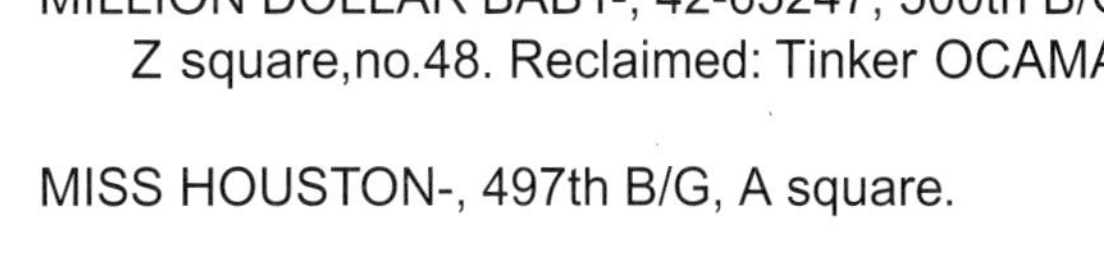

MILLION DOLLAR BABY-, 42-65247, 500th B/G, 883rd B/S, Z square,no.48. Reclaimed: Tinker OCAMA. 10/04/54.

MISS HOUSTON-, 497th B/G, A square.

MRS.TITTYMOUSE-, 42-65212, 498th B/G, 875th B/S, T square, no.42. Shot down by "Flak" on 04/07/45 over Urban Tokyo.

MISSION TO ALBUQUERQUE-, 42-24849, 500th B/G, 881st B/S, Z square, no.3. reported missing on 03/16/45.

THE MOTLEY CREW-, 73rd B/W.

NEW GLORY-, 497th B/G, 870th B/G, A square, no.31. Aircraft Commander/Pilot: Warren Delker. With two engines out and the airstrip at Isley Field socked in by inclement weather, she flew on into Iwo for a week's worth of re pairs.

(LEFT) MRS TITTYMOUSE-, 42-24649, 498th B/G, 875th B/S, T square 47. On December 18, 1944, on mission to Nagoya (mission no. 13) to bomb target no.193, the Mitsubishi Aircraft Engine Plant. The no.3 engine was smoking on the way into the target area. They feathered the number three engine after the bomb run so as not to alert the Japanese fighters that their B-29 had been hit. It was noted that their no.3 fuel transfer pump had been shot out, and they couldn't transfer 700 gallons from the number three fuel tank. When they arrived back on Saipan they had only 20 minutes of fuel remaining. The B-29 crashed on landing, shearing off the wings and breaking the fuselage into four large pieces. It's incredible, but all of the crew walked away from this one. (Campbell) (RIGHT) MRS.TITTYMOUSE-, This is the remains of the B-29 after her crash on 12/18/44. All of the crew walked away from this one. (via J. Heyer)

MUSN'T TOUCH-, 42-24657, 500th B/G, 883rd B/S, Z square, no.45. Ditched on 01/09/45 on return from raid over Tokyo. (via J. Heyer)

NINA ROSS-, 42-24689, 500th B/G, 881st B/S, Z square, no.9. Reclaimed: Tinker, OCAMA, 09/11/50.

OLD IRONSIDES-, 42-24436, 500th B/G,882nd B/S, Z square, no.28. Reclaimed: Pyote AB, TX, 12/21/49.

OREGON EXPRESS-, 44-69969, 498th B/G, 873rd B/S, T no.11. Final: unknown

PACIFIC PIRATE-, 499th B/G, 873rd B/S, V square no.22. Final: Unknown.

PACIFIC UNION-, 42-24595, 497th B/G, 869th B/S, A square 2. rammed by a Japanese fighter, ditched while returning from a mission to Nagoya 01/14/45.

PASSION WAGON-, 42-63524, 498th B/G,875th B/S, Z square, no.52, Reclaimed: Pyote AB, Texas, 09/11/50.

OUR BABY-, 42-24597, 497th B/G, 869th B/S, A square, no. 10. Flew 17 combat missions, 2 enemy fighters destroyed. Final: Unknown. (Campbell Archives)

PACIFIC QUEEN-, 42-63429, 500th B/G, 882nd B/S, Z square, no.35.Reclaimed: 07/14/49. The letters are red and the queen wears a crown of gold. (Campbell)

PATCHES-, 42-24624, 498th B/G, 875th B/S, Y square, no.44. Redesignated and modified to a TB-29 after 48 combat missions and 873.25 applicable flying hours. Reclaimed: Pyote AB, Texas, 09/11/50. (Hill)

PEACE ON EARTH-, 42-63412, 497th B/G, 870th B/S, A square, no.25. right and left side views. (J. Heyer)

POISON LIL 499th B/G, 877th B/S, V square, no.10. (Watts)

PONDEROUS PEG-, 42-63431, 497th B/G, 871st B/S, A square, no.44. Aircraft Commander/Pilot: Major Fred Trickey. B-29 was lost in a mid-air collision with Dixie darling, a square no.45 ser. no. 42-24808 on 02/25/45. They were returning from a raid over the Tokyo dock and urban area, and the residential area was nearly completely destroyed in the resulting firestorm. The mid-air was attributed to poor visibility due to rain. On an earlier mission Maj. Trickey brought "Peg" home with just 3 engines, losing another engine just prior to their landing at Iwo. (via T. Carmichael)

POCAHONTAS-, 42-24601, 498th B/G, 873rd B/S, T square, no.23. Aircraft Commander Pilot: Lt Webster. Flew the first mission and the last mission against the Japanese Empire for a total of 56 combat missions. Corporal Guillermo Hernandez had the honor of painting the artwork.

PRIDE OF THE YANKEES-, 42-24676, 500th B/G, 882nd B/S, Z square, no.24.Aircraft Commander/Pilot: Cecil E. Tackett flew aircraft in from the states on November 6, 1944. Her first mission over the Japanese Empire was on November 27, 1944, mission no.8, Tokyo and the Dock area sector. During her career she flew 61 combat missions, 3 POW supply drops, and went through 16 engine changes. On January 23, 1945, mission to Nagoya (Mission no.21,[the secondary target this trip]) she lost two engines on the same wing and still made it back to Saipan. Pride of the Yankees made it back to the states with three crewmen, but was later scrapped as surplus and war weary. She was the only B-29 to make it back to Saipan twice on only two engines. Corporal Henry Johnson applied the artwork to this B-29—he was nicknamed the "Drowsey Swede." He had named the B-29 in honor of the Hollywood baseball movie starring James Stewart. (M. Hill)

PRIDE OF THE YANKEES-, This is a view of the battle damage sustained on the January 23, 1945, mission to Nagoya.

PRIDE OF TUCSON-, 42-65370, Salvaged at Davis Monthan on 07/14/54. T square. (via J. Heyer)

PUNCHIN'JUDY-, 42-65219, 500th B/G, 881st B/S, Z square, no.10. Reclaimed: Tinker OCAMA. 03/31/51. 50 combat missions. (Hill)

PUNCHIN'JUDY-, 42-65219, this later view shows the ball and barb insignia of the 73rd Bomb Wing. 500th B/G, 881st B/S,T square, no.10. Reclaimed: Tinker: 03/31/51. (Campbell Archives)

(LEFT) RAMBLIN ROSCOE-, 42-24664, 500th B/G, 882nd B/S, Z square, no.23. During the Tokyo raid on April 13, 1945 (mission no.42) they bombed the arsenal area. 10.7 square miles of city burned out due to this night incendiary attack. Japanese fighters shot up two of her engines, as well as damaging the main landing gear. The B-29 made it back to a night landing on Iwo, but she hit a truck and went through a tent before an embankment brought Roscoe to a sudden halt. This is a frontal view of the results. (Campbell Archives) (RIGHT) RAMBLIN'ROSCOE- 42-24664,500th B/G, 882nd B/S, Z square, no.23. This is a view of the right hand side of Roscoe after her rough landing on April 13/14, 1945. (Campbell Archives)

RAMBLIN'ROSCOE-, 42-24664, 500th B/G, 882nd B/S, Z square, no.23. Flying next to the Constant Nymph, on mission to bomb Tokyo, early in April of 1945. (Watts)

RAMP QUEEN-, 42-63513, 499th B/G, 877th B/S, V square,no.5. B-29-26-BA. This B-29 was shot down over the Tokyo Arsenal on 05/25/45. (W. Walrond)

RAUNCHY RAMBLER-, 500th B/G, Z square, no.56. Seen here in the bombing mission over Yokohama on 29 May 1945.

READY-, 42-24751, 500tH B/G.

RED HOT RIDER-, 42-65338, 497th B/G, B-29-31-MO, A square. Reclaimed: Davis-Monthan 05/10/54. (M. Hill)

RAIDEN MAIDEN-, 42-63522, 498th B/G,873rd B/S, T square,no.9. Reclaimed: Pyote AB, TX,09/11/50.

RAMBLIN'ROSCOE II-, 42-93649, 500th B/G, 882nd B/S, Z square. 4-166

READY BETTIE-, 499th B/G, 878th B/S, V square no.37.

READY TEDDY-, 497th B/G, A square.

RIPPLE SPRINGS-, 500th B/G,883rd B/S.

THE ROC-, 499th B/G, 878th B/S, V square, no.33. Final unknown.

ROUND TRIP-, 499th B/G, 878th B/S, A square, no.26. Was destroyed on the ground during a Japanese air attack on Saipan, December 7, 1944. A bomb blew the flight deck right off of this Superfortress. (J. Heyer) 4-175

ROUND TRIP-, on December 7,1944, the Japanese sent fighters and bombers to attack Saipan, Round Trip. A square no.26, seen here, took a hit in the cockpit, instantly shearing it off from the rest of the Superfortress, almost as neat a cut as the blade at Davis-Monthan. The B-29 had been sitting on the hardstand—lucky for the crew they weren't rotating out on a mission when the attack came. (J. Heyer)

ROSALIA ROCKET-, 42-34656, 500th B/G, 881st B/S, Z square, no.1. Abandoned on return from Tokyo, 12/03/44.

ROUND TRIP-, A head-on view of this B-29 shows just how vulnerable they are when hit by a bomb. (J. Heyer)

ROVER BOYS EXPRESS-, 499th B/G, 878th B/S, V square, no.27. Shot down by fighters on the January 27, 1945, mission to Tokyo's urban Dock area, mission no. 22. 5 crewmembers survived the POW camp there in Tokyo, and were liberated on August 29, 1945. Aircraft Commander/Pilot:"Snuffy" Smith. Their Wichita built B-29 was no.771. The crew was kept at the infamous Kampei Tai in solitary confinement, then moved to the Omori POW camp at the southern edge of Tokyo. Upon their release they were taken aboard the hospital ship "Benevolence", resting at anchor in Tokyo Bay.

RUSTY DUSTY-, 499th B/G, 878th B/S, V square.

RUTHLESS-, 42-94027, 498th B/G, 873rd B/S, T square, no.1. Reclaimed: 08/19/54.

SALLY DELLE-, 44-61623, 498th B/G, 873rd B/S, T 12/16. Reclaimed: 09/28/54.

SAND BAG-, 500th B/G, Z square.

SATAN'S SISTER-, 499th B/G, V square.

SATAN'S SISTER II-, 42-63453, 499th B/G, 877th B/G, V square, no.4. Reclaimed:06/30/46.

SEA BISCUIT-, 497th B/G, A square.

SALVO SALLY-, 42-24699, 499th B/G, 877th B/S, V square, no.9. Ditched on 04/28/45 mission to bomb Izumi Airfield. (R. Pickett)

SENTIMENTAL JOURNEY-, 44-70147, 498th B/G, 874th B/S, T no.31. The Flight Engineer—George Wallace—is a State Governor today. On display at Pima Air Museum, Tucson, Arizona. (D. Stroud)

SHADY LADY-, 42-24619, 497th B/G, 870th B/S, A square, no.23. Flew photo recon missions over the Mitsubishi Aircraft Engine plant, mission no. 12, target no.193, at Nagoya, December 13, 1944. On return from a different mission on a later date, she ran off the runway and into the mud. On the 01/27/45 mission she was shot down over Tokyo. (Campbell)

SHIRLEY DEE-, 42-63443, 500th B/G, 874th B/S, T square, no.37. Reclaimed:Pyote AB, 09/11/50. Seen here flying into target under enemy radar. The only chance of early detection of this flight would be the picket ships off the coast of Japan. (Morrison)

SHARON SUE-, 42-63435, 500th B/G. 881st B/S, Z square, no.3/19. Salvaged: 05/31/46.

THE SILVER STREAK-, 499th B/G, 879th B/S, V square no.55.

SILVER THUNDER-, 500th B/G, Z square.

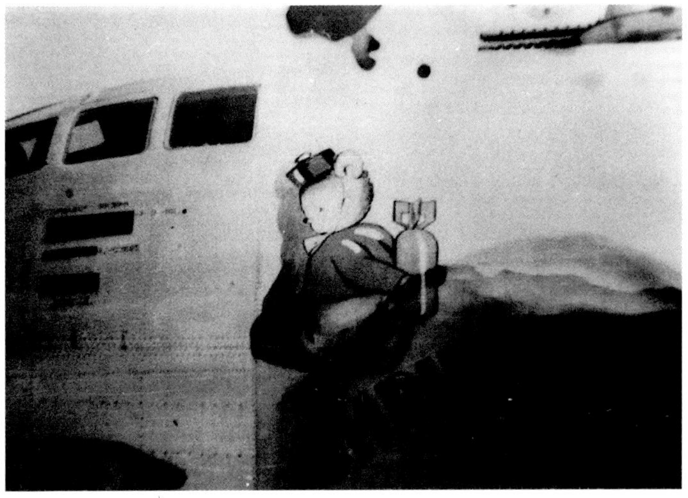

THE SHRIMPER-, 497th B/G, 870th B/S, A square, no.33. Ditched on return from Nagoya mission, 05/14/45. (via J. Heyer)

SKYSCRAPPER-, 42-24599, 497th B/G, 869th B/S, A square,no.9. Aircraft Commander/Pilot: Lt. J.T. Garvin. B-29-41-BW. This B-29 was purchased with war bonds by the employees of Guaranty Trust Bank of New York on November 10, 1944. She flew over Tokyo to gather weather information, as well as to check the accuracy of the Japanese Anti-Aircraft gunners. On November 24, 1944, she was destroyed (BELOW) on the ground by "Zeke" fighters in a strafing attack on Isley Field, Tinian. (Campbell)

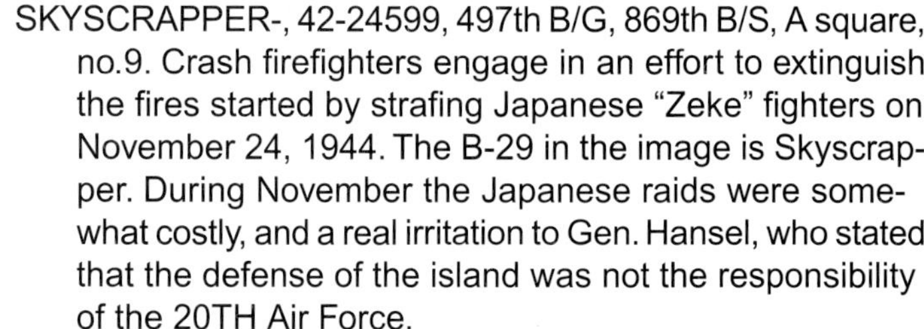

SKYSCRAPPER-, 42-24599, 497th B/G, 869th B/S, A square, no.9. Crash firefighters engage in an effort to extinguish the fires started by strafing Japanese "Zeke" fighters on November 24, 1944. The B-29 in the image is Skyscrapper. During November the Japanese raids were somewhat costly, and a real irritation to Gen. Hansel, who stated that the defense of the island was not the responsibility of the 20TH Air Force.

SKYSCRAPPER II-, 42-63463, 497th B/G, 869th B/S, A square, no.9, On February 20, 1945, the Scrapper was destroyed when a B-29 got out of control and slammed into her empennage, severing the tail section.

SLICK DICK-, 42-24700, 500th B/G, 882nd B/S, V square, no.33. Reclaimed: 12/06/50.

SNAFU-PER-FORT-, 42-63435, 500th B/G, 881st B/S, Z square, no 3/19. Reclaimed: 05/31/46.

STAR DUSTER-, 42-24782, 499th B/G, 878th B/S, V square, no.31. Class 26, 06/17/54.

SLEEPY TIME GAL-, 42-63469, 498th B/G,874th B/S, T square no.33. Reclaimed:

SOUTHERN BELLE-,42-63478, 498th B/G, 874th B/S, T square, no. 35. Reclaimed: 09/11/50. (Campbell Archives).

SPECIAL DELIVERY-, 42-24628, 497th B/G, 870th B/S, A square, no.29. Aircraft Commander/Pilot: Ed Campbell.

STAR DUSTER-, 42-93858, 497th B/G, 870th B/S, A square. Had miniature stars to mark her missions. The name of the respective target would be centered in the star. (J. Heyer)

STING SHIFT-, 44-61699, 500th B/G, 882nd B/S, Z no.30. Reclaimed: 05/10/54. (Hill)

STRIPPED FOR ACTION-, 42-63466, 497th B/G, 870th B/S, A square,no.32. Reclaimed: 12/6/50. (Campbell Archives)

SUPINE SUE-, 42-24653, 500th B/G, 883rd B/S, Z. The International square, no.42. 1st B-29 in the Figure. 500th B/G to arrive on Saipan, McClellan. 08/25/50.

SU SU BABY-, 42-24721, 500th B/G, 881st,B/S, Z square, no.46. Ditched on 03/07/45 mission to bomb the Tokyo Urban area, was on weather patrol and ran out of fuel. Out of a crew of 12, 8 were rescued, but 2 died later. Aircraft Commander/Pilot: Capt. Theodore Holmes (Hill)

SU SU BABY-, 42-24721, seen here at rest while undergoing service and maintenance checks. In the Western Pacific there were a lot of natural elements that gave grief to the Superfortress, not the least of which was corrosion from saltwater. (G. James)

SUPER WABBIT-, 42-65220, 499th B/G, 877th B/S, V square, no.28. missing presumed shot down over Tokyo, on November, 27, 1944. (via B. Davis) 4-209

"SWEAT'ER OUT'-, 42-63471, 497 th B/G, 871st B/S, A square,no.47. Aircraft Commander/Pilot: Walker. Reclaimed: 09/11/50. (via B. Davis)

TAILWIND-, 42-24761, 500th B/G, 345th B/S, Z square,no.51. Reclaimed; Pyote AB, TX, 09/15/53. (M. Bacon)

TANAKA TERMITE-, 42-24749, 498th B/G, 874th B/S, T square,no.29. Flew 60 missions before being sent home as war weary in August 1945. Reclaimed: Pyote AB, TX, 06/24/54. (J. Heyer)

SWEET ELOISE-, 499th B/G, 878th B/S, V square. This B-29 deserves to be mentioned. The name isn't on the cockpit section, but rather along the tail gunner's compartment. The tail gunner was confirmed to the status of Ace. He had 5 confirmed kills and 2 probables. He was the top scoring tailgunner in the Pacific. His wife was named Eloise. He was John Floyd Sullivan, shooting down his first "Zero" fighter on the 1st mission over Tokyo, November 24, 1944.

SWEET SIXTEEN-, 44-61666, 498th B/G, 873rd B/S, T no.16. Abandoned over Iwo on 09/07/45 on returning from a mission to bomb Toyokawa Arsenal.

SWEET SUE-, 498th B/G, 875th B/S, T square no.42. Abandoned over Iwo.

TALE OF TEXAS D0-, 497th B/G, A square.

TEN UNDER PARR-, 497th B/G, A square.

TERRIBLE TERRY-, 42-63425, 497th B/G, 870th B/S, A square,no.41. Formerly "The Dragon Lady".Reclaimed:11/01/48.

TEXAS DOLL-, 42-24627, 497th B/G, 870th B/S, A square,no.27. She saw two crews through their required missions. Delivered to Saipan by Capt. James Arnold on 10/29/44, then passed on to Aircraft Commander/ Pilot: Lt. Edward Cutler. Reclaimed: Pyote AB, TX, 09/11/50. (Campbell)

TEASER-, 42-63526, 497th B/G, A square. This B-29 was ditched on return from the Nagoya mission on 03/24/45.

TERRIBLE TERRY-, (aka)
THE DRAGON LADY-, 42-63425, pictured here after losing the port inboard prop. This aircraft is equipped with the new 4-gunned top turret. She was renamed to Terrible Terry when the 73rd Bomb Wing's Barb and ball was applied. Reclaimed:11/01/48. (Campbell Archives)

THREE FEATHERS-, 42-24671, 500th B/G, 883rd B/S, Z square,no.49. Reclaimed: Tinker, OCAMA. 10/04/54. 12 "Hump" trips, 3 combat missions shown. (B. Davis)

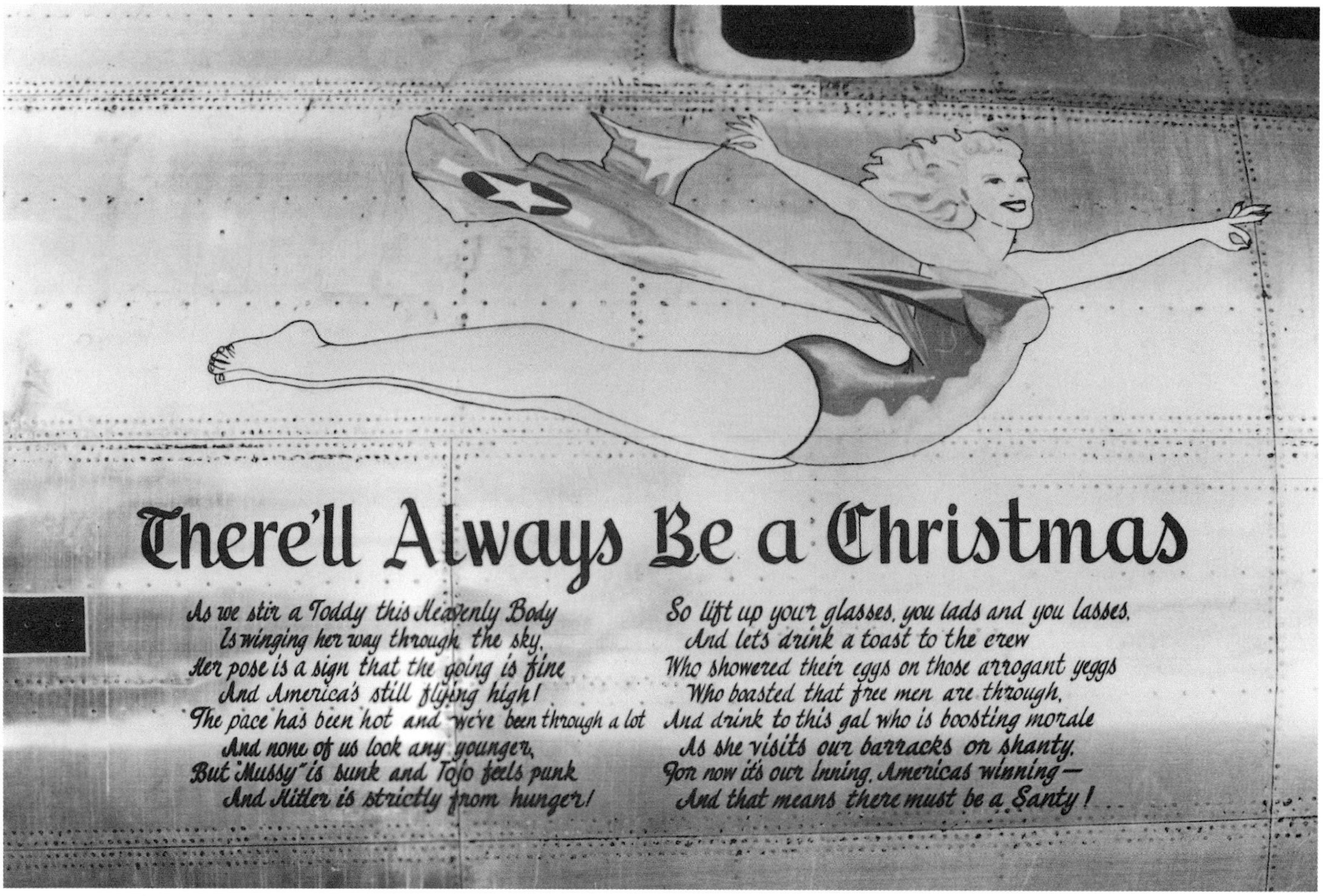

THERE'LL ALWAYS BE A CHRISTMAS-, 42-24643, 500th B/G, 881st B/S, Z square,no.5. Reclaimed: Tinker, OCAMA. 09/11/50. (Campbell)

THUMPER-, 42-64623, 497th B/G, 870th B/S, A square,no.21. Flew 40 missions over the Japanese Empire. (Davis)

THUMPER-, 42-64623, 497th B/G, 870th B/S, A square,no.21. Seen here after going home with 40 missions to her credit.

THREE FEATHERS III-, 500th B/G, 883rd B/S, Z square.

TOKYO LOCAL-, 42-24687, 500th B/G, 882nd B/S, Z square,no.26. Ditched 12/13/44 on return from mission to bomb Nogoya's aircraft industrial engine plant. After turning away from the target area she dropped out of formation with one engine windmilling and another trailing smoke. Aircraft Commander/Pilot:Charles Grise and crew were lost.

TOKYO LOCAL-, 42-24587, 500th B/G, 882nd B/S, Z square,no.26. Final: unknown.

TOMMY HAWK-, 42-24755, 498th B/G, 873rd B/S, T square,no.28. Reclaimed: Pyote AB, TX,09/15/53.

TUMBLING TUMBLEWEEDS-, 42-93959, 498th B/G, 875th B/S, T square,no.55. Reclaimed: Pyote AB,TX, 09/11/50.

TWENTIETH CENTURY LTD.-, 500th B/G, 881st B/S.

THUNDERHEAD-, 42-24641, 497th B/G, 871st B/S, A square,no.43. Reclaimed:Hickham 11/10/48.

TOKYO TWISTER-, 42-24682, 499th B/G, 877th B/S, V square,no.5. On 01/27/45 she crashed on Saipan after returning from mission to Tokyo's Aircraft Engine industrial complex. (B. Davis)

TORCHY-, 42-24646, 498th B/G, 874th B/S, T square,no.27. Reclaimed: McClellan 01/05/50. (Bill Davis)

UMBRIAGO,DAT'S MY BOY-, 42-63447, 499th B/G, 879th B/S, V square,no.50. Ditched 12/13/44 on return from bombing the Aircraft Engine Industrial Works at Nagoya.

UMBRIAGO III-, 499th B/G. V square.

UNCLE TOM'S CABIN-, 42-24642, 498th B/G, 874th B/S, T square,no.25. Rammed three times over Tokyo on 12/27/44—the target was the Musashino aircraft factory.

VANISHING RAE-, 44-69706, 498th B/G, 875th B/S, T square,no.53.

WABASH CANNONBALL-, 42-24743, 500th B/G, 882nd B/S, Z square,no.25. Reclaimed: Davis-Monthan, 05/10/54.

WAR WEARY-, 42-24633, 499th B/G, 877th B/S, V square, no.6. Reclaimed: Pyote AB, TX, 09/11/50.

WILLIE MAE-, 42-24663, 498th B/G, 875th B/G, T square, no.43. Reclaimed: Pyote AB, TX, 09/11/50.

WUGGED WASCAL-, 42-24658, 499th B/G, 877th B/S, V square, no.3. Ditched on the 01/09/45 mission to bomb the Tokyo aircraft engine industrial complex.

TWENTIETH CENTURY SWEETHEART-, 73rd B/W.

WADDY'S WAGON-, 42-24598, 497th B/G, 869th B/S, A square,no.5. Ditched on return from mission to Tokyo, 01/09/45. Aircraft Commander/Pilot:Waddy Young, a graduate of Oklahoma University at the outbreak of hostilities. The artwork depicts a caricature of his crewmen. (Campbell Archives, OKC.)

WHEEL'N'DEAL-, 42-24604, 497th B/G, 870th B/S, A square,no.24. Missing in action due to weather strike on 04/13/45. (Campbell Archives) 4-244

WEREWOLF-, 42-63423, 497th B/G, 870th B/S, A square,no.28. Exploded on 01/27/46.(Campbell Archives)

THE WICHITA WITCH-, 42-24654, 498th B/G, 874th B/S, T square, no.30. Destroyed on the ground at Tinian December 25, 1944, by strafing Japanese fighters. (Campbell Archives)

YANKEE MADE-, 42-24651, 499th B/G, 879th B/S, V square,no.41. Reclaimed: Tinker on 09/11/50.

During the months of November and December 1944, the Japanese, in a last final attempt to stem the flow of bombers out of Iwo and Tinian, took to throwing steady strafing attacks on the B-29s at their home bases. The last major attack was on December 25, 1944, Christmas night. These raids inflicted a fair amount of damage, but were unable to stop the saturation bombings.

During these strafing attacks, at night the skies would be lit up with anti aircraft fire. Some of the Fighters got through, but they paid a price. (J. Heyer, USMC)

Lloyd Avery's Irish Lassie was the survivor of two consecutive rammings by Japanese fighters on January 27, 1945.

B-29s of the 500th Bomb Group unload their lethal cargo over Yokohama, May 29, 1945. The bombs for this mission were the M47A2 incendiary type bombs. They generated a great deal of heat and started numerous fires wherever they fell. (via J. Heyer)

This B-29 of the 497th Bomb Group ran off the end of the runway at Motoyama Field on return from the March 10, 1945, Tokyo Raid. (via Bill Davis)

These B-29s of the 499th Bomb Group are flying through what was referred to as "Intense Flak". The little black clouds of smoke are much more menacing than they look. Nagoya was the target, and it had the reputation of being, "the city that would not die". (Campbell Archives)

These B-29s of the 498th Bomb Group are passing a very familiar landmark, Mt. Fuji. This reference point was well known by any and all B-29 crews who participated in the different Tokyo missions. (via Bill Davis)

These 498th Bomb Group B-29s are post April 1945 ships. Marked with the larger, more visible markers, they drone into the target area at medium altitude. They are from the 873rd Bomb Squadron. T no.5 is Joltin Josie, and T no.6 is Lucky'Leven'. (via Gary James)

In the upper left corner, a lone Superfortress from the 9th Bomb Group flies high over the Island of Tinian. This island saw more B-29s at one time than any other place in history. (OCAMA/HO-Tinker)

With Mt. Fuji as a scenic backdrop, these B-29s of the 498th Bomb Group are again headed in towards Tokyo. T square 21 (the lower left B-29) is Lassie Come Home. (via Morrison)

With fires raging below, another wave of B-29s comes in to keep pounding the target. The saturation bombing leveled and blackened mile after mile of the Japanese Empire, The B-29 in the center left of image is A no.10, and goes by the name "Our Baby". (Morrison)

When Allied ground forces began to enter the former Japanese Empire, they were able to see first hand the havoc and destruction the bombers applied to Japanese factories, cities, and other targets. This roofless storage hangar at the Nagoya industrial aircraft factory is an example. (Campbell Archives)

When the B-29s unloaded their salvos of bombs on Japanese shipping, the view here explains it all. This "sitting duck" is well bracketed by the spread of bombs as it vainly tries to escape it's fate. (Campbell Archives)

Here we get a close up look at a Nakajima fighter. This fighter was captured and now bears the insignia of the Chinese. (Campbell Archives)

These Japanese,"Tony" class fighters were a real pest to the bomber formations. With their ramming techniques refined to an art they could easily slice through a tail or rudder and cause major damage to the B-29s, and, in many cases, bring the Superfortress down. (Campbell Archives)

During the strafing attacks on Saipan during the months of November and December 1944, the Japanese Zero fighters would form up and come in hot and heavy, causing as much damage as possible. Here we see a flight of "Zero" fighters departing on a raid, and getting a royal send off from their ground crews. (Campbell Archives)

A "Zero" fighter takes to the air on another mission. Whether it is to be a ramming mission, an intercept, or if it is on its way to strafe Saipan is not known. But the clean lines of this fighter made it almost unbeatable in the earlier years of the war. (Campbell Archives)

BAKA BOMB-one of the many adversaries in the night skies over the Japanese Empire. A Suicide weapon first developed for use against our ships, it was turned towards the B-29s. This rocket-propelled bomb was flown to within a few miles of the target by a mother ship—usually a "Betty Bomber"—and then released. It carried 500 pounds of TNT. It was only 19 feet 10 inches in length, and it had a range of 55 miles and flew at speeds up to 535 miles per hour. The first captured Bakas were found on Okinawa, as seen here. The rocket at night was a luminous glow, eerie in appearance, and first thought to be an aircraft being shot down in flames, but the speed was much too fast. One account by a tailgunner stated that he felt like he was being chased by a ball of fire. The Baka's exhaust was the mysterious ball of fire. (Campbell Archives)

The 73rd Bomb Wing and her Groups, Squadrons, Pilots, Copilots, and Crewmen made a tremendous contribution to the 20th Air Force during the Second World War. Already in the Marianas, the 73rd had a head start on the bombing campaigns against the Empire of Japan. There were many victories, but those victories all had a price. The lives of our men in the air were put at risk almost daily. Many of the heroic acts of these men went unrecorded in history. The most important factor to remember about these men is that they were Americans all, and they felt the calling.

Ground crewmen align fuel drums on Tinian. The Superfortress being serviced is from the 427TH bomb Group. This type of hard labor was a daily routine on the bases in the central and western pacific. (Campbell Archives)

Two B-29s flying high over the overcast. Some dark acrid smoke is coming up through the solid white cloud cover, and above in the stratosphere you can make out the jet stream. (Morrison)

Row after Row of B-29s make ready for their POW supply drops. The barely visible tail indicators show Group markings from nearly every Bomb Wing. (Morrison)

On Guam as on Saipan, when the Americans took over there were bits and pieces of the former occupants everywhere. This Nakajima fighter abandoned in a rush to pull out, stresses the attrition the Allies were causing on the Japanese. (Campbell)

Sgt. Elmer Moore stands next to this downed Japanese fighter on Guam. The Japanese had lost many aircraft and were to lose many more. (Campbell Archives)

At war's end the Allies were to come upon many a scene like this one. Damaged bits of the Japanese Air Arm lay in ruin from one end of the Japanese Empire to the other, including the satellite islands and domains. (Campbell Archives)

More damaged and discarded Japanese fighters, once proudly serving the Japanese Empire, sit in disarray and neglect. Their purpose denied, their cause defeated. (Hill)

LITTLE GEM- Having returned to the states as war weary, she sits proudly with many of the men and women who had worked on her, supported, and financed her. (Bob Snodgrass)

Chapter 5:
THE 313th BOMBARDMENT WING MINING, DAVEY JONE'S LOCKER, AND THE ATOMIC BOMB

The 313th Bombardment Wing, the third B-29 Wing to be formed, was activated on April 23, 1944. They trained and prepared their Groups for combat op erations, and began setting up operations at North Field, Tinian, on December 24, 1944.

The 313th had 4 Bomb Groups, as did the majority of the other Bomb Wings. They were the 6th Bomb Group, the 9th Bomb Group, and two newly formed Groups, the 504th & 505th Bomb Groups. Their B-29s started arriving at North Field, Tinian, in December, and continued to arrive into February of 1945. Their first mission, which was actually more of a training mission, was against Truk and Japanese occupied Maug.

Their markings would be a large black circle, with the Group's assigned letter centered in the circle. "R" for the 6th Bomb Group, "X" for the 9th Bomb Group, "E" for the 504th Bomb Group, and "W" for the 505th Bomb Group. In May of 1945, the 509th Composite Group was added to the 313th Bomb Wing. They also added two new squadrons, the 393rd Bomb Squadron and the 320th Troop Carrier Squadron.

The 320th TCS started arriving with C-54s at Tinian on May 29, 1945.The mission of the 509th Composite Group was to deliver the first Atomic Bomb to the Empire of Japan. Therefore, all of their operations were shrouded in secrecy.

To facilitate this, they all used the markings of the 6th Bomb Group, an "R" inside a circle. In late March of 1945 the 313th Bomb Wing started an active mining campaign against Japanese shipping. Every harbor, channel, and water mass close by would be mined, both in Japan and along the coast of Korea. This aerial blockade was history's largest and most successful aerial blockade.

In the last six months of the war, more Japanese shipping tonnage was sent to the bottom by aerial mines than any other force, including the U.S. Navy's Submarine Fleet. Records indicate that as of August 10, 1945, between 700,000 & 1,000,000 tons of Japanese shipping had been either sunk or damaged by mines laid by the 313th Bomb Wing, with a total of 14,000 mines dropped. These results shortened the war considerably.

The Squadrons assigned to the 313th were as follows: as of 27 January 1945, the 6th Bomb Group had the 24th Bomb Squadron, the 39th Bomb Sqdn. and the 40th Bomb Squadron. The 9th Bomb Group had the 1st Bomb Squadron, the 5th Bomb Squadron, and the 99th Bomb Squadron on 25 January 1945. The 504th Bomb Group, as of January 16th, 1945, had the 398th Bomb Squadron, the 421st Bomb Squadron, and the 680th Bomb Squadron, which arrived in June of 1945. The 505th Bomb Group's squadrons had arrived a little earlier, and they assumed their duties on December 30, 1944. They were the 482nd Bomb Squadron, 483rd Bomb Squadron, and the 484th Bomb Squadron.

OPPOSITE: BAINBRIDGE BELLE-, 504th B/G, 5th B/S. The pin-up appears to be almost nude, but has a very scanty swimsuit on. Based at North Field, Tinian. (W. Walrond)

AIRCRAFT of the 313th BOMB WING (VERY/HEAVY)

ANNE GARRY III-, 6th B/G, 39TH B/S. Aircraft Commander/ Pilot: Arthur M. Clay. On May 26, 1945, with two engines lost due to hits by "Flak", she returned to Iwo where the crew bailed out over home turf. Clay was the only crew-member to get wet that day. He turned the stricken B-29 back out to sea, set the auto-pilot, and bailed out. Then, a P-61 "Blackwidow" night fighter shot the crewless B-29 to ribbons till she plunged into the sea.
Anne Garry was a B-17, and Anne Garry II was Clay's 2nd ship, a B-24 Liberator he flew as a flight instructor. Named after Clay's mother's maiden name, Anne Garry III had 33 combat missions and sank two enemy ships during her career.

ANNE GARRY IV-, 6th B/G, 39th B/S. Aircraft Commander/ Pilot: Arthur Clay. This was Clay's fourth aircraft. While being flown on mission over Japan with a different crew aboard, the B-29 was shot down.

ANNE GARRY V-, 6th B/G, 39th B/S. Aircraft Commander/ Pilot: Arthur M. Clay. Clay's final ship, this Superfortress most probably fell victim to the salvage blade, because by that time the war had ended.

B.A.BIRD-, 42-93896, 9th B/G, 1st B/S, Reclaimed: Pyote Field, Texas, 09/11/50.

BANANA BOAT-, 44-69802, R, 6th B/G, survived WWII but was a combat loss in Korea ,09/12/52.

BATAAN AVENGER-, 44-69753, R, 6th B/G, Salvaged: 09/ 06/49.

BATTLIN'BETTY-, R, 6th B/G. Carries the Group's Pirate centered in a triangle insignia—common to all aircraft in the group.

BATTLIN' BONNIE-, 42-24907, X, 9th B/G, 1st B/S, No.15. Reclaimed: 05/10/49.

BALL OF FIRE 42-65344, 505th B/G. (M. Hill)

BATTLIN'BONNIE II-,44-87737, X, 9th B/G, 1st B/S.No.15. Surveyed: 06/ 02/52. (Witt)

BETTER-N-NUTIN-, 42-24524, X, 9th B/G.25 hump flights & 27 bomb missions, 8 to the heartland of Japan. (J. Root)

BIG ASS BIRD-, 9th B/G, flew 22 combat missions, returned to U.S. as war weary.

BIG MIKE-, 313th B/W

BIG STINK-, 44-27354, X, 509th Composite Group (C/G) No.90, 393rd B/S. Reclaimed: Tinker, AFB, 10/10/54.

BIG TIME OPERATOR-, 42-24791, X, 9th B/G, 1st B/S. Aircraft Commander/Pilot: Capt. E. Shenefiel (Wichita) The nose section is on display at Boeing Seattle museum. Final: Robbins, 04/28/46 to 10/31/50. Scrapped: 12/06/50 Flew 46 missions, 2 aborts.

BIG WHEEL, The-, 42-65283, X, 9th B/G, 5th B/S, No.33. Reclaimed: crashed from Shimonoseki 03/31/45.

BLIND DATE-, R, 6th B/G, 24th B/S. Lost on mission over Tokyo,1945.

BUCCANEER-, R, 6th B/G.

CABOOSE-, X, 9th B/G.

CHARLIE'S HAUNT-, X, 9th B/G.

CHIP'S NIP CLIPPER-, X, 9th B/G

COUNTRY GENTLEMAN-,42-24793, W, 505th B/G, 482nd B/S, No.1. After bombing the Nikajima Plant at Ota, Feb. 10, 1945, this B-29 was damaged when its brakes failed upon landing. MIA-05/14/45.

CORAL QUEEN-, E, 504th B/G.

COX'S ARMY-, 42-63544, X, 9th B/G, 5th B/S, No.26. Aircraft Commander/ Pilot: Capt. Cox. (Bell) 31 combat missions, 6 aborts. Final: Hill AFB, 01/01/48 to 01/04/51. Scrapped: 01/04/51.

BOCKSCAR-, 44-27297, 509th C/G, 393rd B/S. Aircraft Commander/Pilot: Capt. Fred Bock. On July 24, 1945, scored a direct hit on the Sumitoma Aluminum Plant, resulting in a ripple effect throughout the plant. Maj. Charles Sweeney piloted "Bockscar" on August 9, 1945 to deliver "Fatman", the 2nd Atomic Bomb, released over Nagasaki. One of only two aircraft to have ever dropped an Atom Bomb during wartime. Named for Capt. F. Bock. A/C. (J. Heyer)

CULTURED VULTURE-, 42-24901, L, 6th B/G, 39th B/S, No.25. Participated in March 1945 bombing mission to Tokyo, Mission # 7. The bomb mission destroyed 15.8 square miles, 10 percent of Tokyo. There were no casualties over the target on this mission. Reclaimed: 07/15/52.

DANGEROUS LADY-, 42-24823, W, 505th B/G, 483rd B/S, No.25. Reclaimed: Pyote Field, TX, 09/15/53.

DARLING DONNA III-,42-24820, X, 19th B/G, 99th B/S. No.34. (Wichita) 43 combat missions. This B-29, very low on fuel, made a one engine landing on Tinian, 06/05/45, on return from mission # 47 (the Kobe Urban Area). Combined forces destroyed 2.9 square miles, 25 percent of Kobe. There were heavy fighter attacks against the bomber force, and 16 enemy fighters were destroyed, while 7 B-29s were damaged. Reclaimed: 09/15/53.

DARLING DONNA II-, X, 19th B/G. 99th B/S, No.34. Seen here returning from mission to land. In the foreground, the hulk of what once had been a mainstay in taking the island, this tank sits as a monument to the U.S. Marines who gave their lives to take this tiny Atoll.

DAVE'S DREAM-, 44-27354, X, 509th C/G, 393rd B/S. No. 90. Dropped A Bomb during the Bikini Island tests, was one of the 5 "Silverplates", the name given to modified B-29s that could carry an Atomic Bomb. Dave's Dream dropped a Fat Man bomb on 73 ships anchored off Bikini, severely damaging 9 and sinking 5 of the ships. Reclaimed: 10/10/54.

DESTINY'S TOT-, 42-65284, X, 9th B/G, 1 & 5 B/S. No.19 & 34. Aircraft Commander/Pilot: Capt. C.L. Collins. (Martin) 40 combat missions, 6 aborts. Also flown by William L. Wienert & crew, a lead crew for the 5th B/S. Escorted Sheafer crew back to Iwo after they received heavy battle damage over Nagoya, April 7, 1945. Reclaimed: Hill AFB, 09/14/54.

DINA MIGHT-, 42-65280, E, 504th B/G, 421st B/S, No. 29. Crashed on Iwo on return from mission to bomb Tokyo, 05/23/45. (M. Hill)

DINAH MIGHT-, 42-65286, X, 9th B/G, 1st B/S, No.9.(Martin) Aircraft Commander/Pilot: Lt. L.G. Butler.Was first B-29 to land on Iwo Jima,03/10/45. This piece of real estate was expensive, for over four and a half thousand Americans died. The little island started earning dividends when, two weeks later, there was an island ditching due to a faulty fuel pump. Malo's crew was flown to Guam for a news conference that was widely broadcast throughout the United States. Flew 42 combat missions, 1 abort. Final: Aberdeen 05/267/46. (Hill)

"DOC" SAID ALL I NEEDED WAS AFFECTION-,42-65266, E, 504th B/G, (G. James)

DOTTIE'S DILEMMA-, 42-24796, X, 9th B/G, 1st & 5th B/S. No.31. 34 combat missions, 5 aborts. went off of runway on landing, summarily scrapped. Started her career with the 9th B/G as no.16. Surveyed: 07/06/45. (Campbell)

"DRAGON LADY"-, 42-93892, X, 9th B/G, 99th B/S,(Renton). Flew 41 combat missions, with 6 aborts. Flying Herrington to Mather, lost two engines and was forced to land at Amarillo Army Air field. Lost another engine out of Mather and returned to Amarillo AAF again. Final: OCAMA/Tinker, 06/28/50 to 08/28/50. Scrapped: 09/11/50.

The DEACON'S DELIGHT-,42-24818, K, 505th B/G, 484th B/S. B-29 ditched on 02/10/45.

DEARLY BELOVED-, 44-70069, R, 6th B/G, 40th B/S, No.59. (The Ramp Tramp) 24 combat missions, 9 were stenciled with milk bottles denoting "milk runs".

DEUCES WILD-, 44-69809, R, 6th B/G.

DIRTY GERTIE-, L, 6th B/G.

DOC'S DEADLY DOSE-, 42-24780, E, 504th B/G. Completed 44 combat missions.

DOTTIE'S BABY-, W, 505th B/G, 485th B/S. Aircraft Commander/Pilot: Paul Mason flew the roughest Tokyo mission to date. Mason had almost all his instruments shot out by heavy "Flak", and the whole crew made it back to home base.

EARLY BIRD-, 42-63556, X, 9th B/G, 5th B/S, No.25. Reclaimed: 09/11/50.

EARLY BIRD-, 44-86303, L, 6th B/G,

EL PAJARO DE LA GUERRA-, 42-24874, L, 6th B/G, 24th B/S. Reclaimed: 09/22/53.

ENOLA GAY took to the air at 02:45 AM, August 6, 1945. She began her bomb run from an altitude of 31,600 feet. Her speed was 328 miles per hour. At 09:15 AM, the history of aerial warfare would be changed forever—at least far as it was known at present.
The first Atomic Bomb was released over the target, "Hiroshima", Japan. The nuclear age had begun. "Little Boy" was the name of the weapon. "Fat Man" was the name of the Atomic Bomb dropped on Nagasaki. The "Manhatten Project" had been successful. Final: Smithsonian Institution, Washington, DC.(Campbell Archives, OKC.)

ENOLA GAY-, 44-86292, R, 509th C/G, 393rd B/S, No.82. Named after Pilot, Paul Tibbits' mother. Col. Tibbets ordered the name put on. This B-29 was guarded at all times.

EARTHQUAKE McGOON-, 42-24686, L, 6th B/G, 40th B/S, No.51. Reclaimed: 09/15/53. (Watts)

THE ERNIE PYLE-, 44-70018, E, 504th B/G, These two views of Ernie Pyle show first the completed, painted, and named B-29 in flight. This image gives the reader a good look at the ground scanning radar dome on the belly of the aircraft. (Walrond)

ERNIE PYLE'S MILKWAGON-, L, 6th B/G. Named in honor of War Correspondent & Writer Ernie Pyle, who wrote of "Brave Men". He was, of course, referring to the U.S. Servicemen in the Pacific. He was Killed by a sniper in the S.W. Pacific during World War II. (D. Fisher)

THE ERNIE PYLE-, 44-70018, E, 504th B/G, Ernie Pyle stands on the left of the B-29, posing for his own photo with his portrait on the nose. His name has yet to be added. (W. Walrond)

LEFT & OPPOSITE: FLAGSHIP-, 42-63504, E, 504th B/G, 398th B/S, No.2 (4 views) was adorned with characters of the crewmen painted at each of the crewmembers' stations. The insignia for the Seabees was also painted on her fuselage. (Bob Snodgrass)

FOREVER AMBER II-, 42-69839, L, 6th B/G, 40th B/S, No.4. Was hit by "Flak" on the Kobe mission, tearing a gaping hole in the right side and tearing out the rear bomb bay. Against all possibilities, she made it back to Saipan and landed safely, never to fly again. (J. Heyer)

FLAK ALLEY SALLY-, 42-24878, L, 6th B/G, 39th B/S, No.33. Diverted to Iwo due to low fuel with 5 other B-29s in March of 1945 on return from the Kobe mission.

FRENCH'S KALBAZIC WAGON-, 44-70011, X, 9th B/G, 99th B/S, No.54.

FULL HOUSE-, 44-27298, Arrow, 509th C/G, 393rd B/S, No.83. Aircraft Commander/Pilot: Capt. Ralph Taylor. This B-29 hit the target at the Sumitoma Copper Refinery the day the "Hiroshima" bomb was dropped. Full House was checking out the secondary targets at Kokura and Nagasaki. On August 9, 1945, she was the standby ship on Iwo.

CITY OF GAINSVILLE-, R, 6th B/G, Aircraft Commander/Pilot: James Maguire. Flew 23 combat missions.

GOD'S WILL-, 42-24831, X, 9th B/G, 1st B/S, No.2. Aircraft Commander/Pilot: Capt. Dean A. Fling. Name was chosen after a mission over Truk in the Carolines. The art work which adorned this B-29 was a Gold Cross and a gleaming Silver Sword on a Purple Shield. The B-29 flew 34 combat missions with 4 aborts. On June 5, 1945, mission to Kobe, GW, was bounced by Japanese fighters. The cockpit rapidly filled with smoke, the results coming from materials which had been ignited by the projectiles fired by the fighters. The junction box over the pilot's head had been pulverized, causing a loss of communication with the remaining crew stations. There was a huge hole in the nose above the bombardier's head. Engines 1 & 2 had to be feathered. The crew was credited with two Japanese fighters shot down and two probables. Upon landing at Iwo, both left tires blew out, causing the B-29 to veer into a volcanic ashen bank beside the runway. The entire crew survived to return home. Final: Pyote, Texas.

GRAND SLAM-, L, 6th B/G, 40th B/S.

GRIDER GAL-, 42-24884, R, 6th B/G, 39th B/S, No.36. Aircraft Commander/Pilot: Capt. Charles Besore. Painted with the Bust of Pirate Jean Lafitte, reflecting back on the Group's long time service in the Panama Canal Zone in the early 1920s and 1930s. No other art was allowed at this time, yet names were added onto the streamers. This B-29 had 43 combat missions and 3 aircraft victories to her credit—2 Japanese and 1 American. Reclaimed: 08/02/54. 5-61 &5-61A

HEAVENLY FLOWER-, 42-94025, X, 9th B/G, 99th B/S. No.51.

HIGH "EH" DOC !-, ..-..823, K, 505th B/G, 483rd B/S.

GOIN'JESSIE-, 42-24856, X, 9th B/G, 5th B/S, No.30. Aircraft Commander/Pilot: Capt. J.D. Fleming (Wichita) dropped the two-millionth ton of bombs during World War II, and flew 50 combat missions with 0 aborts. (M. Hill)

GOOD DEAL-, 42-24852, E, 504th B/G, Artwork was applied by a U.S. Marine named Scott. Some of his other works are Island Queen, Dina Might, and Satan's Lady. Reclaimed:07/07/48.

THE GREAT ARTISTE-, 44-27354, L, 6th B/G, 39th B/S, No.89. Assigned to 509th Composite Group. Aircraft Commander/Pilot: Maj. Charles "Chuck" Sweeney. Loaded with blast gauges and other equipment, and engaged as the instrument ship on the Hiroshima mission. Recorded all critical data and the effects of the actual bomb detonation. Repeated her performance on the Nagasaki mission. The great blinding flash stunned the crew, as did the strange colored sky, which was illuminated by a purplish white light. The mushroom cloud was red and white at the top, gray and black at it's base, climbing higher on up past that of the Great Artiste. Salvaged: Goose Bay. (W. Watts)

"HADES EX ALTO" 505th B/G, 483rd B/S, no.41. Hell from Below-, a crew shot, and a shot that they took of her (RIGHT) at the end of the runway after a slight miscalculation. (Strekel)

HERD OF BALD GOATS-, W, 505th B/G, 482nd B/S. No.14. (J. Heyer, USMC)

HONORABLE SAD SAKI K, 505th B/G. Ben Kuroki, a Nebraska born Japanese American, flew as a gunner. He was noted as a man with great courage.

HONORABLE TNT WAGON-, 42-63484, W, 505th B/G, 484th B/S, on May 7, 1945, ran into stiff opposition when the 505TH bombed Ota Airfield. 50 to 60 fighters swarmed all over them, and 2 B-29s were lost. TNT's gunners claimed 3 fighters shot down, an "Irving", a "Jack", and a "Tojo". (Campbell)

INDIAN MAID-, 42-24806, E, 504th B/G, was painted by Navy Seabees on Tinian. Reclaimed: 11/07/50. (G. James)

ISLAND QUEEN-, E, 504th B/G.

HON.SPY REPORT-, 42-24876, X, 9th B/G, 99th B/S, No.52. (Wichita) 39 combat missions, 4 aborts. Aircraft was damaged from Caldwell, and crashed on take-off 05/19/44. First 9th B/G aircraft to achieve 400 hours on all four engines. Final: Robbins 07/26/46 to 10/31/50. Scrapped:12/ 6/50

HOUSTON FLYER-, X, 9th B/G.

IN THE MOOD-, 42-24826, 314th B/W.

INDIANA-, 42-63546, X, 9th B/G, 99th B/S. 9 missions 0 aborts. B-29 lost on Kobe mission 03/16/45.

INDIANA II-, 42-94010, X, 9th B/G, 99th B/S. 34 combat missions 2 aborts. Final: Tinker OCAMA

IRISH LULLABY-, 42-24830, R, 6th B/G, 24th B/S.

ISLAND GIRL-, W, 505th B/G. 482nd B/S, No.5.

JABBITT-, R, 509th C/G.

JABBITT II-, R, 509th C/G.

JABBITT III-, 44-27303, R,509th C/G. on August 5, 1945. While the first Atomic Bomb was on its way to Hiroshima, Jabbitt III was enroute to Kokura and Nagasaki, the secondary targets.

JAKE'S JALOPY-, 44-69985, X, 9th B/G, 99th B/S, No.53. (Wichita) 29 combat missions, 0 aborts

McClellan, Scrapped: 09-14-48.

JACKPOT-, 42-24797, K, 505th B/G, 484th B/S Aircraft Commander/Pilot: Lt. Warren. On March 16, 1945, after a combined mission over Kobe and Nagoya. Out of 290 B-29s, the only loss was Jackpot. With two engines shot out, they limped away from the target to an area about 250 miles off the coastline, where she finally had to ditch.

KRO"S KIDS-, 42-24788, L, 6th B/G.

JO/INDIANA-, 42-63546, X, 9th B/G, 99th B/S, No.39.

MIA Kobe, 03/16/45.

JOLLY ROGER-, 42-63444, R, 6th B/G.

JOOK GIRL-, 42-65225, W, 505th B/G Crashed Feb.10, 1945, crashed take-off for a mission to Ota for the 2nd strike, and the 2nd Empire mission.

JUDY ANN, The-, 42-94025, X, 9th B/G, 99th B/S (Renton) 35 combat missions, 2 aborts. Final: Unknown

JUKE'S JALOPY, X, 9th B/G.

KRISTY ANN-, 42-93886, X, 9th B/G, 1st B/S, No.6. (Renton) 41 combat missions,1 abort Reclaimed: Tinker 06/28/50. Scrapped: 09/11/50.

LADY ANNABELLE-, R, 6th B/G..

LADY JAYNE-, 44-69874, X, 9th B/G, 5th B/S,No.21. (Wichita) 25 combat missions, 3 aborts. Final: Pyote Field, TX, 12/ 31/46 to 09/22/53. Scrapped: 10/21/53.

LADY JEAN-, L, 6th B/G. 39th B/S. Aircraft Commander/Pi lot: Jack Henshaw.

LADY LUCK-, R, 6th B/G.

LASSY TOO-, E, 504th B/G.

LIL'IODINE-, 42-24875, X, 9th B/G, 1st B/S, No.7 Aircraft Commander/Pilot: Lt. M. Hardgrave(Wichita). 6 combat missions, 0 aborts. On mission no. 7, March 9, 1945, to bomb the Tokyo Urban area, this B-29 was lost due to lack of fuel, having to ditch. Entire crew was rescued.

"LAGGIN" DRAGON-, 44-86347, Q, 509th C/G, 393rd B/S. No.95. Reclaimed: 09/14/54.

LAGGIN' WAGON-, 44-65390, 509th C/G, was also assigned to 98th B/G in Korea.

LADY BETH-, R, 6th B/G.

LIFE OF RILEY, The-, 42-65241, E, 504th B/G. Ditched on return from Nagoya on March 25, 1945. (M. Hill)

LIL'IODINE II-, 44-69748, X, 9th B/G,1st B/S, No.3. Aircraft Commander/Pilot: Lt. M. Hardgrave (Wichita built). 6 combat missions, 0 aborts. B-29 was lost on 03/24/45 mission to Nagoya (mission #12), the Mitsubishi Aircraft Engine Plant. This plant was bombed 7 different times to achieve the final results of 94 percent destruction. Crew MIA.

LIMBER RICHARD-, 44-70072, X, 9th B/G, 99th B/S, No.55. (Wichita) 30 combat missions, 1 abort. Final: Mt. Home AFB, 12/23/53 to 07/18/54. Scrapped.

LITTLE EVIL-, 42-94025, X, 9th B/G, 99th B/S, No.51. Reclaimed: 08/19/54.

LITTLE JEFF-, 44-69855, L, 6th B/G, 40th B/S, No,65. Salvaged: 04/01/49.

LIVE WIRE-, 42-24853, X, 9th B/G, 1st B/S, No.10. (Wichita built) 2 combat missions,0 aborts. Reassigned, crashed on Iwo 04/25/45.

LONG WINDED-, 42-63509, X, 9th B/G, 99th B/S, No.50. (Bell built) 21 combat missions, 1 abort. Aircraft Commander/Pilot: Lt. J.R. Lewis. B-29 lost on May 22, 1945, (mission #42) mining the Shimoneski Straits. Crew had to bail out, and only 3 were rescued by a U.S. Navy submarine.

LOOK HOMEWARD ANGEL-, L, 6th B/G. Aircraft Commander/Pilot & mission leader: Maj. John Layson. On July 15, 1945, mission to mine Rashin, had to fly on extra power in order to complete their mission as planned. This seriously cut their fuel reserves. Their problems soon multiplied when they had one engine cut out and another engine commence to backfiring violently. Maj. Layson guided his B-29 to Okinawa and was the first B-29 to land on the Bolo fighter strip.

LUCKY LADY-, 42-24863, E, 504th B/G, 398th B/S, No.12. (J. Heyer)

MARY ANNA-, 42-65253, K, 505th B/G, 482nd B/S.

LIL'SPOOK-, 44-86346 W, 509th B/G.

MISS MINOOKY-, 42-24764, X, 9th B/G, 5th B/S,No.43.

MONA-, ..-..283, W, 505th B/G, 483rd B/S.

MYA'S DRAGON-, 42-94042, L, 6th B/G, 39th B/S, No.40. Reclaimed 08/19/54.

LUCKY LADY-, 42-34584, X, 9th B/G,5th B/S,No. flew 10 trips over the "Hump", 13 bombing missions and 2 enemy fighters shot down on her scoreboard. A fine record.

LUCKY LEVEN-, 42-93951, X, 9th B/G, 1st B/S,No.8. (Renton built)

LUCKY "LEVEN"-, 42-93956, X, 9th B/G, 1st B/S, No.8. (Renton) 37 combat missions, 6 aborts. Final: Davis Montham AFB Arizona. Reclaimed: 05/10/54.

LUCKY STRIKE-, L, 6th B/G, 39th B/S. Lost on mission to Tokyo.

MAN O'WAR II -, 42-63511, X, 9th B/G, 1st B/S,No.17 31 combat missions,1 abort.(Bell) Final: Lowery 8-23-45 to 07/31/46 Scrapped.

MAN O'WAR II-, 44-69975, X, 9th B/G, 1st B/S,No.1 transferred to Army 05/23/46.

MARIANNA BELLE-, 44-69883, X, 9th B/G, 1st B/S, No.1 Aircraft Commander/Pilot: Capt. Roy F. Nighswonger. (Wichita built) 35 combat missions, 4 aborts. B-29 lost on 08/07/45 over Iwo when crew had to bail out because of severe battle damage received over Toyokawa, Japan.

MIA From Kyushu Air Field.05/07/45.

MARY ANNA II-, 44-69964, W, 505th B/G. Shot down over Tokyo, 05/25/45

MAXIMUM LOAD-, 42-63563, X, 9th B/G flew an incendiary bombing mission to Tokyo using the M-47 incendiary bombs on April 13, 1945.The fire bombing missions were quite an effective tool due to the damage that was inflicted to wooden structures by fire bombings

MISS AMERICA "62-, 42-65281-, L, 6th B/G, 24th B/S.No.11 Reclaimed Post 1954.

MISS MI-NOOKIE-, 44-69764, X, 9th B/G, 99th B/S.No.43. (Wichita built) 39 combat missions, 3 aborts. Final: OCAMA-Tinker, 06/30/46 to 07/27/48.Scrapped: 07/27/48.

MY NAKED-, 44-63725, R, 509th C/G, 393rd B/S.

NECESSARY EVIL-, 44-86291, R, 509th C/G, 393rd B/S, No.91. Salvaged: 07/14/54.

NIP FINALE-, X, 9th B/G.

NECESSARY EVIL-, 44-27291, X, 509th C/G, 393rd B/S, No.91. was the first camera ship to follow the Enola Gay on the first dropping of the Atomic bomb on Hiroshima. Aircraft Commander and Pilot: Maj. George Marquardt. Reclaimed: Hill AFB, 08/19/54. (M. Hill)

NIP NEMESIS-, 44-69733, X, 9th B/G,5th B/S,No.24. (Wichita built) 37 combat missions, 2 aborts. Final: Tinker 06/30/46 to 06/28/48. Scrapped: 07/ 28/49.

9TH SEABEES-,

OLD FAITHFUL-, L, 6th B/G, 40th B/S. Lost on mining mission,03/09/45.

PAPPY'S PULLMAN-, E, 504th B/G.

PASSION WAGON-, 42-63524, K, 505th B/G. Also served with the 73rd B/W, 498th B/G, 875th B/S as T square 53.

NIP CLIPPER-, 42-63512, X, 9th B/G, 5th B/S,No.23 Aircraft Commander/ Pilot: Lt. Geo. Keller. Keller was killed when his B-29 was shot down by "Flak" over Yawata 08/08/45 on Shimonoseki mission. Remainder of crew bailed out and were captured and sent to POW Camps.(Bell built). (Hill)

NEXT OBJECTIVE-, 44-27299, K, 509th C/G, 393rd B/S. No.86. Aircraft Commander/Pilot: Lt. Ralph DeVore. The little fat men symbols denote the "Fat Man" missions that this B-29 worked in conjunction with on the Bikini Island tests. Salvaged: Biggs Field, 05-26-49.

OLD 574-, 42-63574, X, 9th B/G, 99th B/S,No.41 (Bell built) 38 combat missions, 3 aborts. Final: Hill AFB, Feb 28, 1946. Seen here after take-off, with the cemetery and Old Glory flying proudly in the sky. Scrapped 01/04/51.

OLD 900-, 42-24900, X, 9th B/G, 99th B/S. (Wichita built) 46 combat missions, 2 aborts. Final: Pyote Air Field, TX, 1948 to 1953, Scrapped:09/23, 1953.

THE ONE YOU LOVE-, 44-69727, E, 504th B/G, During the Korean war, she was assigned to the 98th B/G where her name was changed to "Hot to Trot".

OMAHA ONE MORE TIME-, 42-24851, E, 504th B/G. Surveyed:04/12/45

PACIFIC PLAYBOYS-, 44-24704, K, 505th B/G, 482nd B/S.

PADRE & HIS ANGELS-, XX-XX839, K, 505th B/G,483rd B/S. After mission to bomb Japan's heartland, B-29 received severe damage to control surfaces and landing gear was damaged, forcing the aircraft to make a wheels up landing. The instability of the controls made control of the B-29 next to impossible to land easily, the results of which we see here. (M. Bacon)

PASSION WAGON-, 42-94043, X, 9th B/G, 1st B/S, No.12. Aircraft Commander/Pilot: Capt. J.Q. Payne (Renton built) 32 combat missions, 2 aborts. Final: Howard AFB, Panama. Scrapped 1949.

THE PEACEMAKER-, L, 6th B/G, 40th B/S. Lost on mining mission 03/27/45.

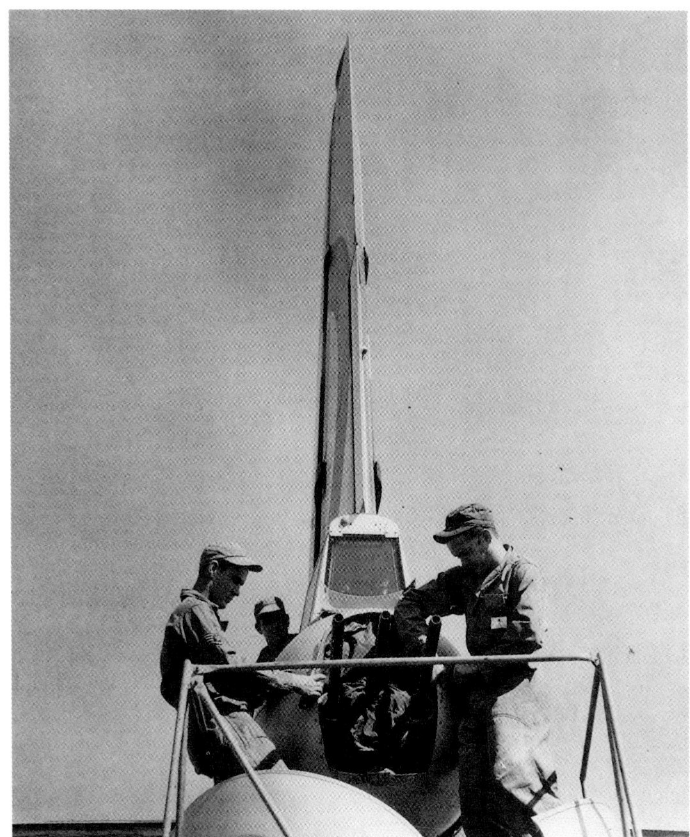

PURPLE HEARTLESS-, 44-69760, X, 9th B/G, 5th B/S, No.20. (Wichita built) Armorers checking out the business end of "Heartless", one can see how menacing this sight can be. 44 combat missions, 2 aborts. Final: Lowery AFB, 03/11/49 to 05/24/49. Scrapped:05/24/49. (John "Socks" Heyer USMC)

READY TEDDY-, 42-63561,X, 9th B/G, 5th B/S, No.29. On May 25, 1945, mission to mine the Shimonseki Straits, was forced to land at Kadena on return leg of the mission, which at this time was a dirt fighter strip. The B-29 blew a tire, but there was no other damage to the aircraft. 43 combat missions, 3 aborts. Final: Memphis Tenn. 05/26/46. (James)

REAMATROID-, 44-69672, L, 6th B/G, 39th B/S, No.33. Flew mining missions to seaports in Korea, staging these missions at Iwo. In August of 1945 made POW supply drops, PW SUPPLIES was stenciled in large letters under the wing. The B-29 bears the large white disk with red streamer, used by the entire Group.

SITTIN PRETTY-, 42-24881, E, 504th B/G. Aircraft Commander/Pilot: Capt. Worde. 16 combat missions. On May 29, 1945, on mission to bomb Honshu Island and the city of Yokohama, the B-29 was hit in the number 2 engine and the B-29 had momentary loss of control and veered to the left underneath the other B-29s in the formation, just as they were releasing their bombs. As luck would have it, none of the bombs hit Sitting Pretty. The Pilot had to reduce power on the no.3 and no.4 engines to straighten out their stricken Superfortress. In normal conditions one engine can pull a B-29 in flight, but not in the condition she was in. The crew had to bail out. B-29 crashed into a hill on the Chiba peninsula and was seen to explode. The crew was captured and taken to Ofuna POW Camp. They were liberated on Sept.1, 1945 and loaded into a C-54 cargo plane to start their long Journey home. (Campbell Archives)

PATCHES-, 42-24822, X, 9th B/G, 5th B/S, No.18. Later changed to No.33.(Wichita built) 33 combat missions, 4 aborts. Sustained damage over Nagoya and landed at Iwo on 04/07/45. Flew again on 05/24/45. Final: Davis Montham AFB, AZ, where she was scrapped: 05/10/54.

PEACHY-, 42-94508, E, 504th B/G, 482nd B/S.

QUEEN BEE-, 42-24840, X, 9th B/G, 1st B/S,No.3. Flew 14 combat missions,3 aborts. Crew bailed out 04/29/45, 380 miles North of Iwo. All rescued except Radar Navigator. (Submarine Rescue)

RATTLE N'ROLL-, 44-61803, R, 6th B/G, 40th B/S, No.55. Salvaged at Kelly AFB, 06/30/49.

SAD TOMATO-, 42-65285, X, 9th B/G,5th B/S, No.22. (Martin built) Flew 40 combat missions, 6 aborts. Flew numerous "Super Dumbo", SAR (Search and Rescue) missions. Final: Davis Montham AFB, AZ. 10/29/45. Scrapped: 05/10/54.

SASSY LASSY-, 42-24867, K, 505th B/G, B-29 was shot down by fighters over Ota, Japan, February 10, 1944. Ota was home for the Nickajima Aircraft plant which built the Ki-84 fighter.

SATAN'S LADY-, 42-24779, E, 504th B/G, Shot down 04/25/45.

SHASTA-, 44-41549, L, 504th B/G, 24th B/S, No.2.

SLAVE GIRL-, 44-27307, B-29-35-MO, R, 6th B/G, 39th B/S. Reclaimed:Harmon,08/05/48. (Campbell Archives)

SLICK'S CHICKS-, 42-24784, K, 505th B/G, 483rd B/S. Lost in mid-air collision with another B-29 on mission to Ota on February 10, 1945. Both aircraft were destroyed. This B-29 had been dedicated to the 92nd Naval Construction Battalion. (M. Hill)

SNUGGLEBUNNY-, 44-69667, L, 6th B/G, 39th B/S,No.32. Flew 85 combat missions during WW II, and another 55 during the Korean war with the 98th Bomb Group for a total of 140 missions. (M. Bacon)

STRAIGHT FLUSH-, 44-27301, 509th C/G,393rd B/S, No.85. flew as a weather ship on the Hiroshima mission to drop the first Atomic Bomb. Salvaged: Davis Montham AFB, 07/14/54. (Campbell)

THE SPEARHEAD-, 44-69975, X, 9th B/G,1st B/S, No.1. Aircraft Commander/Pilot: Capt. Dave Rogan. 25 combat missions, 1 abort. Dedicated to the 5th Marine Division, whose men fought and died to take the Island of Iwo Jima. This B-29 was previously named "Man O'War II". Final: Aberdeen Proving Grounds in Maryland, used as a ground target and eventually scrapped on 05/23/46. (Heyer USMC)

THE SPIRIT OF F.D.R.-, 44-69846, K, 504th B/G, 398th B/S, No.4. limped back to Tinian with more than half the tail shot off. Completed over 20 combat missions. F.D.R. was later lost on a low level incendiary mission on 11/10/44. (Campbell)

STRANGE CARGO-, 44-27300, 509th C/G, 393rd B/S, No.73. Aircraft Commander/Pilot: Lt. Joseph Westover. Bombed the Mitsubishi Heavy Industrial complex on July 24, 1945. Final: Unknown. (Campbell)

THE STARDUSTER-, 42-94067, X, 9th B/G,5th B/S, No.35. (Renton built) Flew 28 combat missions, 1 abort. Final: Pyote AB, TX, 06/23/54. (M. Hill)

THUMPER-, 42-63536, E, 504th B/G, from the Disney cartoon classic Bambi one of several B-29s with the same name. (M. Hill)

SHE HASTA-, E, 504th B/G.

SKY BLUE-, W, 504th B/G.

SOME PUNKINS-, L, 6th B/G, 24th B/S, No.13.

SPEAGLE EAGLE-, L, 6th B/G,

SPIRIT OF MINNEAPOLIS-, X, 9th B/G.

SPOOK-, 44-86346, 509th C/G, 393rd B/S.

SWEET JENNY LEE-, X, 9th B/G.

SWEET SUE-, 44-70112, X, 9th B/G, 1st B/S,No.5. (Wichita built) Flew 16 combat missions no aborts. Final: Kelly AFB, 11/09/50. Scrapped: 09/19/54.

T-N-TEENY-, 42-65278, X, 9th B/G, 1st B/S, No.5.

T-N-TEENY II-, 44-69920, X, 9th B/G, 1st B/S, No.3. 5-171

THUNDERIN'LORETTA-, 42-24913, X, 9th B/G, 1st B/S, No.13. (Wichita built) flew 22 combat missions, 3 aborts. Suffered severe structural damage due to thermal, crashed 05/19/45.

TINNY ANNE-, 44-69811, X, 9th B/G, 1st B/S, No.7. (Wichita built) Flew 13 combat missions, 2 aborts. crashed 05/27/45, hit by "Flak" over Shimonoseki Straits, MIA.

TINNY ANN-, L, 6th B/G.

TOJO'S NIGHTMARE-, 44-70124, R, 6th B/G, 40th B/S, No.60.

TRIGGER MORTIS-, L, 6th B/G, 39th B/S, No.28.

TOKYO-KO-, 42-24859, X, 9th B/G, 1st & 5th B/S No.17 and 32. Flew 38 combat missions, 5 aborts Reclaimed: 05/07/54. Final: Robbins AFB, Scrapped: 05/07/54. (M. Hill)

TOP SECRET-, 44-27302, 509th C/G, 393rd B/S, No.72. Salvaged: Davis Montham AFB AZ. 07/14/54. This B-29 was used in the Bikini Island Bomb tests. (Campbell Archives)

TRIGGER MORTIS II-, R, 6th B/G.

TWENTY-NINTH USNCR-, E, 504th B/G,

UMBRIAGO-, 42-63545, X, 9th B/G, 5th B/S. No.28. Aircraft Commander/Pilot: Lt. Sullivan (Bell built) B-29 lost on mission no. 21, April 15, 1945, to bomb the Kawasaki Urban Area. Destroyed 2.15 square miles, 44 percent of city. There was heavy "Flak" and fighter cover. 4 crews were shot down.

UMBRIAGO II-, 42-94041, E, 504th B/G, (Renton built) 7 combat missions, 3 aborts lost 07/26/45, target unknown.

UP AN' ATOM-, 44-27304, K, 509th C/G, 393rd B/S,No.88 Reclaimed: Hamilton, 09/14/54.

VIRGINIA DARE-, X, 9th B/G.

WARSAW PIGEON-, 44-69849, X, 9th B/G, 5th B?S, No.27. (Wichita built) Flew 35 combat missions, 2 aborts. Final OCAMA- Tinker AFB, 06/30/46. Scrapped:10/04/54. 5-189

20th CENTURY LIMITED-, 44-61797, X, 9th B/G, 5th B/S. (Renton built) 6 combat missions, 1 abort. Final: Smoky Hill. Scrapped:12/04/52. (Walrond)

THE UNINVITED-, 44-69754, X, 9th B/G, 99th B/S, No.42. flew 40 combat missions, 4 aborts. Had wheels up landing in late September, as seen here. Sent to Clark AB, PI. Condemned: 04/19/46. (Campbell Archives)

VISITING FIREMEN-, E, 504th B/G, 680th B/S,No.66 (M. Hill)

WHITE HUNTRESS-, 42-24776, L, 6th B/G, 39th B/S, No.57. Veered off runway in landing accident, was repaired and flew again. The positioning doesn't look too promising, but the ground crews and other attached servicemen could deal with this minor problem. Final: Tinker 05/05/54.

THE WOLF PACK-, X, 9th B/G, also served in Korea war with same artwork. (Bacon)

THE WORRY BIRD-, L, 6th B/G. (W. Watts)

WILLIAM ALLEN WHITE-, 44-70078, W, 505th B/G. Salvaged: 04/24/47.

WILLIAM ALLEN WHITE-, 44-70121, X, 9th B/G, 99th B/S, No.50 7 combat missions,1 abort. was reassigned. Final: Pyote Field, TX, 09/25/53.

THE WOLF WAGON-, R, 6th B/G.

WAMBLI-, 313th B/G. shows 8 bomb missions, two into the Japanese Heartland. (Hill)

This view of North Field, Tinian, the largest air base in the world, was home to literally hundreds of B-29s. Each B-29 had a hardstand for dispersal purposes. Then there were visiting B-29s on the ramp and aprons. You can see miles of B-29s inside their protective revetments. (Campbell Archives).

From atop this grassy knoll overlooking North Field you can see all the B-29 activity. The B-29 in the foreground is just turning up and sending her complementary spray of dust and dirt into her wake. The B-29 in the foreground is named Reamitroid, and was assigned to the 313th B/W, 6th B/G, 40th B/S, ser. no. 44-69672. She is on assignment to the 509th C/G and bears the circle "R" on her tail with the no.33. In this photo there are B-29s for as far as the eye can see. (Campbell Archives)

Not enough thanks can be expressed to the "Little Friends" This P-47N Thunderbolt is based at le Shima with the 318TH Fighter Group. With the coming of long range drop tanks, to give the Jug more range, the B-29s would have fighter escort in their shorter missions out of Guam and Tinian.

One of the B-29 gunners is seen here cleaning the barrel of one of his .50 Cal. machine guns. They had to make sure the guns were in top condition for each mission to assure that they would all function properly when needed.

This view of a B-29 on Tinian from the 509TH composite Group shows the clean lines of the Superfortress. On closer inspection you can see the Plexiglas blisters on each side of the B-29 used by the central Fire Control Gunner to sight these two menacing .50 Cal. machine guns on the center line of aircraft.

This B-29, seen here at Isley Field, Tinian, is somewhat of a mystery. The aircraft bears a symbolic piece of artwork dedicating her to the 38th Seabees detachment. This was a common practice for the B-29 crews out of thanks and well-earned respect for the job they had done building and maintaining their airfield.

When a B-29 fell from the sky, the results were almost always the same, the only variable being "Fire". The evidence here reveals no carbon scoring that would be present in a crash with fire. Only the window frame is identifiable in this scene from a crash site, as one of the ground personnel gives the wreckage a once over.

When the B-29s came back from many missions with damage inflicted by aerial combat, sometimes the damage was apparent, and other times not. In shot up tires or wheels, brakes sometimes failed, and other times, well, the runway just wasn't long enough to come to a complete stop. This shot taken at Tinian gives a look at a pretty big job ahead (getting this aircraft repaired), but she flew again and was later lost when she had to ditch 150 miles off the coastline. The crew was rescued from the former B-29 "Jackpot" after being adrift for two days.

This B-29 of the 504th B/G. 398th B/S, veered off the runway on Tinian on return from a mission. This crash was worse than many of the accidents of this sort because the no.1 engine in the left of the image seems to have broken down from its mount, possibly causing damage to the main spar of the aircraft.

On return from a mission to bomb Ota on February 7, 1945, this B-29 crashed on landing. Once a B-29 started burning almost all one could do was help save the crew. The B-29s would burn very hot and very fast.

On a lighter side, many signs and murals were made to make a humorous note to getting the word or explanations out to our men. This mural depicts the complete contents of a mission, from mission briefing to mission completed.

Another B-29 over the edge of the runway. The damage to the right wing is evident as the outer 8 feet of wing is crumpled pretty badly. The volcanic rock and coral was extremely hard on the B-29s in these kind of landings.

This is a frontal view of the same crash. One would imagine that the tail gunner got a big thrill, since it appears that he was left high and dry.

The side view of this B-29 of the 505th B/G, 482nd B/S shows it met with the same grief as a lot of the other B-29s that either overshot their runway or had mechanical failures of one kind or another, and wound up with the nose down. Most were repairable, but in a lot of cases there were major structural members stressed outside the limits and tolerances allowed.

After a B-29 became irreparable, then came the salvage stage. Anything of use would be cannibalized off of the existing airframe, engines, spare parts, assemblies, propellers—anything that could be used to keep the other B-29s in a state of airworthiness. Guns, Turrets, and wheels and tires—anything of use. Then what was left would end up like this, in the scrap pile. This kind of image is saddening to those of us who love the old aircraft.

American aircraft weren't the only aircraft to end up in a dump sight. These remnants of Japanese aircraft left over from before the Americans took the island were pushed out of the way to make room for the bombers that would replace the smaller fighters that had previously occupied the field.

The "Conga Line". These B-29s are rowed up and readied for the POW supply drop campaign at the closing days of the war and extended into September of 1945. All of the squadrons, wings, and bomb groups would take an active role in this campaign. The word on the lips of our men at arms was that nothing was too good for our boys.

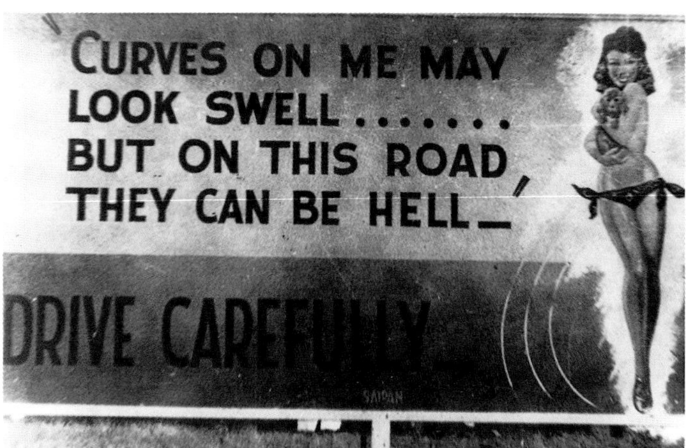

ABOVE AND FOLLOWING: These four images were common to the roads in and around Saipan. These sultry reminders were cheery as well as informative, and the soft cell approach seemed to lighten the mood on the islands.

This aerial photo shows the pre-strike photo of the Kokubu Airfield from about 10,000 feet. The main runway is visible, and the spiral roads next to the air field seem quiet and undisturbed just prior to the 9TH bomb Group's mission.

Smoke and debris bellow up after the first bombs detonate on Kokura. Closer inspection will reveal smaller smoke plumes at top and center of photo.

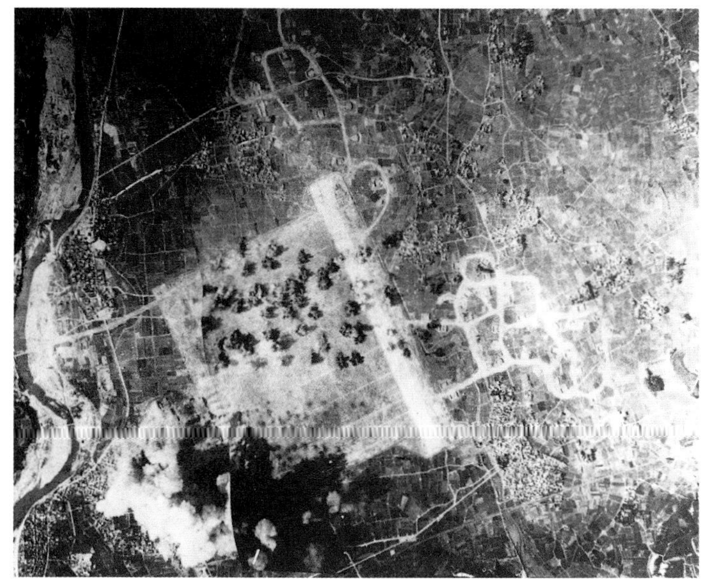

April 20, 1945, the 19TH B/G bombed the Kokubu Air Strip from 12,000 feet. One can see the bombs going off on target, centered in the square area beside the runway. This area was used to park and service the Japanese aircraft based there.

There were several occasions when B-29s would unload bombs on ships of the Japanese Navy. This Japanese Cruiser is in an effort to take evasive action to avoid the high explosive rain falling on her in this view.

The mining and bombing of Japanese shipping continued until the war's end. This Japanese Cruiser is rocked by the bombardment as she narrowly escapes a direct hit.

Close to the close of the war, scenes like this were up and down the coastline of Japan and Korea where the Japanese had tried to intensify cargo shipments. The remains of this freighter are a silent testament to the effectiveness of a well-planned mining and bombing campaign.

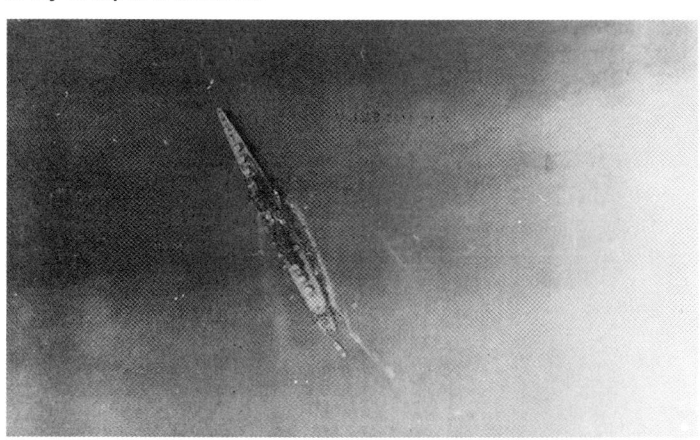

This is an aerial view of the Missouri as she steams for Tokyo Bay. The terms of the Potsdam conference, in all probability, have already been served on Hirohito and his General Headquarters. I feel this is evidenced by the fact that in this view there is no convoy or escorts close to the old Battlewagon, nor are any picket ships visible.

ENOLA GAY & BOCKSCAR

ENOLA GAY and LITTLE BOY: THE HIROSHIMA ATOMIC BOMB

ENOLA GAY CREW

Col. Paul Tibbets	Pilot
Capt. W.S. Parsons	US Naval Weapons Officer
Maj. Thomas W. Ferebee	Bombardier
Capt. Robert A. Lewis	Co-Pilot
Capt. Theodore J. VanKirk	Navigator
Lt. Jacob Beser	Radar-Countermeasures
Lt. Morris R. Jeppson	Assistant Weapons Officer
S/Sgt. W.E. Dusenbury	Engineer
Sgt. Robert R. Shumard	Aircraft Gunner
Sgt. Joe A. Stiborik	Radio Operator
PFC. R.H. Nelson	Central Fire Control Gunner

BOCKSCAR AND THE "FAT MAN": NAGASAKI ATOMIC BOMB

BOCKSCAR CREW

Maj. Charles Sweeney	Pilot
CDR. F.L. Ashworth, USN	Weapons Officer
Capt. James F. VanPelt	Navigator
Lt. Charles D. Albury	Co-Pilot
Lt. Jacob Beser	Radar Countermeasures Officer
Lt. Philip M. Barnes	Assistant Weapons Officer
Lt. F.J. Olivi, Assistant	Co-Pilot
M/SGT. John D. Kuharek	Flight Engineer
S/Sgt. Edward R. Buckley	Radar Operator
Sgt. Albert T DeHart	Central Fire Control Gunner
Sgt. Raymond G. Gallagher	Aircraft Gunner
Sgt. Abe M. Spitzner	Radio Operator
Capt. Kermit Beahan	Bombadier

ENOLA GAY-, 44-86292, Col. Paul Tibbets (2nd from left) poses with members of his crew of the Enola Gay, named for his mother and painted the night before the historic mission. This B-29 was to be the first Superfortress to drop an Atomic Bomb on a specific populated target. (TAFB)

This photograph of Col. Paul Tibbets shows a man with a sense of humor. He had been seriously concerned with the "Manhattan Project" all along, and had taken his assignment very seriously.

North Field, Tinian, Enola Gay returns from her history making flight. Upon landing the B-29 would taxi to an obscure section of the field and await the technicians who would examine her and check for any signs of radioactivity. The crew would have to stay on board this aircraft till that task was completed.

This image reveals the total devastation wrought on Hiroshima. Very few structures are left standing, some tree trunks minus branches, and the city a barren wasteland. Quite a testimony to the force of the Atomic Bomb.

BOCKSCAR-, 44-27297, this picture was taken after the war and after this aircraft's participation in the Bikini Island tests. She is seen here at the storage are of Davis Montham AFB after her reclamation. The plane was named after the Aircraft Commander: Fred Bock. He had flown numerous missions over the Japanese heartland in this B-29, but was not the Pilot during the mission August 9, 1945, to bomb Nagasaki. Major Charles Sweeney was at the Yoke for that mission.

The remains of a once bustling factory in Nagasaki. This image, after the Nagasaki "Fat Man" bomb's devastation, shows the factory as well as the surrounding area gutted and laid to waste.

ENOLA GAY-
After VJ day the 509th C/G changed from circle R to the visible arrow in a circle. This view was taken sometime after the bombing of Hiroshima.

The forward fuselage and cockpit section as she sat for many years in the Paul Garber Facility in Suitland, Maryland. She has since been re-assembled and restored. Let the true history be printed, without prejudice or false innuendo, so it can be there for all to learn from. (Dan Stroud)

Close-up view of the tailgunner's compartment off of the Enola Gay prior to her restoration. You get a good, close look at the panel hatch window and the twin .50 caliber machine guns as well. (Dan Stroud)

This is not the real Enola Gay, but a section of a B-29 set up in Hollywood for the making of the movie about the events that led up to the bombing and the actual bombing of Hiroshima. Two such movies have been made, an older movie with actor Robert Taylor called "Above and Beyond", and a more recent movie, "Enola Gay", with actor Patrick Duffy in the role of Paul Tibbets. This section of B-29 is in Santa Monica, California. (Dan Stroud)

POST WAR AND THE 509th COMPOSITE GROUP

This is a view of the right side of Dave's Dream, the B-29 that dropped the Atomic Bomb during the Bikini Island Tests. She is one of the original "Silverplates" B-29s modified to carry the Atomic Bombs, and had the starring role on "Able Day". (Higgens)

This B-29 has the low visibility matte black undersurface of the 314th B/W and the insignia for the 509TH Composite Group. (Hill)

This natural metal finish bears the insignia for the 509th composite group, and is sitting after the war as assigned to the Crossroads Project.

The initial concussion and shock wave of the Atomic Bomb on "Able Day". There were 73 ships at anchor off of Bikini. Five ships were sunk, and another nine severely damaged.

In this image of the Bikini Island A-Bomb explosion, the compression and shock wave is starting to dissipate. The cloud, however, is still climbing.

The shock wave is gone, and the cloud is still blooming up over the Pacific.

The Mushroom Cloud, at a considerable distance from the F-13 photo ship, is just starting to bloom in this photo taken at about 10 miles distance and 30,000 feet altitude.

The mushroom cloud is gone, and the water and what little debris there was has fallen back into the sea. A cloud of steamy vapor clings to the surface of the Pacific as results are still being recorded. The lack of debris due to the weight and size of ships and their heavy construction, as well as no earthen mass that the vacuum caused by the explosion could draw up into the cloud would account for the lack of purple coloration during the blast.

Chapter 6:
THE 314th BOMBARDMENT WING
THE EMPIRE BUSTERS

The 314th Bombardment wing was activated on April 23, 1944, and started her (Very Heavy) bomber wing career at Peterson Field, Colorado. The same day four activatied Groups were assigned to the 314th Bomb Wing. The four Groups assigned included the 19th B/G, famous for being the only Heavy Bomber Group in the Philippines at the outbreak of World War II. Flying early production Model B-17s, labored fiercely to stop the Japanese advancement in that theater. The 29th B/G, the 39th B/G, and, finally, the 330th Bomb Group were also added.

The first of the 314th Bomb Wing began arriving at North Field, Guam, in the middle part of January 1945. The 19th and 29th Bomb Groups carried out their first bombing mission on February 25, 1945, on a raid against Tokyo. The 39th Bomb Group and 330th Bomb Group began to arrive on North Field, Guam, on February 18, 1945. They were not destined to start their bombing campaigns against the Japanese until early April of 1945.

The 314th's B-29s came to Guam unmarked except for their National insignia and serial numbers, but that was quickly remedied. The wing's tail marking was to become a large black square with the center of these squares masked out to form large, natural metal (aluminum) finish letters for Group markers. Therefore, the square identified the wing, and the letter denotes the Group: "M" for the 19th Bomb Group, "O" for the 29th Bomb Group, "P" for the 39th Bomb Group, and "K" for the 330th Bomb Group.. The squadron aircraft and individual aircraft were also to carry numbers near to the rear of the fuselage in the same manner as the other Superfortress aircraft of the 20th Air Force. Lead aircraft were also marked with identifiers, a vertical black band denoting the flight leaders painted on the vertical stabilizer (tail). Group/Wing numbers were painted on the outboard engine cowlings. The 19th Bomb Group had three squadrons, the 28th B/S, the 30th B/S, and the 93rd Bomb Squadron. All three squadrons earned the Distinguished Unit Citation (DUC) for their bombing campaigns against the Japanese and mission participation over Kobe, Japan, and were activated Feb. 12, 1945. The 29th Bomb Group also had only three squadrons, the 6th B/S, the 43rd B/S, and the 52nd Bomb Squadron. The three squadrons and group received two Distinguished Unit Citations, and were activated Feb.15, 1945. The 39th Bomb Group's assignments were the 457th B/S, 485th B/S, and the 459th Bomb Squadron, and they were activated on 12 April 1945. The Group and three squadrons assigned received two Distinguished Unit Citations as well for their participation in the bombing campaign against Tokyo and the Japanese Empire. In all, the 314th Bomb Wing flew 64 missions during their six months of bombing the Japanese homeland.

THE

Royal & Rugged Order of

EMPIRE BUSTERS

Be it known that

______ 2ND. LT. 0-931697
NAME RANK ASN.

... Having visited the Japanese Emperor a total of 24 times in his capacity as B-29 BOMBARDIER to pay his respects with H.E., incendiaries, and C-ration cans,
Having helped clear the Tokyo slums and having aided in the spring plowing,
Having repeatedly furnished free target practice for His Majesty's AA batteries and honorable Kamikaze Corps
And having pondered many long hours on the age of the water buffalo out of which in-flight lunches are made
Is hereby, and without benefit of T.O. vacancy, inducted into

THE ROYAL & RUGGED ORDER of EMPIRE BUSTERS
330TH GROUP CHAPTER

In testimony thereof, I do hereby set my fist and chop this V-J day of 2 SEPTEMBER 1945.

BIG GEAR'S FIST

This humorous certificate bears some seriousness. Given to members of the 314th Bomb Wing, it first tells the crew member's name, rank, and service No., how many missions, and the position of the crew member. The certificate is outlined in bombs that represent all the missions that the 314th Bomb Group flew.

ARKANSAS TRAVELER-, 330th B/G, 52nd B/S.

BABY SAN-, O, 50. 29th B/G, 6th B/S. MIA.

BABY'S BUGGY-, 42-93964, K, 330th B/G, 458th B/S. K-52. Aircraft Commander/Pilot: William C. Wilson, crew No. 901. 22 combat missions.

BATTLIN'BETTY-, 44-69847, 0, 29th B/G,

BATTLIN'BETTY II-, 44-69847, O, 29th B/G,

BATTLIN BULLDOZER-, 42-93908, K, 330th B/G, 458thB/S, K-31. Aircraft Commander/Pilot: Duwayne Baker. Crew No. 814. 26 combat missions, 0 aborts.

BIG GASS BIRD, The-, 42-93896, K, 330th B/G, 1st B/S. (Renton) 32 combat missions, 2 aborts. Received structural distortion on mission to Kawasaki, 4-16-45. Final: Pyote, Texas, 05/01/47 to 08/28/50. Scrapped: 09/11/50.

BATTLIN'BONNIE-, 42-24907, K, 330th B/G, 1st B/S, No.15. 40 combat missions, 6 aborts, Final: OCAMA, Tinker. Scrapped: 08/28/48.

CITY OF ALBUQUERQUE-, P, 330th B/G, 29th B/S. Carried the APQ-13 Radar, a ground scanning radar which scanned and rotated 360 degrees, designed by Denver Modification Center.

CITY OF ATLANTA-, 0, 29th B/G,

BEATS ME-, 42-93943, K, 330th B/G, 458th B/S,K-30. Aircraft Commander/Pilot, Jerome Blanchard. Flew 13 combat missions off of Guam. Crew then returned to U.S. to attend lead crew training. Upon return to Guam they were assigned to aircraft K-34, "Beats Me Too".

BEATS ME TOO-, K, 330th B/G, 458th B/S. K-34. Aircraft Commander/Pilot: Jerome Blanchard. 13 combat missions.

BEHREN'S BROOD-, 42-93955, K, 330th B/G, 458th B/S, K-37. Aircraft Commander/Pilot: Arthur Behrens on June 1, 1945, B-29 took a direct hit by Flak over Osaka. Behrens killed. With most of controls shot away, Lt. Robert Woliver struggled for over 4 hours to return to Iwo. Once over Iwo the crew managed to bail out in two passes over the island. 9 combat missions, Beherns went down with a/c.

BESTY-, K, 330th B/G

BIG DICK-, K, 330th B/G.

BIG WHEEL, The-, 42-65283, K, 330th B/G, 99th B/S.(Martin) 8 combat missions, 2 aborts. This B-29 crash landed on Tinian on return from mission March 30, 1945. All but radar operator killed.

BUSTY BABE BOMBER-, K, 330TH B/G, 458th B/S, No.44 Aircraft Commander/Pilot: Robt. A. Hall 11 combat missions, North Field, Guam.

CABOOSE-, 314th B/W.

CENSORED-, P, 39th B/G, 60th B/S. No.11. Participated in nearly 70 percent of all of the Group's missions. 33 combat missions against the Japanese Empire.

CHERRY-THE

HORIZONTAL CAT-, 42-63564, O, 29th B/G. 52nd B/S MIA. Shot down by "Flak" March 9, 1945, on night incendiary raid over Tokyo.

CITY OF ARCADIA-, 42-93925, O, 29th B/G, 43rd B/S. Reclaimed: 07/24/54. The 314th Bomb Wing adopted a map of the United States in an effort to try to commemorate some of the cities who had crew members in the wing. The map and pennant with the City's name was on the right hand side of the aircraft. Most of the B-29s in the 314th had other names or artwork on the port side of the aircraft.

CITY OF BAKERSFIELD-, 44-69680, M, 19th B/G, 28th B/S, No.2. Transferred to Royal Air Force 03/10/50, was officially off U.S.A.F. inventory.

CITY OF BATTLE CREEK-, M, 19th B/G.

CITY OF BIRMINGHAM-, K, 330th B/G, 458th B/S.

CITY OF BROOKLYN-, M, 19th B/G.

CITY OF BUFFALO-, M, 19th B/G.

CITY OF BURLINGTON-, 42-65304, M, 19th B/G, 30th B/S, No.27. Crash landed on test flight.

CITY OF CHARLOTTESVILLE-, M, 19th B/G,

CITY OF CHATTANOOGA-, 42-94062, K, 330th B/G, Reclaimed: 04/20/54.

CITY OF CHICAGO-, 42-94003, M, 19th B/G, 28th B/S, No.12. Reclaimed: 07/14/54.

CITY OF CINCINNATI-, O, 29th B/G. Aircraft Commander/ Pilot: Bob Morris. Took part in the Kawasaki mission and other missions to Japan.

CITY OF CLIFTON-, 42-65308, M, 19th B/G, 93rd B/S. No.45 Reclaimed: Hill AFB. 11/17/53.

CITY OF COVINGTON-, 44-69875, O, 29th B/G, 6th B/S. Surveyed:05/17/50.

CITY OF DALLAS-, 42-24883, M, 19th B/G, 28th B/S. No.7. Missing in action: 05/08/45.

CITY OF DETROIT-, M, 19th B/G.

CITY OF FLATBUSH-, 44-69682, M, 19tH B/G, 28th B/S. No.4. Salvaged: 05/14/51.

CITY OF FLINT-, 44-61676, O, 29th B/G.Reclaimed:06/17/53

CITY OF FORT GIBSON-, 44-69762, O, 29th B/G, 52nd B/S.

CITY OF FORT WORTH-, K, 330th, 457th B/S, No.3 Aircraft Commander/Pilot: Jackson S. Wallace. 23 combat missions. Guam.

CITY OF GAINSNILLE-, K, 330th B/G, 459th B/S, No.65. Aircraft Commander/Pilot: Travis Budlong

CITY OF GALVESTON-, P, 39th B/G. Abandoned 1945, circumstances unknown.

CITY OF LONG BEACH-, O, 29th B/G.

CITY OF GRIFFIN GEORGIA-, 44-7780, O, 29th B/G, 6th B/S. No.16.

CITY OF HERSHEY-, K, 330th B/G,458th B/S.No.39.

CITY OF LAREDO-, p, 39th B/G, 60th B/S. This aircraft was equipped with the latest radar bombsight and navigational aids. Completed 8 combat missions at war's end.

CITY OF LEXINGTON-, M, 19th B/G.

CITY OF LINCOLN-, 44-70103, M, 19th B/G, 28th B/S. No.7 Salvaged: 11/15/47.

CITY OF OKLAHOMA CITY

CITY OF LOS ANGELES-, 42-65302, O, 29th B/G, 52nd B/S. No.37. Commemorates Sgt. Henry "Red" Erwin. The only member of the 20th Air Force to hold the Congressional Medal of Honor. On April 12, 1945, he threw out a flare from his B-29 bare handed, saving everyone's life. Reclaimed: Hill AFB, 11/17/53.

CITY OF LYNN-, 44-61664, K, 330th B/G, 459th B/S. Aircraft Commander/Pilot: Robt. W. Gunther. 7 combat missions. was an unassigned aircraft.

CITY OF MAYWOOD ILLINOIS-, N/A

CITY OF MEMPHIS-, 42-93917, M, 19th B/G,93rd B/G,No.50. Aircraft Commander/Pilot: John Handwerker On April 13, 1945, mission to bomb Tokyo, their B-29 was hit by both "Flak" and aerial assault by fighters, taking hits. They were able to make it back to North Field base on Guam on two engines. While taxing to the hardstand the No.4 engine up and quit. On closer inspection of the B-29, they found holes in the bomb bay doors, nose, and fuselage, and also holes in the wings, rudder, elevators, and ailerons. She had really taken a beating. On May 3rd, 1945, Lt. John J. Handwerker was awarded the Silver Star for his gallantry in action. Reclaimed: McClellan AFB. 06/22/49.

CITY OF MILES

CITY-, 44-69962, 0, 29th B/G.

CITY OF MILWAUKEE II-, M, 19th B/G, 93rd B/S. Aircraft Commander/Pilot: William S. Underwood. Lt. Bob Kuhns, Co-pilot. On March 10, 1945, on an incendiary raid over Tokyo, the crew nearly lost their lives. Badly shot up by the intense "Flak", they had to limp back to Iwo Jima on two engines. They landed at Iwo Jima only to be shot at by Japanese Snipers still on the island. Lt. Kuhns stated "Someone always pays for those of us that get through." This is, of course, true on any target mission. On a later mission the Japanese fighters found their mark. Just after releasing their bomb load, 3 20mm cannon shells hit the left wing gas tank, and one exploded, starting it on fire. Luckily, the fire extinguished itself, but the B-29 was losing fuel. They lost their No.1 engine due to the fuel transfer system being hit. The Superfortress made it back to Iwo on two engines that were acting up all the way. On landing they fell short of the runway due to darkness and slid to a stop half in the soft dirt of the Island and half in the sea. The crew was able to get out the left side of the B-29, but on the right side of the aircraft was a 50 foot drop into the sea below.

CITY OF OAKLAND-, 44-69872, M, 19th B/G, 30th B/S, No.36. (Wichita) Based at North Field, Guam. B-29-65-BW. was named after an old Humphrey Bogart movie. Flew 35 missions with the same crew and the same engines she had arrived in the theater with, still running fine. Had 0 aborts, one of only three to complete this feat. This B-29 also goes by the name "Whites Cargo". (McClellan)

CITY OF OGDEN-, 0, 19th B/G, 30th B/S,No.21. Reclaimed: Hill AFB, 11/17/53.

CITY-, 42-24917, 0, 29th B/G, 6th B/S, No.8. Also went by the name "NIPP-ON-ESE". Had a rather nasty crash as seen here on North Field, Guam, 1945.

CITY OF ORLANDO-, 44-69689, M, 19th B/G, 28th B/S,No.10 Reclaimed: 06/27/54.

CITY OF OSCEOLA-, K, 330th B/G, was inadvertently shot down by a P-61 "Blackwidow", Northrop Aircraft Company's Night Fighter, on 06/01/45.

CITY OF PALM BEACH-, 314th B/W.

CITY OF PATERSON-, 0, 29th B/G.

CITY OF PHILIDELPHIA-, 314th B/W.

CITY OF PITTSBURGH-, M, 19th B/G,

CITY OF LINDSEY-, 42-94023, O, 29th B/G, 43rd B/S. Reclaimed: 08/19/54.

CITY OF RICHMOND-, 42-65309, M, 19th B/G, 93rd B/S, No.43. Salvaged: 05/31/45.

CITY OF QUAKER CITY-, 44-70016, K, 330th B/G,

CITY OF SAN FRANCISCO-, K, 330th B/G, 458th B/S, No.29. Aircraft Commander/Pilot: Raymond Smisek. 26 combat missions. (M. Hill)

CITY OF SAN JOSE-, K, 330th B/G, 457th B/S, No.14. Aircraft Commander/Pilot: Robt. I. Locks. 11 combat missions.

CITY OF SANTA MONICA-, 42-65303, M, 19th B/G, 30th B/S, No.24. Reclaimed: Pyote, TX.

CITY OF SEATTLE-, 314th

CITY OF SPOKAINE-, 44-70018, circle E on TDY to 504th B/G. Salvager: 04/24/47.

CITY OF TOLEDO-, P, 39th B/G.

CITY OF TULSA-, 44-69815, M, 19th B/G, 28th B/S, No.11.

CITY OF WICHITA-, M, 19th B/G.

COLLEEN-, 42-93955, K, 330th B/G, 458th B/S, No.32. Aircraft Commander/Pilot: Carl R. Bauer. Crew no.809, 12 combat missions. B-29 crashed into jungle at end of runway and went over cliff after aborting from Tamashita mission June 22, 1945. Heavy rain and poor visibility with one engine out caused the crash. Only the CFC Gunner survived.

CUE BALL-, K, 330th B/G, 458th B/S. Aircraft Commander/Pilot: Clyde T. Higginston. 20 combat missions. On 1 mission the B-29 had a runaway prop, and it went out from the engine and folded over the top. Bail out orders were give, and some did. Order was canceled because prop fell off. Those who had bailed out were lost and never found.

DON'T WORRY ABOUT A THING-, K, 330th B/G,457th B/S, No.5. Aircraft Commander/Pilot: C.C. Wolvine 15 combat missions.

EARLY BIRD-, 42-63556, K, 330th B/G, 5th B/S, (Bell) 44 combat missions, 7 aborts. Final: OC/AMA Tinker AFB, Oklahoma, 6/30/46 to 8-28-50. Scrapped: 09/11/50.

EIGHT BALL, The-, 44-70070, K, 330TH B/G, 1st B/S. 35 combat missions, 2 aborts. Final: Tinker, OCAMA, 06/30/46 to 03/31/48. Scrapped: 03-31-48.

ERNIE PYLE, The-, 44-70118, K, 330th B/G, 458th B/S, No.38. Aircraft Commander/Pilot: James Walker. Named in honor of the famous War Correspondent, Ernie Pyle, killed in the Pacific by a Japanese Sniper. Pyle wrote of "Brave Men". He was referring of course to the servicemen whom he came to love and admire and who adored him , his wit, and his honest commentary on the war that was at hand. 21 combat missions.

"FAINTER No.1"-, P, 39th B/G, 60th B/S, No.7. Aircraft Commander/Pilot: Capt. Chester Juvenal. On the May 10, 1945, bombing mission to Otake, Japan. 132 Superfortress bombers participated in this mission. The camera was accidentally left running after the bomb run and totally by accident filmed all the ships that were at the Kure Naval Base. It was to provide our Headquarters Intelligence an invaluable tool since it filmed nearly the entire Japanese Navy, and because at the time of the mission no one knew where the Japanese Navy was! Kure was just across the inlet from Otake. The Japanese were alive and well on the Inland Sea. We took a hit in our number 3 engine. Losing oil rapidly, we decided to stop at Iwo—the mission over Otake had been a success.

FANCY NANCY-, K, 330th B/G, 1st B/S. Aircraft Commander/Pilot: Maj. Lewis C. McMahon.

FEATHER MERCHANTS-, K, 330th B/G, 459th B/S, No.64. Crew 913, Aircraft Commander/Pilot: Mortimer E. Stevenson, Jr. 29 combat missions.

FIRE BUG-, 42-63566, O, 29th B/G, 52nd B/S, No.43. North Field, Guam, 1945. Reclaimed: 12/06/50.

GENERAL ANDREWS-, 44-69888, P, 39th B/G. Named in honor of General Frank Andrews. He was a visionary and was able to foresee the power and practicality of long range bombardment. General Andrews was killed in the crash of a B-24 Liberator on 4/27/45, on its first mission. Over the target she was damaged by "Flak" and a phosphorous bomb caught one of her engines on fire over Kurshira Airfield. While struggling to reach the coastline to try to ditch the stricken B-24, the wing crumpled back. Going into a violent spin, the B-24 crashed into the sea. Three crewmen were able to successfully bail out and were later rescued by the submarine U.S.S Gato.

GERM, The-, K, 330th B/G, 475th B/S, No.6. Aircraft Commander/Pilot: Ralph Erwin. 20 combat missions.

GRYM GRYPHON-, 314th B/W.

HAPPY SAVAGE-, K, 330th B/G, 457th B/S, No.2 Aircraft Commander/Pilot: John 'Jack' A. Matthews. 20 combat missions.

HEAVENLY-, 42-69696, M, 19th B/G, 30th B/S. No.29. Salvaged: 07/27/48.

HEAVENLY BODY-, 44-69997, K, 330th B/G, 458th B/S, No.35. Aircraft Commander/Pilot: Foster B. Huff. Crew # 811. 21 combat missions.

HERE TO STAY-, 42-69786, K, 330th B/G, 459th B/S, No.53. Aircraft Commander/Pilot: Charles E. Tibbs. Crew no.902. Flew 21 combat missions.

INFANT OF PRAGUE-, K, 330th B/G, 459th B/S, No.67. Aircraft Commander/Pilot: Owen J. Flanagan 19 combat missions. Crew flew K-60 without a hit for 18 missions, but on their eighth mission were badly damaged by "Flak' over Nagoya. With 2 engines out, bomb bay doors un able to close, only basic instruments, no guns, gas tanks leaking gas into the bomb bay, and with fire and 2 tires flat, the B-29 still got back to Iwo safely.

JANIE-, 44-86438, K, 330th B/G, 458th B/S, No.30. Aircraft Commander/Pilot: R.M. McDonald. 22 combat missions.

JE REVIEN-, K, 330th B/G, 457th B/S, No.11 Aircraft Commander/Pilot: Fred West. crew no. 708, 23 combat missions.

JUG HAID II-, 42-24650, 0, 29th B/G.

JUNGLE FOLLY-, P, 39th B/G.

JUNGLE JOLLY-, P, 39th B/G, 60th B/S. Over Osaka, the B-29 had made two full circles over the target area. She was flying this mission with a new piece of radar jamming equipment, and performed this mission as a pathfinder. Was the 1st B-29 over Osaka, and when the damage assessment photos arrived the following day the photos showed the effects of their mission. 88 percent of Osaka had been destroyed or severely damaged beyond repair. There were no direct hits on any of the B-29s flying this mission.

KNIPP'S VS NIPS- K, 330th B/G, 458th, B/S, No.32. Aircraft Commander/Pilot: Richard F. Knipp. Crew no.815, flew 26 combat missions.

KOEHANE"S KULPRITS-,42-69774, K, 330th B/G, 459th B/S, No.54. Aircraft Commander/Pilot: Lawrence T. Koehane Crew no.903, flew 22 combat missions, and 4 with a different crew for a total of 26 overall missions completed.

LANCER-, P, 39th B/G, 62nd B/S.

LADY JANE-, 42-65363, K, 330th B/G, 459th B/S, No.56. Aircraft Commander/Pilot: Robt. E. Strong. Crew no. 912. Flew 30 combat missions.

LIBERTY BELLE II-, P, 39th B/G.

LIGHTNING LADY-, 42-6801, K, 330th B/G, 459th B/S, No.58. Aircraft commander/Pilot: Earl C. Wheelock. Crew no.917, 27 combat missions.

LONESOME POLECAT-, 42-4059, K, 330th B/G, 459th B/S, No.61. Aircraft Commander/Pilot: Karl W. Stalnaker. Crew no.905, completed 28 combat missions

MASON'S HONEY- 314th B/W, 29th B/G. 6th B/S. Aircraft Commander/ Pilot: Col. Robert L. Mason, the 29th's Group Commander, from the 23rd of July 1945 until war's end. (M. Hill)

LORD"S PRAYER-, 44-69914, O, 29th B/G. 26 combat missions.

LUCKY STRIKE- 42-94029, K, 330th B/G,457th B/S,No.16. Aircraft Commander/Pilot: Vivian E. Lock. On "Sunset Project", back to the U.S. this B-29 crashed on tiny "Johnson Island" enroute. Special orders dated Nov.4, 1945, put the crew on a plane to Hamilton Field, California. 26 combat missions.

LOVELY LETA- 314th B/W.

MARY KATHLEEN-, 42-69814, K, 330th B/G, 458th B/S, No.33. Aircraft Commander/Pilot Frederick A. Rice. Crew no.802, flew 27 combat missions.

MAXIMUM LOAD-, M, 19th B/G.

McNAMARA'S BAND- K, 330th B/G, 457th B/S, No.13. Aircraft Commander/Pilot: Charles J. McNamara. Crew no.701, flew 29 combat missions.

MISS BEHAVIN'-, 44-69685, M, 19th B/G, 28th B/S, No.01. Reclaimed; 10/04/54.

MISS TAKE-, K, 330th B/G, 457th B/S, No.07. Aircraft Commander/Pilot: James W. Bradford. 23 combat missions with this crew #1, also Aircraft Commander/Pilot: John D. Dickenson, with crew # 2. 11 combat missions. Relief crew for Bradford. Aircraft's total—34 combat Missions.

MOTLEY CREW-, K, 330th B/G, 459th B/S, No.62. Aircraft Commander/Pilot: John Stoddard. 28 combat missions. Crew # 910.

MY GAL-, K, 330th B/G, 459th B/S, No.8. Aircraft Commander/Pilot: Thompson Hiles, Jr. This aircraft was taken from crew after 8 to 10 missions because of some factory wiring being for special equipment.

MY GAL II-, K, 330th B/G, 457th B/S, No. 14. Aircraft Commander/Pilot: Thompson Hiles, Jr. 14 combat missions.

NO BALLS ATOLL-, 42-93925, 0, 29th B/G, 43rd B/S, No.20. Transferred to U.S. Navy, Off Inventory 04/26/54.

OILY BOID-, 42-24912, 0, 29th B/G, 6th B/S. Aircraft Commander/Pilot: Lt. Chas. Shaffer. Lt. Schaffer got his stricken aircraft home, riddled with "Flak" holes, from their mission over Tokyo. Earlier in the mission the turbulence from the fires below had put the "Boid" into a dive from which they were able to pull out at about 1,000 feet. B-29 reclaimed. Scrapped:10/21/47.

OL'BOOMERANG-, K, 330th B/G, 458th B/S, No.27. Aircraft Commander/Pilot: John P. Wells. 22 combat missions.

OL' SMOKER-, K, 330th B/G, 794th B/S, No.59. Aircraft Commander/Pilot: Richard P. Cox. Pilot and crew named this aircraft after their first mission. A/C was lost on a mission with a different crew.

'NIP ON ESE' NIPPER-,42-24917, O, 29th B/G, 6th B/S. The "Nipper" survived 40 combat missions over Japan, taking part in two thirds of all combat missions flown by the 29th B/G. Crashed on Tinian when landing gear hit an embankment and collapsed on November 2, 1945. Due to heavy amounts of damage, the B-29 was returned to the U.S. as war weary. Reclaimed: McClellan. Scrapped: 06/22/49.

OL'SMOKER II-, 42-65370, k, 330th B/G, 458th B/S. Aircraft Commander/Pilot: James F. Lawrence. 23 combat missions, crew no.906. This B-29 was out of service for an engine change. Lawrence took K-59 "Smoker" on mission that was lost on a later mission. Lt. Cox and crew renamed this aircraft.

OLD SOLDIER'S HOME-,42-69766, K, 330th B/G, 459th B/S, No.57. Aircraft Commander/Pilot: Francis P. Heid. Crew no. 915, 12 combat missions. This crew was sent back to the states to become a lead crew. On their return to Guam, the war was nearly over and they didn't fly any additional missions.

OUR BABY-, K, 330th B/G, 457th B/S, No.12. Aircraft Commander/Pilot: Bobbie L. Johnson. Crew no.704, 24 combat missions. On third mission had engine shot out over Tokyo, dropped their bombs, and returned to Saipan with very little fuel remaining.

OUR BABY-, K, 330th B/G, 457th B/S, No.12. Aircraft Commander/Pilot: Richard M. Barthels, crew no.709. 7 combat missions. The crew was returned to states for lead crew training.

OUR GAL-, 44-61932, M, 19th B/G, North Field, Guam. Also served in Korean War with the 98th B/G, 343rd B/S, of Strategic Air Command. Surveyed:11/23/51.

PARKER'S VAN-, 44-70003, M, 19th B/G, 28th B/S, No.12. Salvaged: 07/28/48.

PRINCESS PAT II-, 44-70103, M, 19th B/G, 28th B/S, No.7. Salvaged:11/15/47.

PRINCESS PAT III-, 44-83974, M, 19th B/G, 28th B/S, o.15. Salvaged: 01/24/50.

PLUTO-, K, 330th B/G, 457th B/S, No.9. Aircraft Commander/Pilot: Donald R. Freeman. 26 combat missions over Japan with crew no.1. Crew 2 flew an additional 11 missions with this aircraft for a total of 37 combat missions.

READY BETTIE-, K, 330th B/G, 457th B/S, No.4. Aircraft Commander/Pilot: Hermann Lee Smith. 21 combat missions.

REBEL'S ROOST-, K, 330th B/G, 458th B/S, No.37. Aircraft Commander/Pilot: Adrian B. Crimmins. 19 combat missions.

RISING STAR-, 314th B/W.

SALT CENSORED RESISTOR-,42-65307, M 19th B/G, originally went by the name "Salt Peter Resistor", but was too racy for the command and had the Peter "Censored". On March 8, 1945, returned to Saipan with low altitude radar photos of Tokyo and urban dock areas. (Campbell)

ROUND ROBIN-, K, 330th B/G, 458th B/S, No.42. Aircraft Commander/Pilot: Walter L. Ormond. Was returned to U.S. at war's end and based in California.

SHE WOLF-, K, 330th B/G, 457th B/S, No.5. Aircraft Commander/Pilot: Robt. J. Willman crew no.705, 7 combat missions.

SHILLELAGH-, K, 330th B/G, 457th B/S, No.10. Aircraft Commander/Pilot: Richard O'Neill. 18 combat missions.

SLICK CHICK-, 42-24906, M, 19th B/G, 93rd B/S, No.42. Aircraft Commander/Pilot: Chas. Lucas. Reclaimed: 10/04/54.

SENTIMENTAL JOURNEY-, 44-70016, K, 330th B/G, 458th B/S, No.40. Aircraft Commander/Pilot: Les E. Gilbert On June 7, 1945, A/C Richard Knipp bombed Osaka, dropping 12,510 pounds of bombs from 21,200 feet. The elapsed time of the mission was 14.45 hours. Flew a total of 33 combat missions. Quaker City is painted on the right side of this B-29 which is on display at the Pima Air Museum. (Dan Stroud)

TROJAN SPIRIT-, seen here at North Field in early 1945. (K. Roberts)

SNATCH BLATCH-, 42-65302, O, 29th B/G, 52nd B/S. Aircraft Commander/Pilot: Maj. Tony Simeral. This B-29 also served as the observation ship on March 9, 1945, mission over Tokyo. Flew as a pathfinder aircraft fully armed but minus a bomb load. Reclaimed: Hill AFB, 11/17/53.

SOUND AND FURY-, 44-69678, M, 19th B/G, 28th B/S, No.5. Reclaimed: 06/08/54.

STAR DUST-, K, 330th B/G, 458th B/S, No.36. Aircraft Commander/Pilot: Earl W. Meyers, crew no.803, 31 combat missions.

WHITE'S CARGO-, 44-69872, M, 19th B/G, 30th B/S, No.36. B-29-65-BW, also called City of Oakland. Based at North Field, Guam. Was named after the old Humphrey Bogart movie. Flew 35 combat missions with the same "entire" crew and with the same engines she had arrived on Saipan with, still running fine. Had "0" aborts, one of only 3- B-29s to achieve this record. (McClellan)

SWEET CHARIOT-, Y, 501st B/G.

TEN UNDER PARR-, 42-69741, K, 330th B/G, 459th B/S, No.51. Aircraft Commander/Pilot: John E. Parr. Crew no.904, 26 combat missions.

THROBBING MONSTER-, K, 330th B/G, 459th B/S, No.63. Aircraft Commander/Pilot: Talmon Mager, 26 combat missions.

THUNDERBIRD-, 42-63570, O, 29th B/G, 6th B/S, No.7. Reclaimed:

UNINVITED, The-, O, 29th B/G.

VIVACIOUS LADY-, K, 330th B/G, 459th B/S,No.59. Aircraft Commander/Pilot: Larry Scruggs, 24 combat missions.

WANGO BANGO-, 44-87653, M, 19th B/G.

WE DOOD IT-, 44-69860, M, 19th B/G, 30th B/S, No.14.

WILLFUL WITCH, The-, K, 330th B/G, 458th B/S, No.39. Aircraft Commander/Pilot: Richard B. Brown. Crew no.816, flew 25 combat missions.

YANKEE DOLL-AH-, 42-65371, K, 330th B/G, 458th B/S, No.28. Aircraft Commander/Pilot: Howard McClellan. 30 combat missions.

In this image we see almost all of the B-29 Superforts of the 29th Bombardment Group. Sitting in their hardstands, the service vehicles are all making their rounds while other activities take place, such as engine maintenance, inspections, and fueling operations—all in a days work.

It takes a generous amount of fuel to fill the "Superfortress". Row after row of stacked 55 gallon fuel drums wait to be emptied into the B-29s for their trips to the Japanese Empire.

Here we see a 330th B/G B-29 parked behind a P-61 Blackwidow. The other B-29s belong to the 9th Bomb Group.

With an almost solid overcast, these B-29s of the 29th Bomb Group drone on towards their target for the day's mission—Tokyo.

This 330th B/G B-29 is at the ready. Next to her is a B-29 of the 29th B/G, and in the distance you can see Mt. Surabachi. These aircraft are at Iwo Jima.

Smoke from the already burning target rises above the clouds as another wave of B-29s moves in on the target area. drone on towards their target for the day's mission—Tokyo.

On missions to bomb Tokyo one could see Mt Fuji, seen in the rear lower half of this image.Tthese 2 B-29s belong to the 330th B/G and the 29th Bomb Group.

Another 39th B/G B-29 as seen from the pilot's position, is releasing its load of bombs over the target. This scene was familiar to all of the pilots, co-pilots, and bombardiers flying in the Superfortress.

Three B-29s from the 19TH bomb group fly past Mt. Fujiyama on their way towards Tokyo. Mt. Fuji, as the volcano is called, was a landmark for the bomber crews to set their radar bombing equipment up with on missions into the Tokyo area.

B-29s of the 19th Bomb Group salvo their bombs in a massive saturation as many hundreds of tons of bombs fall on targets. Osaka, Tokyo, Yokahama—no matter which target, they all got the treatment. Saturation bombing was equivalent to a scorched earth type of campaign.

A side view of a Superfortress from the 39th B/G as she is releasing her bombs over the target area in a daylight raid on the Japanese Empire.

As seen from the bomb bay, the bombs have been unleashed on the Hitachi plant below. Still free of smoke and debris, this aerial view will soon be changed to black and gray smoke, and most of the lines you see dividing the different areas will no longer be clearly visible.

Returning to base was many times a treacherous occasion with different degrees of battle damage. It was sometimes hard to know just how bad your B-29 was damaged. This B-29 of the 19th Bomb Group, 30th Bomb Squadron crashed on 11-2-45. The B-29 broke apart and started to burn. The B-29 was serial number 44-70092.

Another view of the same B-29, ser.# 44-70092, reveals just how bad the crash was. The fuselage was broken off and away from the rest of the aircraft.

The last and final view of 44-70092 shows that the chance for survivors is near to hopeless. The crushed and burning remains of what was once a proud bomber lay useless & broken.

This B-29 ran off the hard-packed runway and the results can been seen quite easily. The engines are tilted all the way to the ground, the wing main spar most likely bent or broken. This crash was on May 10, 1945, 19th Bomb Group, 30th Bomb Squadron. The chances for surviving this one were pretty good.

There were cases of damage which were not as severe. Here one can see visible damage to the leading edge of the left wing. Though it will take some time to repair, the Superfort will fly and bomb again.

This is an aerial photo of the Omura Air Field, which was bombed by the 314th B/W on May 4, 1945. 10 B-29s took off on the mission, and all 10 B-29s bombed the primary target, dropping 43 tons of bombs. They were over the target for only three minutes at an altitude of between 18,000 and 18,500 feet. No B-29s were lost, and one enemy aircraft shot down. All 10 B-29s returned to Iwo from mission no.141. Close inspection of the photo shows hangars and repair barns, and aircraft scattered all over the parking areas, as well as single engine and multi-engined Japanese aircraft. (Campbell Archives)

Another B-29 crash on North Field, Guam. This Superfort was Ser.# 42-65304, and crashed May 29, 1945. High landing speed and no brakes or hydraulic pressure caused many an image such as this. Once off the landing strip, the surrounding grid was very rough, with large lava rocks and hard terra firma.

The tail, or vertical stabilizer as it is appropriately called, was one of the largest sections of B-29 ser.# 42-65304 after its crash on May 29, 1945. The charred and wrinkled skin is evidence of the extreme heat generated by the burning aviation gasoline.

Even though the 314th Bomb Wing only bombed the Japanese Empire for somewhat less than a year, they helped to accelerate the ultimate end of the hostilities. Many brave men died, and I am certain that all who grew to know these men and to love these men will miss them very much.

Chapter 7:
THE 315th BOMBARDMENT WING
AN END TO THE WAR IN THE PACIFIC

The 315th Bomb Wing (Very Heavy) was the fifth and final B-29 Wing to be assigned to the Twentieth Air Force. Activated on July 17, 1944, they trained in the Midwest and in Puerto Rico. Their arrival in Guam was during April and May of 1945, and, unknown to members of the 315th B/W—and most other servicemen for that matter—they were less than four months away from the end of the war.

The four Bomb Groups assigned to the 315th B/W were the 16th Bomb Group, the 331st B/G, the 501st B/G, and the 502nd B/G. Their main mission or duty was to fly night missions against the Japanese Empire's petroleum industry in the home islands. These B-29s carried new and very special radar equipment, which made a telltale protuberance on the lower belly of the fuselage located between the two bomb bays. This equipment was so secret that no photographs were allowed and very few exist even today.

The markings on the B-29s assigned to the 315th Bomb Wing was a large, black, outlined diamond on the tail. In the diamond was the Group letter designator—(B) 16th B/G, (L) 331st B/G, (I) 501st B/G,(H) 502nd Bomb Group.

Due to the fact that the 315th Bomb Wing almost always flew night missions, the undersurface of some 315th B-29s were painted a matte black. There was also a number on the rear of the empennage, the lowest numbers being allotted to the lowest numbered squadron in the Group. Numbers 1-25 went to the 15th Bomb Squadron, 26-50 to the 16th B/S, and 51-75 to the 17th Bomb Squadron.

They flew their first actual bombing mission on June 26, 1945, and had completed 15 operational missions without hardly any losses at war's end. They flew their last mission (mission number 328) on the night of August 14, 1945, against the Nippon Oil Refinery. The 315th's B-29s were still in flight and returning to Northwest Field, Guam, when their base radio operator gave the announcement that the war was over. The 17th B/S received the Distinguished Unit Citation for actions over Japan from 29 July to 6 August. The 355th B/S received the D.U.C. for action against Japan 22-29 July 1945., as did the 356th B/S and 357th B/S. The 21st B/S received the DUC for action over Japan from 6-13 July 1945, and in the same mission campaign the 41st and 485th Bomb Squadrons also received the Distinguished Unit Citation for their operations from 6-13 July 1945. The 402nd B/S received the D.U.C. for actions taken against Japan from 5 August to 15 August 1945, as did her sister squadrons, the 411th B/S and 430th Bombing Squadrons.

Aircraft of the 315th Bomb Wing

BEEG AZ BURD, The-, 16th B/G, diamond B (Watts)

BETSY-, diam.

BOOMERANG, The-, diam

BUGGER-, 42-63610 331st B/G, 355th B/S, diamond L, No.1, Reclaimed.

BUSHWACKER-, diamond

CHICAGO QUEEN-, diamond

CITY OF MARTINEZ-, 42-63749, 501st B/G, diam. Y, reclaimed Hill AFB, officially off AF inventory 08/19/54

CRAMER'S CRAPPER-, 44-83897, 331st B/G, 356th B/S, diam. L 25. Reclaimed. Officially off USAF inventory 07/08/54.

BELLE OF MARTINEZ-, diam. (D. Thieme)

DODE-, 44-83893, 331st B/G, 355th B/S, Diam. L 4. Reclaimed: 06/24/54 off AF inventory. Seen here while under repairs at Kunming, China, in October of 1945. Capt. A.T. Wilson was liberated from a Japanese POW camp in September of 1945 and was reunited with his two sons, both B-29 Pilots. "DODE" was one of Capt. Wilson's son's Superfortress. (via William H. Hayward)

CABOOSE-, diam. (Watts)

CHICAGO CUBS-, 16th B/G, 15th B/S. Aircraft Commander/Pilot: Lt. Yuska, a native of Chicago. Diam. B (Campbell)

ELLIE BARBARA & HER ORPHANS-, 42-63605, 16th B/G, Diam. B Bell built. Aircraft Commander/Pilot: Ralph Howard. Flew to Guam 04/26/45. B-29B equipped with newer Eagle radar system. Flew her 1st mission 05/05/45 over the Kawasaki Aircraft Factory at Nagoya. Ellie was to fly four more missions during May of 1945—Osaka, Tokyo, Yokohama, and Tamoshina—and managed to get excellent radar photographs of those targets.

FLUFFY FUZZ III-, Diam. This special B-29B was for General Frank Armstrong, the 315th's Wing Commander, with standard modifications plus fuel injection & Curtis-Electric reversible pitch props. General Armstrong flew a radar photo mission and bombed an isolated targot, then flew on to observe his Wing over Utsube on June 26, 1945.

FLUFFY FUZZ IV-, Diam. flew to a record altitude (47,910 feet) while carrying a 1,000 kilogram bomb.

FLUFFY FUZZ V-, Flew non-stop from Honolulu to Manila in March of 1946 as part of the "Marathon Project".

FOR THE LUVVA MIKE-, 331st B/G, Diam. L.

JUGHOUND JALOPY Diam.

LAIDEN MAIDEN, The Diam. L 331st B/G.

LIBERTY BELLE-, Diam. Y 501st B/G, 385th B/S. Aircraft Commander/Pilot: Pete Arnold.

LIBERTY BELLE II-, Diam. L 331st B/G.

LITTLE WHEELS-, Diam.

LUCKY LADY- 44-62304, Diam.

DORIS ANNE-, diam.

FLEET ADMIRAL NIMITZ-, 42-63650, 501st B/G, Diam. Y. Commemorates Admiral Chester A. Nimitz for his support of the 20th Air Force's operations. The "Nimitz" bombed the Utsube Oil Refinery at Yokkaichi, the number 1 target on the 315th B/W's priority list, on June 26, 1945. The "Nimitz" was also equipped with the new AN/APQ 7 "EAGLE" radar. Northwest Field, Guam, June 15, 1945. Admiral Nimitz standing to the left in this photo. B-29 was reclaimed and off official inventory on 03/31/51. (Campbell Archives)

"JUS'ONE MO'TIME"-, Diam. Y 501st B/G. B-29B.

GRIMWOOD'S GREMLINS-, Diam. (Hill)

LOADED DICE-, 42-63688, Diam. B no.7, 16th B/G, 15th B/S, based at Northwest Field, Guam. This B-29B was the only aircraft damaged on the first "Eagle" radar bombing mission, with a small hole in the right rear bomb bay door. The target was the Utsube Oil Refinery at Yokkaichi, Japan. Number 1 on the 315th's target priority list, June 6, 1945. (Hill)

LOVELY LETA-, Diam. The matte black undersurface, common to the 315th B/W, is evident here, but they were careful not to mar Leta in Guam, 1945. (D. Thieme)

MIASIS DRAGON-, Diam. Shows 10 missions to her credit. The fire breathing dragon applied over the black undersurface commanded a lot of attention. (Hill)

MOONSHINE RAIDERS-,44-61815,Diam.L, 331st B/G, Salvaged:07/10 1952. The character shown here seems to be quite the worse for wear, what with guarding all that moonshine.(Witt)

NIGHT PROWLER-, Diamond (Watts)

NIGHT ROAMER-, Diamond Y, 501st B/G. Crew is ready for final check out. (Watts)

PACUSAN DREAMBOAT-, 44-84061, made a historic flight, setting a non-stop distance record of 8,198 miles from Guam to Washington, D.C., late in 1945—she was stripped of all armament, and the tail turret was enclosed. Note the "Andy Gump" nacelles on the lower portion of the engines. (Campbell Archives)

"NOAH BORSHUNS"-, Diamond (Watts)

POM POM-, Diamond

ME WORRY ?-, Diam.

MIZPAH-, Diam.

MY NAKED-, 42-94042, Diam. Y, 501st B/G, 485th B/S. Reclaimed: Tinker AFB, off inventory 09/14/53.

NEUTRAL SPIRITS-, Diamond

NIPPONESE NUISANCE-, Diamond

OH BROTHER-, Diamond H, 52. 502nd B/G, 430th B/S.

OH BROTHER-, Diamond H, 32. 502nd B/G, 411th B/S.

OLE MATUSALUM-, Diamond

PUNCH N JUDY-, Diamond

SALOME!WHERE SHE DANCED-, 44-83893, Diamond L, 4, 331st B/G, 355th B/S. Under the Where she Danced are listed targets and mission dates she danced at (Bombed): Amagasaki, Kawasaki, Shimatsu, Ube, and Akita. Reclaimed: 06/24/54.(Campbell Archives)

RAGGED BUT RIGHT-, 42-63593, Diamond L, 28, 331st B/G, 356th B/S. Reclaimed & off AF inventory 09/11/50.

REGINA COELI-, 44-83906, Diamond B, 16th B/G.

ROAD APPLE-, 42-63600, Diamond Y, 501st B/G. MIA 05/09/45.

ROSE MARIE-, Diamond H, 502nd B/G.

RUDE NUDE, The-, Diamond

SALTY DOG-, 44-83897, Diamond L,25. 331st B/G,356thB/S Reclaimed 07/08/54.

SIZZLING SUSIE-, Diamond

SWEET CHARIOT-, Diamond Y, 501st B/G. Named for a favorite song from the day.

TU YUNG TU-, Diamond

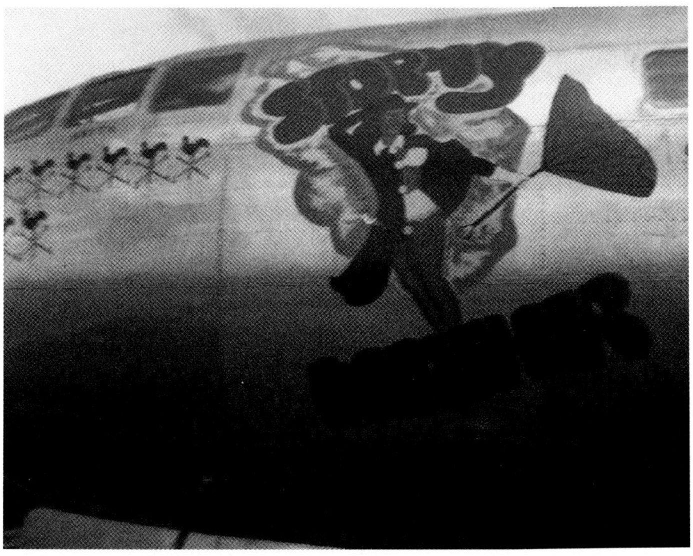

STORMY WEATHER-, This B-29 on Guam in 1945 is assigned to the 315th as a weather recon ship. The weather vanes are a nice touch as a mission marker on Stormy's scoreboard. Her name came from a popular song of the day. (Thieme)

"SCALDED DOG", The-, Diamond, crew posing with B-29B on Guam, 1945. (Campbell)

STRAINED CRANE, The-, Diamond B, 16th B/G. Note how the weather conditions on Guam have made the black painted sections wear down to natural metal. (Heyer)

SHREWD MANEUVER-, Diamond Y, 501st B/G, the artwork is a Wolf in his pinks & greens with silver wings. (Watts)

TEN KNIGHTS IN A BAR ROOM-, Diamond Y, 6.501st B/G, 21st B/S The 10 crew members are depicted in this artwork hoisting a few for the road. (G. James)

TWENTIETH CENTURY FOX-, Diamond Y, 501st B/G, named for the Hollywood motion picture company of the same name.

UNINVITED, The-, Diamond H 502nd B/G.

VICTORY JEAN-, Diamond L,51. 331st B/G, 357th Bomb Squadron.

VIRGINIA DARE-, Diamond

These B-29s are probably at depot level maintenance because of the variety of Bomb Wings present. Shown is a B-29B in the foreground (Diamond B) of the 16th Bomb Group, 16th Bomb Squadron. This Superfortress has the matte black undersurface for flying the night-time incendiary bomb missions over the Japanese Empire.(OC/AMA-Tinker)

Smoke and burning oil rise up into the sky from one of the refineries targeted by the 315th Bomb Wing. Note the oil tank farm in the lower right hand corner of the image. (Fort)

"EAGLE" radar aided in getting a more accurate bomb delivery. Very few of the bomb loads dropped fell short. This photo taken of the refinery in the previous image shows the burning to be more intense, with much more smoke than earlier. (Fort)

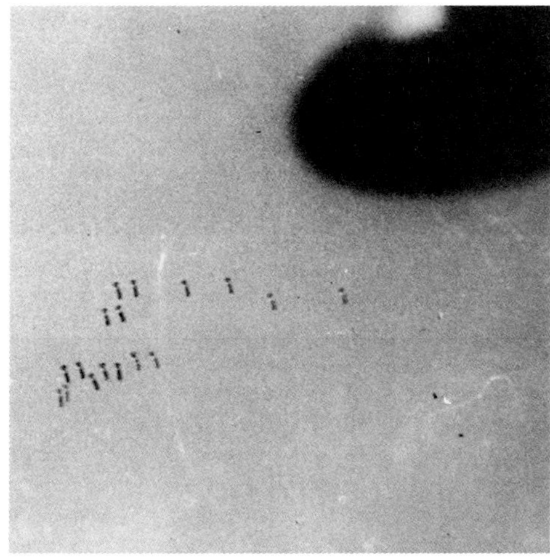

"Bombs away!", the Bombardier would call out to the Aircraft Commander as the view below would equate to the one seen here. These bombs are 1,000 pounders, 18 in number and each capable of creating an immense amount of damage. This particular "salvo" is raining down on the Kawanishi Aircraft Plant. (Heyer)

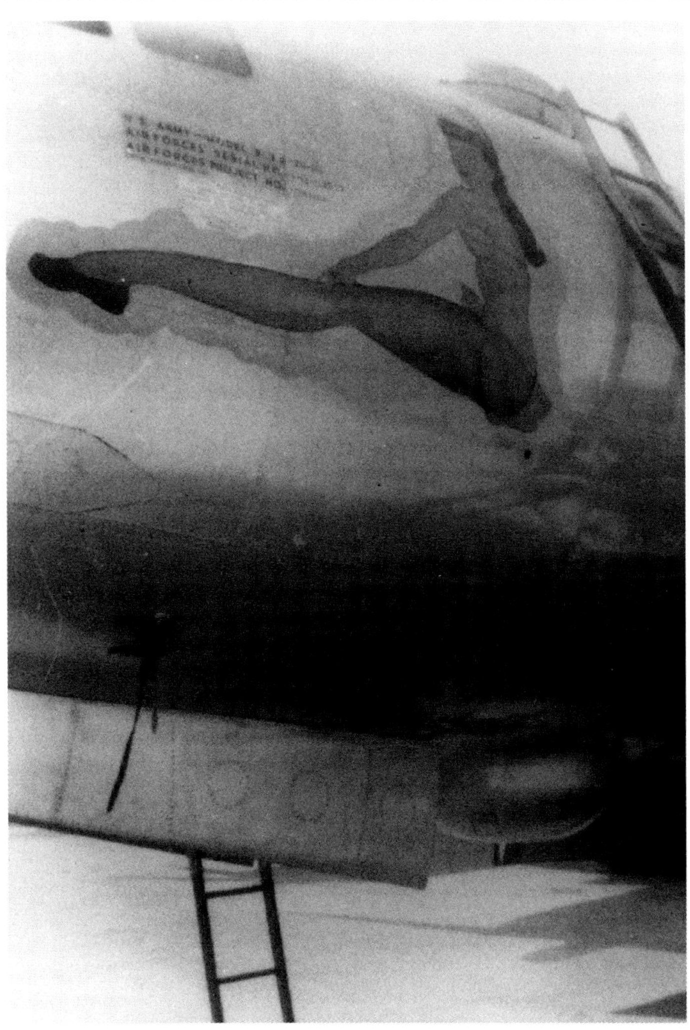

Even though most nose art on the B-29 Superfortress was supported by a name, place, or in some cases a political slogan, a small percentage had just the Classy Pin-up Girl to join the crew and aircraft on their missions. This B-29-25-BA carries the Ser. No.. 42-63517. (Hill)

Much attention has been given to the flying personnel, to their risks, sacrifice and the glamour which is certainly well earned. But many forget to think about the long hours spent before the missions and after the missions, and the hours of work for every single hour of flight. Here we see the engine mechanics working on Miasis Dragon of the 315th Bomb Wing. I'll bet the mechanics seen here were also identifying with the B-29's name at the end of the day's work. (Heyer)

In this maintenance view we see the propeller hub removed and the props fully feathered. Much work and many hours went into upkeep and preventative maintenance to keep the B-29s in top performance for missions. (Hill)

The crew had a lot of small jobs to do getting prepared for a mission, including the loading of bombs by the ordinance personnel, fusing and preparing bombs, and cleaning guns. They also had pre-flight checks of systems vital to the missions, such as radars, pressurization, oxygen, fuel, and navigational equipment, which were all very important to the success of the mission. (Hill)

Chapter 8:
PHOTO RECON:
F-13s WHO SERVED IN XX & XXI BOMBER COMMAND

There were 118 B-29s modified to fulfill the role of F-13. These aircraft were to be used to photograph the target before, during, and after the missions in order to give an accurate accounting and assessment of the damage inflicted on enemy cities, factories, and other targets. This would assist XX and XXI Bomber Commands in planning future strikes.

These specially modified B-29s carried numerous types of photo- graphic equipment. The F-13 was equipped with three K-17 cameras, mounted side by side, one of which was pointed straight down, and the other two pointed outward. There were two K-22 cameras in a vertical mount that was split so as to be able to cover a two mile wide area from 20,000 feet. The sixth camera was a K-18 used for closer range and also wider angle perspectives. The glass covering the camera openings was 3/4 inch thick because of the necessity to pressurize the aircraft. This modification work was done at Denver's Continental Modification Center. Both Renton, Washington, and Boeing, Wichita, worked on the F-13 projects. F-13s costed an estimated $400,000 more than their bomber versions. They also carried full standard armament like the B-29 Superfortress, and they filled their intended role quite nicely.

BELLE OF BIKINI, The-, 44-61822, 16th PRS. The Belle was used on the Crossroads project during the Bikini Island Atomic Bomb tests. She shows 20 photo recon missions. She officially went off of the Air Force inventory on 08/19/54. Reclaimed. (Hill)

DARK SLIDE-, Assigned to the 311th Recon Wing, 3rd PRS. Based on Saipan on Sept. 18, 1944, and TRF to Guam on 01/11/45. Performed photographic, electronic, and weather operations in the Western Pacific from Nov. 1944 until Sept. 1945 during the air offensive over Japan. (Campbell Archives)

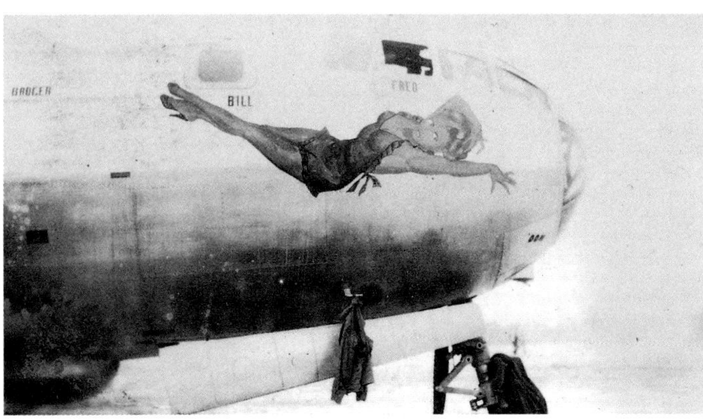

DOUBLE EXPOSURE-, 42-93855, 1st PRS. Worked photo missions with the 58th Bomb Wing in the CBI, 6th Combat Mapping Group. She was salvaged overseas. Seen here at Chengtu, China.

KAMRA-KAZE-, 44-61583, 16th PRS, black square F, was one of the F-13s assigned to the Crossroads Operation, bombing of the Bikini Island Atoll with the Atomic Bomb where she served as a photo ship. Reclaimed.

DOUBLE EXPOSURE-, 42-24877, 3rd PRS. Assigned as a photo ship to the 73rd Bomb Wing, 6th Combat Mapping Group. F-13, F on nose and tail. F-13A-55-BW. Flew 15 combat missions.

OVER EXPOSED-, 44-61999, 16th PRS, Salvaged at Furstenfeldbruch, Germany, on 01/13/50, and officially off inventory.

KAMODE HEAD-, 44-62000, 3rd PRS. The flying outhouse, complete with camera, wings, and properly marked with an "F" for Photo. Officially off of Air Force inventory 08/19/54. Reclaimed.

POISON IVY-, 42-24585, 3rd PRS,6th CMG, assigned to work with 73rd Bomb Wing. Aircraft's name is derived from that of their Crew Chief, Sgt. "Flip" Ivey. F-13-55-BW. Aircraft was lost on a training flight 06/10/45.

SNOOPIN "KID"-, 42-93865, 1st PRS, assigned to 58th B/W, 462nd B/G, CBI. Reclaimed.

BROOKLYN BESSIE-, 42-93854, 1st Photo Recon Sqdn. Pilot: Capt. Arthur Humby Aircraft was on fire over North China and her crew had to abandon her on Feb.2, 1945. The entire crew was rescued by Communist Chinese Guerrillas dressed in stolen Japanese uniforms, and the crew was safely returned to their base.

POISON IVY-, 42-24624, 3rd PRS F. Aircraft Commander/ Pilot Col. Patrick McCarthy, "The Mad Mapper".

QUAN YIN CHA ARA-, 42-93853, 1st PRS, XX Bomber Command, assigned to work with 58th B/W in the CBI. F-13-55-BW. Renton built.

SHUTTERBUG-, 42-93864, F-13A-5-BN, 1st PRS, assigned to the 58th B/W, 462nd B/G, this aircraft was credited with shooting down the first Japanese fighter in WWII by an F-13A photo Superfortress.

TOKYO ROSE-, 42-93852, 3rd PRS, this F-13A was the most famous Photo Superfortress. She went to photograph Tokyo prior to the 1st B-29 bombing mission that was staged in the Marianas in November of 1944. 6th CMG, assigned 73rd B/W. Reclaimed: Davis-Monthan, officially off inventory, 06/27/49. letter F.

UNDER-EXPOSED-, 42-93849, 1st PRS, assigned 58th B/W, CBI. Reclaimed: Warner Robbins AFB, officially off inventory, 04/25/49.

VALIANT LADY-, 42-93870, 3rd PRS, 6th CMG, assigned to the 73rd B/W. Reclaimed.

(LEFT) YOKOHAMA YO-YO-, 42-24621, 3rd PRS, 6th CMG, assigned to the 73rd B/W. F-13A-40-BW. Pilot: Lt. Walter Scheffe, of Enid, Oklahoma. Flew the 2nd Tokyo recon mission and completed an additional 29 missions for 30 missions total. F-13A, was returned to the U.S. for "Combat Strain Studies" at Denver Colorado's Modification Center. While in the U.S. she was placed on display at various "War Bond Drives". Based on Saipan & Guam. On time, one hour after the detonation of the Hiroshima Atomic Bomb "Little Boy', the Yo-Yo's mission was to photograph the destruction and aftermath of the bomb. They approached Hiroshima from around 30,000 feet. The "Mushroom Cloud" had bloomed to 35,000 feet. The crew could see ships blown from their anchors and mooring lines, fires, many damaged bridges, and a lot of smoke. Scheffe stated that when the crew saw the destruction they knew the war would soon be over. When the crew landed back on Tinian, they were directed to an obscure area and directed to stay in their aircraft until the technicians came out and checked their aircraft for radiation. There was none found. The final disposition of Yokohama Yo-Yo is not known. (Scheffe) (RIGHT) YOKOHAMA YO-YO-, We see the tail gunner posing with his window open and all smiles—he must know the end of the war is close at hand. (Scheffe)

YOKOHAMA YO-YO-, Here we see Lt. Scheffe at his position as Pilot, with 20 photo mission markers. He now owns a chain of pharmacies in his home town, Enid, Oklahoma. (Scheffe)

SWEET'N LOLA-, 44-61578, 16th PS, F-13-55-BW, flew on Able Day during "Operation Crossroads", studying the effects of two separate Atomic Bombs, black square F, Reclaimed, 08/19/54 officially off USAF inventory.

TOKYO ROSE-, 42-24621, 3rd PRS, F-13A.

Headquarters. We see in this image the sign out in front of Group Headquarters for the different photo and photo mapping squadrons. (Hill)

The series of mission photos represented here were taken over the Hitachi Engineering works prior to its bombing and destruction, June 10, 1945. The entire 73rd Bombardment Wing participated in the mission. They flew to the island of Honshu. The target was the Kaigan Plant. This brief photo essay will show how the bombing mission progressed from planning to final completion of their task. The percentages of damage, as well as vital statistics, are included.

Hitachi Engineering Works, Kaigan plant just before the bombing mission started, June 10,1945.

497th Bomb Group, 871st Bomb Squadron, 10 B-29s at 19,000 feet. 1st squadron over target.

497th B/G, 869th B/S, 9 B-29s at 20,000 feet. 2nd squadron over target.

498th B/G, 873rd B/S, 11 B-29s at 19,000 feet. 4th squadron over target.

498th B/G, 874th B/S, 11 B-29s at 19,500 feet. 5th squadron over target.

498th B/G, 875th B/S, 11 B-29s at 20,000 feet. 6th squadron over target.

499th B/G, 879th B/S, 8 B-29s at 4,000 feet. 7th squadron over target.

499th B/G, 877th B/S, 8 B-29s at 20,300 feet. 8th squadron over target.

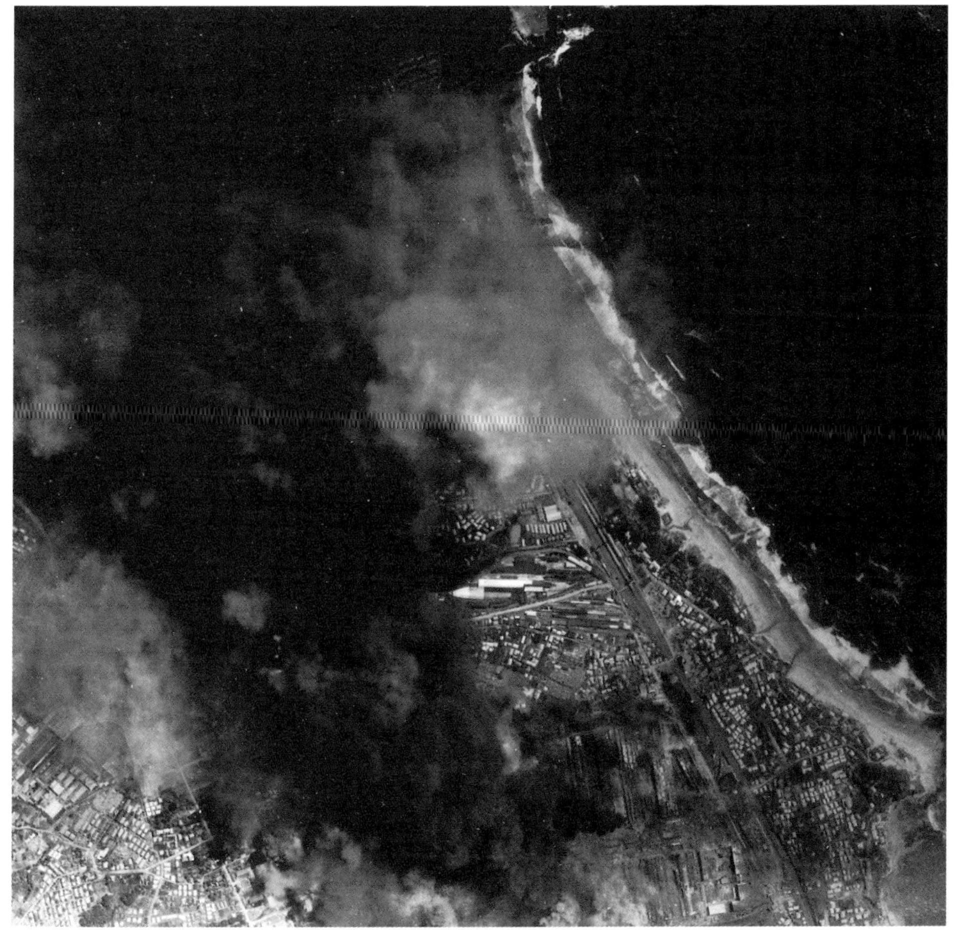

499th B/G, 878th B/S, 8 B-29s at 20,000 feet. 9th squadron over target.

500th B/G, 881st B/S, 10 B-29s at 19,000 feet.10th squadron over target.

500th B/G, 883rd B/S, 12 B-29s at 19,500 feet.11th squadron over target.

500th B/G, 882nd B/S, 11 B-29s at 20,200 feet.12th squadron over target.

The total number of B-29s bombing the target was 118 B-29 Superfortresses.
Number of bombs dropped- 820.
Number of visual hits plotted- 629.
Number of computed hits plotted-191.
Hits within 1,000 feet of AP-594. (73.7 percent)
Hits from 1,000 to 2,000 feet of AP-205 (25 percent)
Hits from 2,000 to 3,000 feet of AP-11 (1.3 percent)
Hits from more than 3,000 feet from AP-10 (1 percent)

Hitachi Engineering works after destruction by 73rd Bomb Wing came to 96.8 percent of all buildings obliterated.

White outlines indicate the original arrangement of buildings in the Hitachi Engineering Works. The success of this type of saturation bombing is preferred, and the results will be followed by many other Japanese factories in the months to come. End: Hitachi Report

Strike photos were the lifeblood for the Bomber Command's Intelligence Network of information about targets and prospective targets. Seen here are a few target photos of more popular targets that were hit and destroyed or severely damaged.

One of the first clear images of Urban Tokyo prior to the bombing campaigns' beginning. This city seems quiet, and at present, undisturbed.

In this image of destruction, we see the whole city of Tokyo at night, with large firestorms in certain areas and smaller fires towards the center of the photo.

Osaka, Japan, during the mission. Much acrid black smoke is being produced in the vicinity of the urban area as a result of the fires started by incendiary bombs.

Nagoya, "The city that would not die". The bombs are still falling towards the target area when this photo recorded the moment. In the top center, you can see that fires are already burning from earlier hits. Nagoya was the primary target for many missions. The Aichi, as well as the Mitsubishi aircraft plants, were located in Nagoya.

Izuni Air Field. A few bombs can still be seen falling towards the target. This photo reveals a clearly timed bomb delivery.

Hamamatsu Urban Area. Bombs were still falling when this image was frozen in time. It's too early to see any existing damage to the target, but the evidence is well on its way.

Night bombing raids and incendiary missions increased with the advent of the "Eagle" radar. Here the city of Matsuyama burns from earlier hits and bombs just starting their fires on this incendiary raid.

The best way to describe this mission is to state that there are many fires and quite a lot of smoke. This mission was Sakai, Japan,.9 July 1945.

Many thousands of photographs like these were taken in all theaters of the war. They were inspected and analyzed over and over again. Much information about the progress being made by the repeated bombing missions was gathered from photos such as these. These images, however, ghastly as they may seem, especially to those unfamiliar with the total devastation of war and aerial bombardment, prove the destructive power as well as the psychological effects of the saturation bombing of strategic targets.

SATURATION BOMBING OF THE JAPANESE MAINLAND

The B-29 Superfortress, Groups, Squadrons, and Bombardment Wings, burned the Japanese Empire to the ground.

Out of 69 cities, 178.2 miles became funeral wastelands. The Japanese industrial might was strangled. Millions of square footage, once producing Japan's war supplies of weapons munitions, equipment, and aircraft were totally destroyed.From high above the Japanese countryside, B-29 bomber crews could see mile after mile of nothing but blackened ash and collapsed structures below them. This concentrated, saturation bombing campaign had dealt Japan a mortal blow. On the incendiary missions to bomb cities like Tokyo, Osaka, Nagoya, and specific other urban target areas, the firestorm reached temperatures of over 1600 degrees F. In Tokyo alone, these raids leveled sixteen miles, incinerated an estimated 130,000 people—two times the amount of people killed by the Atomic Bomb at Nagasaki and the destruction that followed.

The Twentieth Air Force had losses as well, which they had to deduct from their victory over the Japanese Empire. There were 414 combat losses of B-29 aircraft. There were 104 non-combat related losses. There were 10 B-29s lost enroute to the theater from the U.S. A total of 828 B-29 Superfortresses were lost from between April 1944 to August of 1945.

The total tonnage of bombs dropped on the Empire of Japan was staggering. 54,067.00 tons of high explosives, 101,608.00 tons of incendiary bombs, for a total of 5,508,308.00 tons of mass destruction against Japanese targets.

In this entire war, the Japanese people held their own Government to blame, more so than the Americans, for the never ending raids over Japanese cities.

P.O.W. SUPPLY DROPS "MISSIONS OF MERCY"

During the weeks ending World War II, the Twentieth Air Force began a massive campaign. This combination of many missions was for the purpose of supply drops to P.O.W.s. Supplies of food, medicine, and clothing were dropped over P.O.W. camps scattered across China, Japan, and Manchuria—wherever the supplies were needed.

The supplies were dropped in drums by parachute. Usually, the ground crews packaging the supplies would weld 2-55 Gallon drums together with the materials inside, with an attached parachute, so they could be loaded into and dropped from the bomb-bay. The B-29s participating in this operation had large capital letters spelling out "P.W.SUPPLIES". On B-29s with natural metal finish they were black, and on B-29s with black undersurface anti-glare black the letters were white.

A Superfortress carrying precious POW supplies approaches a POW Camp from about 2,000 feet up, ready to salvo the much-needed supplies. (Morrison)

The 55-gallon drum idea was a sound one in principal, although on a few occasions it was reported that the drums, being as heavy as they were, went through the roofs of some of the P.O.W's huts. But, as a whole, the operation went very well. Some of the P.O.W. Camps that received the drops were: the Omori Camp, near Yokohama, where Maj. Gregory "Pappy" Boyington, Commanding Officer of VMF-214's infamous "Black Squadron" was interred; and Tokyo Bay, which had a camp near the Southern end of Tokyo. The Pootung P.O.W. Camp near Shanghai, China, was delivered their supplies on September 6, 1945. One camp had written on the roof of their building "YORKTOWN", which housed the survivors of the U.S. Navy's "Fighting Lady", the U.S.S. Yorktown, which sank during the battle of Midway Island earlier in 1942 on the 7th of June. Fukuoka No.3 Camp, near Tobata, Kyushu, was delivered to on September 13th of 1945. The prisoners at the infamous Omori POW Camp were liberated on August 29th 1945. The POWs at Mudken, Manchuria, were liberated on September 1, 1945. These men were mostly 58th Bomb Wing flight crewmen. There were also camps in Burma with men of the 58th Bomb Wing.

The contents of the supplies was very complete. They consisted of the following parcels: Drawers, Undershirts, Socks, Trowsers, Field jackets, Web Waist Belts, Capt. H. B. T. Shoes, Handkerchiefs, Towels, Shoe Laces, Sewing Kits, Toilet Soap, razor blades, Tooth brushes, Tooth paste, Combs, Shaving cream, and Insect powder. The Medical supplies were complete with instructions for use and rationing.

Coming in very low on this pass over the camp, you can see PW, painted on the roof of one of the POW Camp's Huts. (Morrison)

There were three blocks of No.1, and each contained: 2 cases, Canned Soup; 1 case, Fruit juice; and 1 case, accessory pack. There were three blocks of No.2, and each contained: 3 cases, "C" Rations; 1 case, Hospital supplies; and 2 cases of Fruit.

There was one block of No.3, and each contained: 1 case, Candy; 1 case, Gum; 1, case, Cigarettes; and 1case, Matches.

There was one block of No.5, and each contained:

Located outside cities in suburban areas, you can see from this photo the row after row of P.O.W. quarters. (Morrison)

1 case, Dehydrated soup; 1 case, Vegetable puree; 1 case, Bouillon; 1 case, Hospital supplies; and 1 case, Vitamin tablets.

There was one block of No.7, and each contained: 1 case, Nescafe coffee; 1 Sack Sugar; 1 case, milk; and 1 case, Cocoa.

There was one block of No.10, and each contained 3 cases of Fruit, and 2 cases of Juices.

P.O.W. clearly marked on roofs and in fields, this drop off point should be hard to miss. This particular Camp is Fukuoka, Japan. (Morrison)

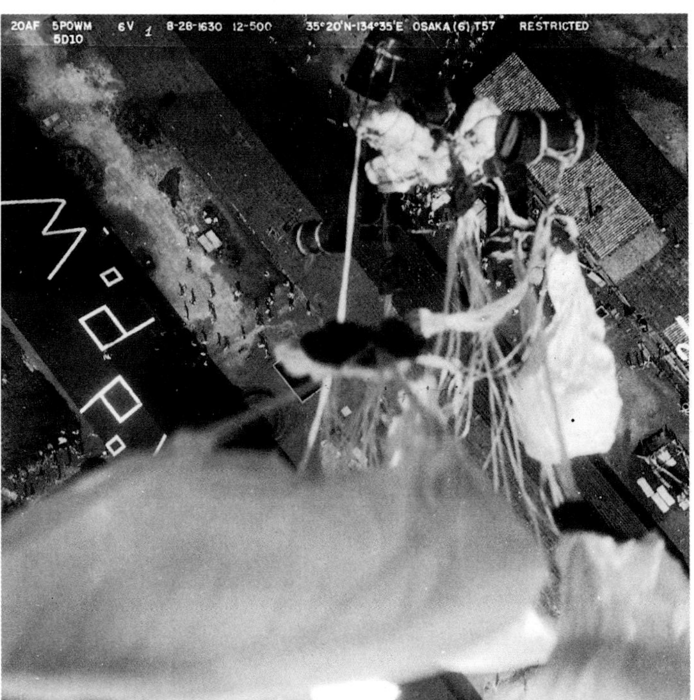

Here is an excellent view of the 55-gallon drum being dropped from a B-29 over the POW Camp at Osaka. On close inspection you can see POWs awaiting their supplies on the ground, standing between their quarters. (Morrison)

This smaller, isolated POW Camp outside Tokyo is receiving their drop, and one can see one 55 gallon drum which has a flared parachute and is free falling. (Morrison)

While the POWs await their supplies on the ground, we can see a message sent to the crew of the B-29 crew from the 300 men in the camp. (Morrison)

The prisoner's quarters were very close together—two 55-gallon drums with their precious cargo and chutes open make their decent to their final arrival point. (Morrison)

These parachutes drift lazily down on this POW Camp. This camp seems to be much smaller than the other camps viewed. (Morrison)

B-29s, row after row, were loaded with P.O.W. supplies, awaiting orders to start engines and take-off. These "Conga Lines" could appear to go on forever. (Bacon)

As the Allied Ground forces arrived, each Prisoner of War Camp was Liberated. From all the happy faces you can tell they know that they'll be going home soon. Hot meals, 3 times a day. Hot showers or cold, "their choice'. A nice soft bed, and best of all, Freedom. The flags seen waving represent the different nationalities of the P.O.W.s. (Official U.S. Navy Photo)

Chapter 9:
GUAM—THE MARIANAS—SAIPAN
THE AIRFIELDS AND UNKNOWN SOLDIERS

During the research on this massive project, I came across some literally unknown and unpublished photos of B-29s which, at this time, couldn't be placed with a Wing, Group, or Squadron.

No author wishes to be considered unknowledgeable or ignorant of his subject, but yet here we are. I feel that it is much more important to give all the B-29s and the men who worked them, flew them, and flew in them their due respect. I apologize for not having the information on these fine pieces of artwork and names, and it goes without saying that they were undoubtedly 20th Air Force, and most probably XXI Bomber Command. It is my sincere hope that the readers, if you have any information on these ships, will contact me through the home office of my publisher and friends at Schiffer Publishing, Ltd., Atglen, PA. I am constantly adding to my archives and need all the help and assistance one can offer to continue bringing these memories back from those valiant years. I have dubbed these unidentified B-29 Superfortresses as, truly, "Unknown Soldiers".

West Field, Tinian. At that time in World War II, the World's largest air base. Home of the veteran 58th Bombardment Wing, as well as home to the 313th Bomb Wing and the 509th Composite Group. (Campbell Archives)

Isley Field, looking in a Northwesterly direction. The 73rd Bomb Wing was based here and launched the 1st Marianas-based mission against Japan. On March 9, 1945, the 73rd Bomb Wing led the 20th Air Force on the Greatest Aerial Assault in history. Most of Tokyo was burned to the ground. (Campbell Archives)

1st SEPARATE ENGINEERING BN- USMC. Many of the Groups in the Marianas paid tribute to the U.S. Marines who captured the islands from the Japanese and whose construction crews came in and made their field ready for the infestation of B-29s that was set to arrive. The teamwork all paid off, and their foothold on the islands helped the 20th Air force to go farther into the Japanese Empire than ever before. (via Bill Davis)

BETT'N BABE-, this is more than likely from the 73rd B/W, although this isn't certain. It was found in a grouping of 73rd Bomb Wing photos at an estate sale, but no additional information is available. (Heyer Collection)

CARLA LANI-, (Battle Baby), seen here with crew as seen in the Marianas. The bomb bay doors are open and ready for the loading of lethal cargo for the Japanese Empire. (B. Davis)

This nice bit of Heraldry is perhaps an unidentified Squadron or Group insignia. The crossed bomb and what appears to be a gun adorns the right side of this Superfortress. (Hill)

CORAL QUEEN-, this B-29A, equipped with the 4 gunned top turret, rests beside a tent city somewhere in the Western Pacific. This is the recon's Coral Queen as referred to in the B-29 listing, but the only certain ID is on the Coral Queen that was assigned to the 73rd B.W. (via J. Heyer)

DEFIANT LASSIE-, This classy femme fatale seems to be later in the war years because of her manner of dress, not mentioned in over 20 different listings of B-29 names. As yet she remains a mystery. (Campbell Archives)

IDIOT'S DELIGHT-, This Superfortress is late-war vintage. The 4-gunned upper turret tells us it's an A model, and the bombs indicate she flew at least 16 missions and shot down three Japanese fighters. The name with letters backwards shows that there was a sense of humor in the Marianas. (Campbell Archives)

LIL' EIGHT BALL-, 42-63521, shows a little man with a little bit of "Flak" going off behind him, and he seems to be behind the eight ball. This B-29 is possibly from the 73rd Bomb Wing. (via G. James)

MAG' DROP MYRTLE-, the artwork shows what is in all appearances a mule in a straw hat. The name infers that this B-29 might have had a problem with magnetos on her engine or engines. This Superfortress is also equipped with the four gunned top turret. (Mark Bacon)

O-0-OKLAHOMA!,-,this B-29A of the XXI Bomber Command is at the ready in Saipan. From the movie musical by Rogers and Hammerstein, we see the surrey with the fringe on top, but perhaps because of the natural metal finish, the two white horses have been exchanged for brown horses. (Campbell Archives)

POT LIMIT-, this late model B-29 carries a full house—4 aces and the Joker. Seen here on Tinian, the B-29 is ready for duty. Bomb bays are open and the props have already been pulled through. (via G. James)

ONE MEAT BALL-, the name on this B-29 assigned to XXI Bomber Command in the Western Pacific is referring to a Japanese Plane. Whenever a crewmember spotted an enemy fighter they would call out over the intercom one of several attention getters. Bandits, or Meatball at whatever position the aircraft might be approaching from. (W. Watts)

SILVER LADY-, the bombs are on their little crates awaiting the process of fuzing and having the fins installed. The living quarters—tents for the most part—are off and to the rear in this photo. This B-29 is missing the top turret, and has no visible missions. Quite possibly a new arrival to the group. (via J. Heyer)

"OUTHOUSE MOUSE"-, perhaps the crew has a feeling when they are aboard their B-29 that they are in the S-House. When aircrewmembers are in constant risk as well as fear of death, most everyone of them will develop an attitude. It doesn't take away from their brave deeds—it simply gives them a way of blowing off steam. (via J. Heyer)

SUCOSHI ? NI !-, a nice bit of artwork and a question in the Asian slang. the only information we have is this is a XXI Bomber Command B-29 and the pilot was named: Lt. W.L. Hildebrandt. The Flight Engineer was Sgt. J.B. Whitner. (via B. Davis)

This B-29 has artwork depicting a little Japanese character being chased by a big bad American Pilot. Mt Fuji is in the background looking down on this event, as she did all the events that transpired around Tokyo. (Campbell Archives)

35 OR BUST- this B-29 is more than likely from the 315th Bomb Wing because of the Black undersurface paint. Even though some B-29s from other Wings and Groups had this scheme, the majority of the 315th's B-29s were painted this way. (via B. Davis)

To add a note, I'd like to mention that many of the B-29s had only a battle number and tail number. For one reason or another, certain Superfortresses weren't blessed with the adornment of art. This should not take away from the duty or mission performed by these fine men and machines, but it made tracking their path down history's runway a bit sticky.

PANCHITO,"THE FIGHTING COCK"-, derived from a popular Walt Disney Cartoon called The Three Caballeros, the name seems to fit the B-29's mission. (Campbell Archives)

Chapter 10:
MEMORIALS:
A TRIBUTE TO ALL OUR FALLEN FRIENDS

It is only fitting to start out with a salute to the U.S. Marines, who gave their lives in the Island Hopping Campaign. The Brave Men who took the Islands of Guam, Saipan, and Tinian, and made it possible for the massive B-29 bases to come into being. This image, with Mount Suribachi in the background, the Marines entrenched, and with the cemetery in the foreground pays fine tribute to the sense of duty, sacrifice, and devotion the men had given their lives for. Our hats are off to each and every one of you. (J.Heyer USMC)

This serene scene is at Tinian. Old Glory flies proudly over the men who lived here, worked here, played here, and because of the war and it's nature, died here. These men were laid to rest for a cause they all believed in, and their memories will live on as to the fine example they set for all Americans and the world to see. (Campbell Archives)

With the Mission as a backdrop, the American Flag is at the center post of this image, set under a blue sky. More American servicemen are at rest. This cemetery is on Guam. (G.James)

An aircraft propeller as a marker, as well as a headstone to mark his final resting place, two of this aviator's friends are paying their respects to a fallen friend. (Sweet)

Row after row of grave markers sit in silent tribute to the fallen U.S. servicemen. This cemetery is on Tinian. There are Flight crewmen, U. S. Marines, Americans, and Heroes all. Joined together in their final resting place, back to whence they had come. (W.Watts)

One of the sisters from the mission prays for the soul of this serviceman who lost his life and was interred to rest here. As the marker reads "Unknown" and as we think of the tomb of the Unknown Soldier in Washington, D.C., at Arlington National Cemetery, we can take comfort in knowing that this man is known to God. (Campbell Archives)

What the native Islanders wanted, what our servicemen wanted, and what they fought and died for has thus been achieved. Somewhere in the Pacific, the guns and bombs are silent. You can feel the warm tropical breeze again, as well as sometimes even hearing it. The drone of the big engines is silent, and the airfields are quiet for now. The war is over. You can relax to the sounds of surf breaking on the beaches from Iwo to Saipan. Peace at last.

Chapter 11:
POST WAR AND THE TRANSITIONAL YEARS

At the end of World War II, many of the B-29s were sent to different Bases and Storage Facilities across the United States. Probably the most well known is Davis-Monthan AFB, near Tucson, Arizona. Certainly the largest, it is still a large aircraft storage and "Boneyard" to this date, and is a home for every type of American built aircraft imaginable. Air Force, Navy, Marine Corps, fixed wing, rotor wing, jet, turbo-prop, and recip. They are all there in the desert solitaire. The aging process for these old dinosaurs is drastically reduced in the dry air, and many of the aircraft are reutilized. Parts and entire aircraft are taken out of their protective spraylat or cocoons. Some are turned into drones and target aircraft, while others may renewed and preserved to replace some of the tired iron our armed services use today.

An aerial view of the B-29 storage area at Tinker shows the Superforts lined up on the taxiway and on the hard deck. This photo was taken on September 10, 1947, a little over a year after war's end. (via OCAMA/ Tinker.)

The B-29s are all gone now at these locations, replaced by newer designs and ideas. The B-29s are still around, though. There are even a few still in flyable condition. "FIFI" of the Confederate Air Force is probably the most well known. Then Fertle Myrtle, once assigned to NACA as a drop ship for the Douglas Sky Rocket and the early X series rocket planes. Pima Air Museum has Sentimental Journey, and Bockscar is at Wright Patterson AFB at the Air Force Museum. Enola Gay is at the Air & Space Museum in Washington, DC, as part of the Smithsonian's collection. Not to mention the many static-displayed B-29s all over the country, including Seattle's Boeing Field, Tinker AFB, Oklahoma, and Offut AFB, Nebraska, at Omaha. They are still around to see and admire. Tinker AFB in Oklahoma City was one of the largest depots for the storage of B-29s at the end of World War II. Pyote Air Base in Texas, sometimes called "Rattlesnake Air Base", served the same role in reclamation and salvage. Many of the Superfortress bombers were stripped of engines and reusable equipment, then put to the scrapper's blade. The Aluminum would then be smelted into new metal for the aircraft which were yet to be.

TINKER AIR FORCE BASE/OCAMA

During the years following World War II, row after row of B-29s were parked and stored at Tinker. The mighty bombers would be towed off of the taxiways and onto the hard deck and left till final disposition was reached.

Some of the B-29s were recalled into the Strategic Air Command to respond to the threat in North Korea. Enola Gay was put into a cycle of modification so she could carry the newer atomic weapons into their test phase during the Bikini Island tests code named "Operation Crossroads." There was to be quite an interesting history developed around the B-29s and their tenure at Tinker.

This second aerial view shows another quadrant of the ramp, taxiway, and hard deck storing even more B-29s Being in the United States and safe...on home soil, dispersal of aircraft was not an issue. (via OCAMA/ Tinker)

A close up of the taxiway at Tinker shows what closely resembles the "Conga Lines" which formed in the Marianas during the "Supply Drop Campaigns" for our POWs interned in Japanese POW Camps. (via OCAMA/Tinker)

This aerial view shows that not just Superforts were stored at Tinker. The main runway No.3 north is bracketed by P-47 Thunderbolts and P-51 Mustangs in the lower left corner of the photo and B-29s closer to the hangar area and maintenance hangars located at the center of the image. (via OCAMA/Tinker)

This aerial view of Tinker, taken on July 15, 1948, shows rowed-up B-29s from the bottom of the field to an area right up to the ramp and hangar area. Even the P-61 Blackwidow nightfighters located on the left edge of the ramp are dwarfed by the sizable amount of Superforts. (via OCAMA/Tinker)

These three B-29s are being serviced, from left to right: KB-29, ser. no.. 44-83591; KB-29, ser.no.44-94029; and B-29, ser.no.42-24879, painted in a high visibility insignia red applied to the vertical stabilizer. These 2-KB-29 aerial tankers were two of the earliest B-29s to be fitted with the in-air refueling booms, the designed test receptacle that was engineered into the 3rd Superfortress. This photo was taken at what is now referred to as the dog leg behind building 3001, the current day rolling line for the Air Force's KC-135 tanker fleet, depot service area. (via OCAMA/Tinker)

During the mid to late 1940s the building (3001 at Tinker AFB/OCAMA) was the home of the B-29 rolling line. B-29s were modified and upgraded, as well as having depot maintenance level modifications applied to the Superforts. (via OCAMA/Tinker)

"ENOLA GAY"- famous for being the first B-29 to drop an Atomic Bomb on Hiroshima, Japan, August 6, 1945. She sits in the hangar at Tinker undergoing modification. The paper placard affixed to her nose reveals that she is being upgraded for the Crossroads Project. Above the placard are five little "Fat Man" stencils indicating 5 tests conducted previously by this B-29. (via OCAMA/Tinker)

One of the propellers of the Enola Gay greets guests of the Tinker Air Force Base Officer's Club and Open Mess. The chances that this prop was mounted to Enola Gay at the time of the August 6, 1945, bombing of Hiroshima are somewhat slim, but still possible. Enola Gay went through a number of engine changes after return to the United States, and it is uncertain which props were the ones mounted at that particular time. The true fact exists, though, that the propeller is in fact off the Enola Gay and that it is a possibility that this prop was on the historic flight. This propeller is now on display next to the B-29 at Tinker AFB aircraft memorial park & garden. (via OCAMA/Tinker)

B-29, ser. no.. 42-24696. This Superfortress had been assigned to the 73rd Bombardment Wing, 500th Bomb Group, 882nd Bomb Squadron. During the war she had carried a Z on the tail, and a number 50 on the empennage. She had carried out both bombing missions and photo missions over the Empire of Japan. The sting is still in place in the tail gunner's position with the twin .50 cal. machine guns and the 20MM Cannon. The little friend parked next to Fancy Detail is a Culver PQ-12 drone. (Campbell Archives via Tinker)

One last look, for this B-29 is in her last days. All but one engine has been removed and half-crated for storage, the turrets are removed, and this Superfortress named 'Bettie Darlin' is next in line for the scrapper's blade. She has a large dent along the cockpit section because of damage which had been inflicted by a tornado on March 20, 1948. (via OCAMA/Tinker)

On March 20, 1948, from 10:10 P.M. till 10:22 P.M., Tinker Air Force Base was attacked, but not in the way one might expect. No terrorist, no bomber or fighter force, yet when released, a force much greater and less able to resist—"Mother Nature". A very large tornado ripped a path from Will Roger's Field ten miles east to Tinker Field. "Miss Daria Hope", a B-29 which, during World War II had been assigned to the 313th Bomb Wing, 9th Bomb Group was, to say the least, "nailed". She was picked up and two aircraft slammed down where she had sat, an AT-11 on the right side and underneath her, and a C-54 on her left side underneath her, she was sentt back to earth. The B-29 suffered very little damage in comparison to her stallmates. Her port inboard prop was bent and her nose gear nearly twisted off, but otherwise there was no other visible damage. Her ser. no. is 44-69764. X, No.43. 5th Bomb Squadron. (via OCAMA/Tinker)

B-29, serial no.44-69764, formerly of the 9th B/G, 99th Bomb Squadron. No.43. went by the name "MISS MI-NOOKIE". Built in Wichita, flew 39 combat missions, 3 aborts. She was reclaimed and arrived at Tinker on 06/30/46. She was ultimately scrapped on July 27, 1948. (via Tinker OCAMA)

From this aerial view of the March 20, 1948, tornado at Tinker AFB, you can see that some aircraft were left untouched, while others were totally destroyed. Picked up, flipped, and slammed upside down onto the ramp. It seems that the C-54/R4D type cargo planes were more susceptible to being flipped, but the damage sustained was very substantial. (via OCAMA/Tinker)

Like a child throwing a temper tantrum, these B-29s were kicked around like toys in a toy box. Three B-29s at the top of the ramp were squeezed together, while the six B-29s in the lower portion of the image were slammed around, tails ripped off and left in a disorderly array of twisted metal. (via OCAMA/Tinker)

Another aerial view of the violent nature of the elements associated with a tornado shows one B-29 upside down in total ruin. The black undersurface would denote that the Superfortress had been previously assigned to the 315th Bomb Wing, and the B-29 almost centered in the image is from the 73rd Bomb Wing, 500th Bomb Group, 883rd Bomb Squadron. Z,no.46. This B-29 went by the name: "SU SU BABY". (via OCAMA/Tinker)

This B-29, painted with a top coating of preservative over what was once a natural aluminum finish, has all manner of aircraft debris scattered about her. This Superfortress has the black undersurface used almost exclusively by the 315th Bomb Wing during WWII, and has the remains of a Fairchild PT-19 strewn about it like so much paper. The prop off of the trainer is even missing. (via OCAMA/Tinker)

A Beechcraft C-45 Expeditor lies on her back under Miss-Mi-Nookie of the 313th Bomb Wing, 9th Bomb Group. This B-29 flanked by a C-54/R4D on the right and left rear of the bomber were left totally inverted, whereas the B-29 sustained bent props, a twisted nose gear, and minor surface damage to the right wing. (via OCAMA/Tinker)

BETTE DARLIN-, serial no. 44-61669, originally went by the name "FLAGSHIP 500th". Assigned to the 500th B/G, 883rd B/S. tail code Z,no.49. Judging by the hastily applied name on the nose which is now present, it was more than likely applied by laborers at Tinker AFB, perhaps as a bit of Graffiti. This B-29 was destroyed on March 25, 1948, at 6:00 P.M. when a second tornado hit Tinker AFB—the second Tornado within a weeks time. The path of this tornado was 1 and 1/2 miles long, and an additional 84 aircraft were hit by the winds generated, 35 of which were damaged beyond repair. One person was slightly injured in this storm. The width of the path of destruction was 200 yards. The estimated damage in this tornado was 6 million, one hundred thousand dollars.

This B-29B, of the 315th Bomb Wing, 16th Bomb Group, 15th Bomb Squadron, Diamond B, no.13. serial no.42-63605, was reclaimed by Tinker AFB at war's end, approx. 1946 time frame. Went by the name "ELLIE BARBARA AND HER ORPHANS". This B-29 had received excellent radar photographs over Yokohama and Tamoshina during May of 1945. The tornado ripped up this section of P.S.P. pierced steel planking and wrapped it around the right wing of this Superfortress. (via OCAMA/Tinker)

Amidst the debris from the March 25, 1948, tornado hit at Tinker AFB, these two B-29s of the 315th Bomb Wing sit in ruin. The rudder was ripped away from the B-29 on the right, as was the trailing edge ailerons and elevators. Not much damage is noticeable to the B-29 on the left. The remains of a PT-26 sit under the B-29 on the left side of the image. (via Tinker AFB/HO)

In this aerial view of Tinker AFB on the morning of March 26, 1948, the damage of the smaller tornado is evident. The B-29 on the ramp is virtually intact, yet the C-54s are all on their backs, except for the aircraft in the upper left corner, which was sheared in half by the high winds generated by the Tornado. The storm on March 20th destroyed 50 aircraft with 50 more damaged—an estimated 10 million dollars in damages to aircraft alone at Tinker. Will Rogers Field in the western part of Oklahoma City received an estimated 6 thousand dollars in damage to aircraft. The winds reached up to 98 miles per hour and the barometric pressure range rose between 28.22 and 22.58 in just a few minutes. The total damages from the two separate storms came to 16 million, 350 thousand dollars. 85 aircraft were damaged beyond repair, and 99 aircraft were seriously damaged. (via OCAMA/HO-Tinker)

On May 3, 1945, another minor accident. It appears that a tow tractor was moving the B-17G, serial no. 42-37765, "Peck's Bad Boy", named for the famous play of the early 1900s, out of the hangar, and didn't notice the B-29 that was taxing up the ramp. The pilot of the B-29 "Klondike Kutie", which had arrived at Tinker from pulling flight tests and weather studies in the cold areas of Alaska, was able to apply brakes and stop. The tow tractor backing the Flying Fortress out of the hangar just wasn't able to stop in time, or didn't see the B-29, and the ensuing accident occurred. It is somewhat humorous to look at the names of the Boeing bombers and the angle at which they came in contact. (Campbell Archives)

This B-29 serial no. 45-21808, is a B-29-96, built at Boeing's Wichita, Kansas, plant in the last year of World War II. This B-29 didn't get to see much action. At war's end she was flown to Keggleman Field, North of the town of Jet, Oklahoma, an outlining practice field for the Air Training Command's program at Vance AFB, Enid, Oklahoma. Both Keggleman and Vance fell under the jurisdiction of Tinker AFB. There at Keggleman, she was used for firefighting as a simulated crash. The remains of the Superfortress were used numerous times and were still at Keggleman Field in the early 1960s. (Campbell Archives)

The clean lines and evenly spaced rivets mark the bombardier's area of this B-29 on static display at Tinker AFB at the North Air Depot Gate. Retrieved from Aberdeen Proving Grounds and restored to her present condition by the Combat Logistics Support Squadron assigned at Tinker, she is one of the most recently restored B-29s today. *see color section. (Campbell Archives)

B-29B-50, serial no.44-84003, sits quietly at rest in the mile long building 3001 at Tinker AFB in 1948, going through Depot Maintenance and Mod. changes. This was an ongoing process. Tinker AFB was the Depot Manager of the B-29s at war's end and up to and including the Korean War. This B-29B was built by Bell in Georgia. This B-29 is from the 509th Bomb Group. (Campbell Archives via Hill)

This dual line-up of B-29 Superforts at Kelly AFB in San Antonio, Texas, shows that Tinker might very well have had the Lion's share of workload for the B-29 fleet, but Kelly was busy with the B-29s as well. Working around the clock, preparing B-29 of Strategic Air Command and the 19th Bombardment Wing for their role in the Korean War. (Kelly AFB/HO).

This KB-29 Supertanker is flying a promotion still for the camera. The refueling boom is in the fully extended position. Although an air refueling was attempted as early as post WWI in old by-planes, state of the art refueling didn't really get going until Boeing's staff of engineers got their hands into it. This KB-29, serial no. 44-86398, B-29-55-MO carries the Radar Dome in the teardrop design. The boom is raised and lowered by a single control cable attached to a hoist extending out of what was once the tail gunner's compartment. (OCAMA/TINKER)

Chapter 12:
THE BEGINNING OF A NEW ERA IN AVIATION HISTORY ROCKET POWERED FLIGHT AND THE MOTHER SHIPS

EB-29-96, serial number 45-21800, was modified to carry the first of the X series rocket planes. The idea was to attempt to penetrate the sound barrier. It was referred to as an invisible wall in the sky and that anyone who tried to penetrate it would die. Some of the test pilots, in fact, did. This image shows the mother ship and two of the new Bell X-1 rocket planes. The B-29, minus the bomb bay doors and plus a few added features would carry the X-1 aloft to a desired altitude over Muroc-cum-Rogers Dry Lake. To load the X-1 and X-1As they first lowered the test vehicle into the pit seen here. The tow tractor would then push the Mother Ship over the X-1, couple up, and literally hoist it into the specially equipped bomb bay. After the EB-29 was airborne the Test Pilot would, "Saddle Up" and close the hatch, and a countdown process would begin, ending in the drop. Capt. (now Brigadier General) Charles E. "Chuck" Yeager was the first to "punch a hole in the sky". Breaking the sound barrier and going beyond the speed of sound. The sound barrier was officially broken on October 14, 1947, by Capt. Charles E. "Chuck" Yeager. Now a Brigadier General, USAF retired. The official recorded speed was Mach 1.06 at 14,000 feet altitude. (via AAFTC/HO, Fred Johnsen)

A side view of the EB-29 shows the cut out bomb bay with the bell X-1 loaded and ready for another test flight. The X-1 had a rocket which was propelled by a mixture of liquid oxygen and fuel. (via Fred Johnsen, AAFTC/HO)

Engines turning and starting to taxi, the EB-29 and one of the earlier X-1 tests is about to get underway. Numerous drops were made to get a feel for the aircraft. Then, the single engine run working up to all rockets being ignited in rapid order to accelerate and boost power. The visible white area under the X-1 is ice which has formed because of condensation around the liquid oxygen tanks. LOX as it is called is in fact so cold in its liquid state that you could dip a fresh cut rose into it, remove the rose, immediately drop the rose to the ground and it would shatter like glass. (via Fred Johnsen, (AFFTC/HO).

The two ships, enjoined, gracefully lift off into the California sky. The X-1 was mounted into the bomb bay area, deep enough so as not to produce drag. (via Fred Johnsen,(AFFTC/HO).

With the EB-29 becoming airborne, the frost on the belly of the X-1 begins to dissipate. They will fly until they can reach their desired altitude before manually releasing the X-1. (Fred Johnson, AFFTC/HO)

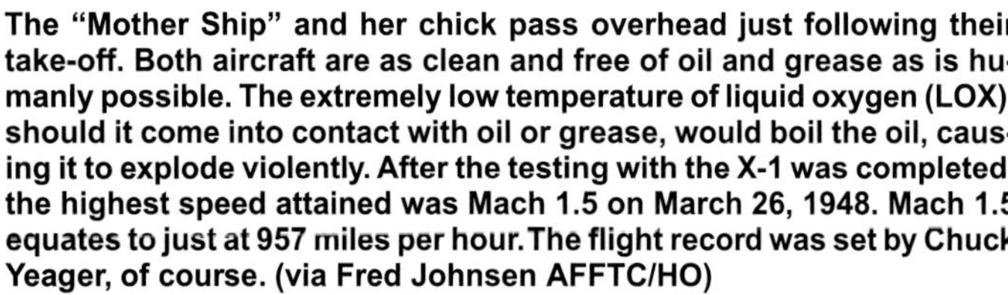

The "Mother Ship" and her chick pass overhead just following their take-off. Both aircraft are as clean and free of oil and grease as is humanly possible. The extremely low temperature of liquid oxygen (LOX), should it come into contact with oil or grease, would boil the oil, causing it to explode violently. After the testing with the X-1 was completed, the highest speed attained was Mach 1.5 on March 26, 1948. Mach 1.5 equates to just at 957 miles per hour. The flight record was set by Chuck Yeager, of course. (via Fred Johnsen AFFTC/HO)

The U.S. Navy also had their flight test center at Muroc (now named Edwards AFB) in honor of Glenn Edwards, who was tragically killed in the crash of the YB-49. The name of the drop ship used by the navy was "FERTILE MYRTLE", and she was to make a record breaking 144 test drops of the Douglas D-558-1 Skystreak and the D-558-2,Skyrocket. These two Naval Aviation experimental aircraft were flown from 1948 to 1956. In one of their supersonic speed research flights, a speed of 1,291 miles per hour was achieved. The peak altitude was 83,235 feet. The NACA mother ship serial no. coded 137 was designated a P2B-1S by the U.S. Navy. Seen here on the ramp at Edwards AFB waiting to power up and go for yet another record. (via Fred Johnsen, AAFTC/HO)

Airborne and high in the atmosphere where the exhaust of engines turns to ice crystals (contrails), the crew and test pilot make ready for the drop. The rocket on the Skyrocket has not as yet been activated. (via Fred Johnsen, AFFTC/HO)

Ignition....the rocket motor is lit off and the test vehicle is ready to drop. A lot of research went into the design and manufacture of the D-558-2, and more information, valuable statistics, and aerodynamic laws of flight would be realized as a result of this venture and the selfless acts of bravery the Test Pilots exposed themselves to on a daily basis. (via Fred Johnsen, AFFTC/HO)

We see Fertle Myrtle's scoreboard of successful drops. A workhorse at the very least, she helped achieve a great deal of information on rocket powered flight. Serial no. 45-21787, she carried a U.S. Naval Bureau no. 84029, since she was acquired by the Navy on May 5, 1947. (via Fred Johnsen AFFTC)

On April 11, 1949, this B-29, serial no. 44-69862, tested a Jet Assisted Take-off.(JATO). The Superfortress starts the initial roll out for take off, then fires the rocket pods, which give a sudden burst of thrust and burn for just enough time to get a heavy laden aircraft airborne. They were used to assist in short take-offs or when the Superforts carried an extra heavy load. The JATO pods could be jettisoned or removed upon landing. (Campbell Archives)

This same B-29, ser. no. 44-69862, lifts into the air after a shorter than usual roll-out. The JATO is about halfway spent at this time in the launch of this Superfortress. (Campbell Archives)

This B-29 is equipped with several unusual systems; the radome on the upper surface of he fuselage and a long, cylindrical tube just aft of the radome. The special equipment is used for air samples in checking radioactive particulate matter in the air at higher altitudes. (Campbell Archives)

A SB-29 of the 5th Air Rescue Squadron, marked in post war insignia and details. She would patrol for downed flyers or souls lost at sea. (Campbell Archives).

This SB-29, serial no.44-62212, is assigned to the search and rescue role. The all-metal rescue boat attached to the bomb bay area is self righting so that, if it were to capsize, it would roll over and correct itself. (via J. Heyer)

This stinger installation was a fixture designed for use on the Northrop Flying wing (the B-35). Because of the flexible housing around the twin 20MM Cannons, its function would be first tested on a B-29 airframe. In this image we only see the stinger assembly. (via Garry Pape)

We see the stinger assembled to the B-29 for functional testing experiments. The cannons are not yet installed, but are mounted on the Superfortress—it looks rather awkward indeed. (via Garry Pape)

OLE MISS VI-, 45-21793, assigned to the All Weather Flying Center, flew research flights in South America in 1946. The National Geographic Society and the Bartol Research Foundation, in cooperation with the Army Air Forces, used this B-29 for Cosmic Ray Research. More of a weather ship with special interior electronics. Seen here at Wright Field in 1946, B-29-90-BW. (Campbell Archives)

PACUSAN-,44-84061, was involved in several record breaking flights. A few short weeks after the war ended, in October of 1945, grossing 149,000 pounds and carrying 13,400 gallons of fuel, Col. Irvine left from Honolulu and flew 10,000 miles over the Arctic Circle to Cairo, Egypt, in 39 hours and 36 minutes. On November 20, 1945, Col. "Bill" Irvine set a new world record by flying from Guam to Washington, a distance of 8,198 miles. Their B-29 had been reduced in weight to 66,000 pounds empty. Gross weight at take-off from Guam was 151,000 pounds. Her speed at take-off was only 145 miles per hour. A short time later, again with Irvine at the controls, she set a new transcontinental record, averaging 451.9 miles per hour. Col. Warren is at Irvine's left. (Campbell Archives via Boeing)

The crew of the Pacusan Dreamboat poses in front of their record breaking Superfortress. (Campbell Archives)

At the end of the Second World War, the United States loaned the British 87 B-29 Superfortresses. Unknown to many, they were crewed by their friends and allies, the Americans. The reason for the loan was to fill a stop-gap while the British Aircraft Establishment worked on the development and testing of their V bombers. The Vulcan is an example. This B-29 flew with 149 Squadron of the Royal Air Force and carries the code WF 512. (Campbell Archives)

The RAF wasn't the only foreign air force to get their hands on the Superfortress. Five B-29s had been forced down in Russia and her provinces during World War II. The crews had been returned with some equipment, such as the Bombsight, CFC Gunner's sights, and other odds and ends. The B-29s interred in Russia were: the Buckin' Bronc, ser.no.44-70136, of the 500th B/G; the General Hap Arnold Special, ser. no. 42-6365, of the 468th B/G; Hog Wild, ser. no. 44-70136, of the 500th B/G; Ramp Tramp, ser. no. 42-6256, of the 462nd B/G; and Ding Hao, 42-6358, of the 468th Bomb Group. The Russians were very taken with the design of the B-29 and created their own version, copied almost rivet by rivet. The Tupolev design was code named "Tu-4", and later the NATO name was "BULL". It is estimated that around 300 "Bulls" were built. Many of that design were sent to the Communist Chinese. The Communist Chinese and Russians also had an AWACS version of the B-29, complete with dish antennae, called the Tu-126 "Moss". A few are still in service. (L. Davis)

During the formation of the Strategic Air Command and the Air Defense Command, the Air Force felt the need to have fighter protection at all times. The FICON PROJECT, as it was called, was the idea that if a fighter aircraft was attached or coupled to a bomber in the formation, it could quickly disconnect, engage the enemy or hostile aircraft, and then recouple with the mother ship. This was tried in several ways, but it turned out not to be practical with aviation technologies growing as fast as they were. The McDonnell XF-85"Goblin", or Bumble Bee as it was sometimes referred to, was one of the classic "bloopers". Only two were built, and they were a little difficult to control when turbulence from the B-29 bounced the little aircraft around like a ping pong ball, almost causing the Goblin to collide with the B-29's underside. (Campbell Archives)

The Goblin was considered a parasite fighter because of the way they attached themselves to the Mother Ship. This XF-85 is sitting on her dolly in the hangar awaiting another test. The size of the craft doesn't help it to look very menacing. (Campbell Archives)

Chapter 13: THE SUPERFORTRESS, SAC, AND THE KOREAN WAR

The Strategic Air Command was formed on March 21, 1946. The mainstay Bomber of SAC at this time was the B-29 Superfortress. SAC only had 9 B-29 Groups, and only 6 of those Groups had aircraft. The B-29 strength reached its all-time high in 1948. The front-line bomber during the Korean war, the B-29 proved her value time and time again. The Superforts did every mission imaginable, from Electronic Counter Measures to Bombing, from Air Sea Rescue to Ferrett missions. The B-29s would even, in some cases, become aces by shooting down the Soviet-built Mig-15 fighters. Two B-29s were to achieve "Ace" status.

ACE IN THE HOLE-, 44-61872, 98th B/G, square H. Reclaimed: 09/13/54. also went by the name: "SAC'S APPEAL". (Campbell Archives)

AL-ASK-HER-, 45-21760, flew in Alaska until rotation back to mainland USA. (Campbell)

AH SOOOooo-, 44-61817, RB-29A, 91st Recon. Squadron at Yokota AB, Japan, 1951. (M. Moffett)

APE SHIP-, 44-86330, 98th B/G, 343rd B/S, square H. Flew missions out of Yokota AB, Japan. Was severely damaged and surveyed on December 18, 1950. (Campbell Archives)

COME ON 'A' MY HOUSE-, 98th B/G, B-29A, based at Yokota AB, Japan, [OUR BABY] in 1951. (via J. Heyer)

ACE OF THE BASE-,

ALLEY OOP-, 92nd B/G, 326th B/S, circle, W.

BABY SAN-, 98th B/G, square H. at Yokota AB, Japan.

BABY'S BUGGY-, 42-24507, 92nd B/G, circle W. Reclaimed: 11/17/53. Flew 22 missions during WWII with the 330th B/G, 458th B/S.

BEETLE BOMB-, 44-69800, 98th B/G, 344th B/S, square, H. Reclaimed:

BIG GASS BIRD-, 44-85400, 98th B/G, 344th B/S, square H. Surveyed: 06/05/52. B-29A, based at Yokota AB, Japan, in 1952.

CHARLIE'S WAGON-, 44-69746, 22nd B/G, circle, E. TRF. to the 98th B/G, square H, where name was changed to "September Song". During WWII she flew with the 500th B/G.

CHIEF MAC'S 10 LITTLE INDIANS-, 44-62186, B-29A-65-BN, 98th B/G, square H, at Yokota AB, Japan, 1951.

CHIEF SPOKANE-, 44-62195, 98th B/G, square H. Unknown [The Red Eraser]

CHIEF SPOKANE-, 44-61925, 98th B/G, square H. Unknown

CHOTTO MATTE-, 44-86400, 98th B/G, 344th B/S, square, H. Surveyed: 06/05/52. Based at Yokota AB, Japan, this Superfortress used "SHORAN" radar to get a radar fix on targets that were in black-outs during night missions.

BEETLE BOMB ER-, 44-69800, 98th B/G, 344th B/S, square H. Served in WWII with the 92nd B/G, named after the Spike Jones' song, "Something to fight for." Reclaimed: (via B. Davis)

CREAM OF THE CROP-, 44-51656, 98th B/G, square H. Reclaimed: 09/13/54. Co-Pilot P.S. Friedrich. First B-29 to bomb enemy during Korean War, on June 28, 1950, targets of opportunity in and around Seoul. This B-29's lavish artwork was censored later in the Korean war by orders of the Group Commander. (P. Friedrich)

CREAM OF THE CROP-, 44-51656, 98th B/G, seen here on hardstand undergoing maintenance. This image was taken after her artwork was censored. (P. Frederich)

DEAL ME IN-, 44-69805, 98th B/G, square H. Originally named: "ACE IN THE HOLE", name was changed at the request of the Unit Chaplin. (Campbell Archives)

DREAMER-, 44-87341, 98th B/G, 343rd B/S, square H. Reclaimed: 08/19/54. (Heyer)

DAIJOBU-, 44-61815, 91st R/G, 91st S.R.S. circle X. Salvaged: 07/10/52. Based at Yokota, AB during 1952, an RB-29A, she had gone by the name: "MOON'S MOON BEAM" when still assigned to the 91st.

DESTINATION UNKNOWN-, 98th B/G, square H. B-29A based at Yokota AB, Japan.

DICKERT'S DEMONS-, 44-86361, 98th B/G, 344th B/S, square H. Reclaimed: 07/14/54.

DOWN'S CLOWNS-, 44-86284, 98th B/G, square H. Reclaimed: 07/14/54. Was shot down by North Korean Mig-15 jet fighters in 1951. Many years later it was discovered that the Migs were flown by Russian pilots. (via Harry Anderson).

FIRE BALL-, 44-62281, 98th B/G, 345th B/S, square, H. Assigned to storage squadron at Davis-Monthan AFB, 09/08/53. (Campbell Archives)

FIREBALL-, 44-62281, 98thB/G,345th B/S, served time in Korean conflict. On rotation back to US, went to DMARC at Davis Montham AFB, AZ. (Heyer)

FLYING PARTS-, 92nd B/G, at Kadena Air Base, Okinawa, August 1950. S/Sgt Jones and S/Sgt, Duvall. (Campbell Archives)

FOREVER AMBLING-, 98th B/G, square, H. At Yokota Air Base, flew with the 58th B/W, 462nd B/G, during WWII. (Campbell Archives)

FRY'IN PAN-, 98th B/G, square, H. Reclaimed: The Aircraft Commander/ Pilot's last name was Fry. (Campbell Archives)

FUJIGMO-, A B-29A, the name abbreviates the slogan,"F___ you Jack, I got my orders." 98th B/G, in Yokota, prior to return to the U.S. reclaimed by the War Assets Dept. (Ethell)

GUARDIANS OF PEACE-, 44-62224, 98th B/G, square, H.

THE GYPSY-, 44-61948, 98th B/G, square, H. Reclaimed: 07/14/54.

HAWG WILD-, 44-61748, 307th B/G, square, Y. On display at the Imperial War Museum in London, England. (Campbell Archives)

HEAVENLY LADEN-, 45-21822, 98th B/G, 344th B/S, square H. At Yokota AB, Japan, 1951. (via J. Heyer)

HEY DOC II-, 98th B/G at Yokoya, square, H.(Hill)

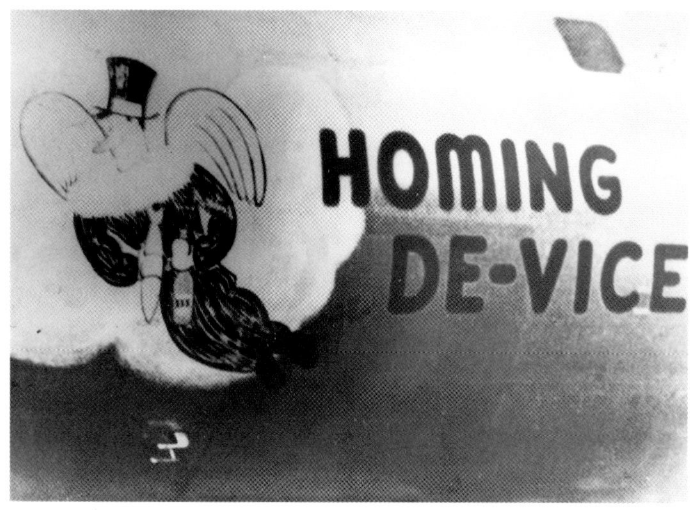

HOMING DEVICE-, RB-29A-55-BO. Assigned to the 91st S.R.S.

HOMOGENIZED ETHELL-, 44-69710, 43rd Air Refueling Squadron, deployed to England in 1949 for 90 days to refuel the 43rd's B-50s that were there on deployment. (M. Hill)

HONEY BUCKET HONSHOS-, 44-61929, 91st S.R.S. RB-29A-55-BO. Omaha built. The characters in the artwork are the crewmen. In Yokota, Japan, in 1950, flew long range recon missions and was flown by 91st squadron against Communist Chinese targets. (M. Moffett)

LAKE SUCCESS EXPRESS-, 44-69980, 98th & 92nd B/Groups. B-29A, the crewmen had their girlfriend's names painted under their crew position on the B-29. Had been based at Spokane Field before deployment to Yokota AB, Japan. (Campbell Archives)

LONELY LADY-, 44-86361, 98th B/G, square, H. (via G. James)

LOS ANGELES CALLING-, 44-86446, 98th B/G, 344th B/S, square H. (via J. Heyer)

MAC'S EFFORT-, 92nd B/G, circle, W. (M. Hill).

MAIS OUI-, 44-86436, 98th B/G, 343rd B/D, square H. (G. James)

THE DUTCHESS 44-93880, 98th B/G, square, H. Reclaimed:

COMBAT READY- 09/27/54. After the Korean War she was sent to the U.S. Naval Weapons Range at China Lake. In 1975 she was sent to Davis-Monthan and scrapped.

HI STEPPER-, 42-65275, 22nd B/G, circle, E. Reclaimed: McClellan, 07/14/54. Flew in WWII with the 58th B/W, 468th B/G.

HOT TO TROT-, 44-69727, 98th B/G, square, H.

HOT TO GO-, 42-65352, 98th B/G, square, H. Reclaimed: Davis-Monthan, 10/01/54.

LADY IN DIS-DRESS-, 98th B/G. square, H. at Yokota AB.

LAGGIN WAGON-, 42-65390, 92nd B/G, square, Y Reclaimed: Davis-Monthan, 11/16/54.

LONESOME POLECAT-, 44-86272, 98th B/G, 343rd B/S, square H. Reclaimed: 07/14/54.

LUCKY STRIKE-, 44-62010, 92nd B/G, 344th B/S, circle, W. Reclaimed: Davis-Monthan, 09/08/54.

M P I -, 44-86247, 98th B/G, 344th B/S, square, H. Surveyed: 01/09/52.

MISS BEA HAVEN-, 44-69805, 98th B/G, square H.

MYAKINAS-, 44-62108, 98th B/G, 343rd B/S, square H. Crashed at Taegu.

MYASIS DRAGON-, 92nd B/G, circle, W.

OLD DOUBLE DUECE-, 42-94022, 91st S.R.S. square, I.

MISS SPOKANE-, 44-27332, 98thN B/G, 344th B/S, square H. Reclaimed: Davis-Monthan, 06/19/55. Was assigned earlier to the 92nd B/G. (B. Davis)

MISSION INN-, 44-61669, 22nd B/G, circle, E. Reclaimed: Castle AFB.

MOON'S MOONBEAM-, 44-61815, 91st R/S, 91st S.R.S. Salvaged: 07/10/52. (M. Moffitt) 13-55

NEVER HOPPEN-, 44-62196, 22nd B/G, circle E. Reclaimed: McClellan, 09/28/54. (via B. Davis)

THE MOOSE IS LOOSE-, 98th B/G, square, H. at Yokota AB, Japan, 1950. (via B. Davis)

NIP ON NESS-, 44-62261, 98th B/G, 344th B/S, square H. Assigned to storage squadron at Davis-Monthan on 08/16/54. was based at Yokota AB, Japan, during Korean war. Seen here before black paint was applied to belly and censorship of the artwork. (G. James)

MULE TRAIN-, 22nd B/G, circle E.

NIP-PON-ESE-, 44-87760, 92nd B/G, circle W. After black paint and nose art changed. (via J. Heyer)

OUR GAL-, 44-61932, 98th B/G, 343rd B/S, square H. Surveyed: 11/23/51. (via J. Heyer)

PHIPPENS PIPPENS-, 98th B/G, square, H. (via J. Heyer)

OUR L'LASS-, 44-61951, 91st Recon. Squadron, square I. Reclaimed:08/26/54. RB-29A-55-BO. Based at Yokota AB, Japan, in the 1950s.(via M. Moffett)

OLD DOUBLE DUECE-, 44-62022, 5th R/S, 91st S.R.S. circle X.

OLD WILD GOOSE-, 44-69771, 98th B/G, square, H.

OUR BABY-, 98th B/G, square, H.

OVER EXPOSED-, 91st Recon, 91st S.R.S., circle X.

PEACE ON EARTH-, 44-61790, 92nd B/G, circle, W. Reclaimed: 07/14/54.

PRIVATE LOVE WITCH-, 44-87741, 98th B/G, square H. Yokota AB, Japan.

RELUCTANT DRAGON-, 44-62253, 98th B/G, 345th B/S, square H. Salvaged: Davis-Monthan, 07/14/54.

PEACEMAKER-, 44-86433, 98th B/G, square, H. (Ethell)

SAC MATE-, 22nd B/G, circle, E. based at Kadena, the name was a play on the Strategic Air Command. (Campbell Archives)

SHACK HAPPY PAPPY-, 98Tth B/G, square, H. Based at Yokota. (J. Heyer)

SNOOPY DROOPY-, used in the Korean war for electronic countermeasures (ECM). Seen here at Yokota AB, Japan, it is believed to have been assigned to the 3rd Radar Calibration Squadron. (J. Heyer)

SHADY LADY-, 42-65357, 98th B/G, 345th B/S, square, H. Reclaimed: Kadena, Okinawa, 02/24/54.B-29-MO (B. Davis)

SO TIRED, 7 to 7-, 44-61727, 91st R/S, 91st P.R.S. square, I. RB-29A-45-BO, flew long range, "Ferrett" missions along the Soviet and Communist Chinese borders during the Korean war. The RBs had two extra crewmen, who operated the ECM equipment, were called "Ravens". (M. Moffett)

SNUGGLEBUNNY-, 44-69667, 98th B/G, 343rd B/S, square, H. Flew 65 missions in WWII, and another 55 bombing missions in Korea for a total of 140 combat missions. (via F. LaPage)

SQUEEZE PLAY-, 44-86415, 98th B/G, 343rd B/S, square, H. Surveyed:10/25/51. B-29A. Yokota AB, Japan. (VIA B. Davis)

T.D.Y.WIDOW-, 44-86335, 98th B/G, 343rd B/S, square, H. Reclaimed: 07/14/54. (Campbell Archives)

TIGER LIL-, 42-94000, 91st R/S, 91st S.R.S. Combat loss 07/11/54. square, I. RB-29A at Yokota AB. Flew over 21 missions against the N. Koreans. (Norm Taylor)

SAC'S APPEAL-, 44-61872, 98th B/G, square, H. Reclaimed: 09/13/54. Had gone by the name "Ace In The Hole", but was changed to SAC'S APPEAL at the request of the Chaplin.

SAD SAC-, 44-61676, 98th B/G, 343rd B/S, square, H. Reclaimed: 06/17/53. Based at Kadena, Okinawa.

SALEM WITCH-, 44-61533, 91st R/S, RB-29A-55- BO. green nose wheel doors and wing tips.

SEPTEMBER SONG-, 44-69746, 98th B/G, square, H.

SHACK RABBIT-, 44-83934, 98th B/G, square, H.

SHEER MADNESS-, 44-61948, 98th B/G, square, H. Reclaimed: 07/14/54.

SHEEZA GOER-, 45-21716, 43rd B/G, 43rd AREFS circle, K.

SKY OCTANE-, 45-21716, 43rd B/G, 43rd AREFS circle, K.

SLOW FREIGHT IV-, 44-61834, 98th B/G, square, H. class 26, 06/17/54.

SNAKE BIT-, 44-86390, 98th B/G, square, H. Surveyed: 07/13/52.

SPACE MISTRESS-, 44-86316, 98th B/G, 344th B/S, square, H, Yokota AB, Japan.

SPIRIT OF FREEPORT-, 44-62060, 22nd B/G, 2nd B/S, circle, E. Reclaimed: McClellan, 09/28/54.

TAIL WIND-, 45-21721, 98th B/G, 345th B/S, square, H. Surveyed:03/19/51.

TO EACH HIS OWN-, 98th B/G, square, H. (via W. Watts)

TREMLIN GREMLINS-, 44-62188, 98th B/G, circle, W. Salvaged: Davis-Monthan, 07/14/54. (via B. Davis)

UNITED NATIONS/JUSTISS FOR KOREA-, 98th B/G, many of the crewmen had a special comment to say and when there was no room to place it anywhere else, the rear section by the hatchway was a good place. (via J. Heyer)

UNITED NOTIONS-, 44-27326, 98th B/G, square, H. Salvaged: 10/25/51. (Campbell Archives)

THE WANDERER-, 44-62224, 92nd B/G, 25th B/S, circle, W. Salvaged: Davis-Monthan, 07/14/54. Named for Lt. Col. Ralph Wanderer, he was up for full Colonel. note: the butterflies are actually Bird Col. Eagles. (via G. James)

WHERE NEXT-, 44-83992, 98th B/G, square, H. Reclaimed: 05/07/54. Served in both Europe and the Pacific in WWII and in the Korean war. B-29A, was Piloted by Lt. J.E Ernest. (via M. Moffett)

THE WILD GOOSE-, 44-69668, 98th B/G, square, H. (via Watts)

WOLF PACK-, 44-86340, 98th B/G, 345th B/S, square H. Reclaimed:06/27/54. In flight on mission to North Korea, October 3, 1951. (Author's Collection)

RB-29A- serial no.44-611727, bears the insignia of the 91st Recon Squadron. Based at Yokota AB, Japan in 1951. (M. Moffett)

THE WORRY BIRD-, SAC, the shell is piercing the bird's tail and the fine print says, "DIS ASS TER". (M. Hill)

WRIGHT'S DELIGHT-, SAC, 98th B/G, tho Chose'n few refers to one of North Korea's main targets, The Choise'n Reservoir. (via Bill Davis)

TODDLIN'TURTLE-, 92nd B/G, was one of the first Groups rushed to the Police Action in Summer of 1950.

TOUCH-N-GO-, 44-87601, 43rd B/G, 43rd AREFS, circle, K. assigned to DET.4 at Yokota AB, Japan.

TOWN PUMP-, 44-27282, 43rd B/G, 43rd, AREFS circle, K. Salvaged: Davis-Monthan, 07/14/54. DET.4, Yokota.

UNDECIDED-, 44-83934, 98th B/G, square, H. Formerly Shack Rabbit.

VICTORY GIRL- 44-87657, 98th B/G, square, H. Had 5-Mig kills to her credit.

During the Korean war, as in most of the wars Americans have fought in, we always have some of the armchair poets and proud men who want to convey their own personal message in their own fashion. This Bomb, destined for North Korea, was personalized by the 548th Technical Recon Squadron. The 345th Bombardment Squadron of the 98th Bomb Wing was to personally deliver the package. This tradition has gone through WW-I, WW-II, Korea, Vietnam, Grenada, Panama, Desert Storm, and now in Bosnia. Wherever we have bombs we will have the "Graffiti". (Campbell Archives)

At the beginning of any mission or deployment there is sometimes the necessity to have a crew's equipment inspected. The crewmembers are all wearing sidearms in their shoulder holsters, and parachutes and other gear is at their feet in precise order. The markings on the B-29 show two large bomb mission markers and another 5 smaller mission markers. These men are preparing for a flight that will take them dangerously close to the Soviet and Communist Chinese Borders. These missions were referred to as "Ferrett" missions. They were crewed by 12 men instead of the normal crew of eleven. The shamrock is the symbol of luck and is also the 307th Bomb Group's heraldry. Provided transitional training for SAC aircrews. (OCALC/Tinker)

The bombing missions in Korea and the Raven and Ferret flights were no picnic. The entire leading edge of the port wing has been torn away from this Superfortress. Other than that this B-29 almost looks intact. The outboard port engine appears to have possibly had a fire, but if so it was extinguished rather quickly because of the lack of evidence of mass deterioration of aluminum on the cowling section of this ship. (via J. Heyer)

This specially modified B-29 has been converted into a KB-29 flying gas station. The refueling boom is lowered, and the thirsty recipient couples up and takes on fuel. The little friend in this image is a Republic RF-84C, which was called the Thunderjet. The F-84 evolved into a Thunderflash, then Thunderstreak, and then later in two models having swept back wings. There was an operator in the former tail gunner's position who would literally fly the refueling boom, as it was called. On close inspection you can see the makeshift wings on the refueling boom. (Campbell Archives)

These B-29s are unloading their lethal cargo on North Korea. The action in Korea lasted for only a short time as compared to World War Two, but a great deal of ordinance was dispersed over Communist Korea and her targets. (Campbell)

This 307th Bomb Wing B-29 is over one of the final targets of the Korean war, the bomb bay doors are open, and this aircraft is on her final towards the target. (M. Hill)

These B-29s are from the 28th Bombardment Group. Seen here in 1948 as they cruise past the famous White Cliffs of Dover. The 28th B/G had been on deployment to RAF Scrampton during August of 1948. (M. Hill)

This B-29 is painted in the colors of Strategic Air Command. The blue sash bearing a sea of stars taxis by the photographer and gives us this brief look. This Superfortress has no armament at all—no turrets, and no guns in the tail section either. (via Mike Hill)

A flight of four B-29s assigned to Air Training Command, as is evident by ATC's insignia on the nose section of each ship. There is no way to be certain as to what the home base is, but during the late 1940's and into the 1950s the B-29s flew many training flights all over the Continental United States, as well as abroad, practicing their approaches to simulated targets throughout the hemisphere. (via M. Hill)

B-29A-50-M0, serial number, 44-61813, 31st Strategic Bombardment Squadron. Circle X. Came in on landing too hot and with too much nose down attitude. Seen here at Johnson AB, Japan, on November 9, 1950. The B-29A overshot the runway as well, which caused too much stress on the fuselage. The aircraft broke into five main sections, the forward cockpit section, the empennage and tail section, the right and left wings, and the engine. This B-29 was a total loss. Luck was with this B-29, as there was only a small fire, and the whole plane was not consumed in flames. (via Col. Mike Moffett)

Another view shows the gaping fuselage as it was torn away. The wings are upside down with landing gear extended. The cockpit section was crushed under the forward section of wing surface. (via Col. Mike Moffett)

The Crash Fire and Rescue Crew is seen here busy at work applying foam to what little remains of the small fire. Returning from the mission and therefore low on fuel is probably what saved the disaster from becoming even worse. The foam is made from hydrogenated animal fat and cows' blood. This mixture mixed with water and sprayed makes a foam blanket which cools as well as smothers the fire. We see the crash crewmen busy at their unpleasant task. (via Col. Mike Moffett)

The fire is out, yet some smoke still clings to the port wing and some rises from the right engine. The B-29 broke so cleanly that the tail section and after fuselage are hardly dented or marred. This picture shows a striking contrast between the cabbage patch in the foreground where the Superfortress started to burrow into the soft earth, and the wreckage a small distance beyond. (via Col. Mike Moffett)

This F-13A-35-BN of the 91st Photo Recon Squadron of the Strategic Air Command's 9th B/W. The 91st was the only photo recon squadron that operated out of the Korean war, and this Photo-Superfortress had a busy time of it. 83 recorded photo reccon missions and still going. (via John Heyer)

This B-29A-50-MO, serial no. 44-86358, seen here while assigned to the 49th Bombardment Squadron, flying the B-29s from 1947 to 1950. Based at Davis-Monthan in 1947, Chatham AFB, GA, May of 1949, and Hunter AFB, GA, 1950. Used mainly as training ships and alert ships for Strategic Air Command's Home Guard. The squadron received the Air Force Outstanding Unit Award in November of 1956 for their activities with B-29s and B-50 aircraft (via G. James)

WATCHIN JO- 45-21717, was attached to the Strategic Air Command in Alaska. She flew patrol missions which were marked with little white polar bears as mission markers. In this image she shows a total of 10 missions completed. Based at Elmendorf AFB, they had the opportunity to evaluate the B-29-90-BWs in the cold Arctic air and winds that are so common to that area of the world. The RB-29s out of Alaska took the responsibility of "Looking Glass" missions, reporting on shipping and troop traffic by the Warsaw Pact countries. (Campbell Archives)

This F-13A-35-BN of the 91st Photo Recon Squadron of the Strategic Air Command's 9th B/W. The 91st was the only photo recon squadron that operated out of the Korean war, and this Photo-Superfortress had a busy time of it. 83 recorded photo reccon missions and still going. (via John Heyer)

With the bomb bay doors open, one can see the hatchway leading from the flightdeck to the bomb bay area. One can also see at the very top of the image the "Tube" which was used by crew members to traverse the length of the B-29s while flying at high altitude while pressurized. (via Dan Stroud)

Chapter 14: THE 19th BOMBARDMENT WING IN KOREA WAR CONTINUES/BOMBING ESCALATES

ATOMIC TOM-, 19th B/G, 93rd B/S, was one of the three (c/slide) B-29s that bombed the Seoul rail station and Han river bridges June 27, 1950, twenty-four hours before President Harry S. Truman officially gave the OK to commence bombing operations. The cat "Tom" of Hanna-Barbera's "Tom and Jerry" adorned this B-29. (via J. Heyer)

BLUETAILFLY-, 42-65272, 19th B/G, 30th B/S, black stripes with blue tips and trim. Was first B-29 in the Far East to complete 100 combat missions. By the time Aircraft Commander/Pilot: Capt. Vito Fierro took her home to the U.S. in 1952, her mission total came to 142. The artwork on the port side of this B-29 shows a cop twirling his nightstick (the 19th Group insignia), very appropriate for the "police action" in Korea. Reclaimed: Davis-Monthan AFB, 08/16/54. (via `Mad" Mike Hill).

BIG SHMOO-, 44-62063, 19th B/G, 93rd B/S, black stripes with red trim. this B-29's name comes from Al Capp's (c/slide) cartoon strip "Little Abner". Seen here at Kadena AB, Okinawa. (via Jeff Ethell)

BUB-, [Beat Up Bastard] 19th B/G, 30th B/S, black (c/slide) stripes with blue tips and trim. A veteran of both WW II and Korea, (via G. James)

BUG'S BALL BUSTER-, 44-61638, 19th B/G, 28th B/S, black stripes with green tips and trim. The artwork on this B-29 really expresses how many of the soldiers and aircrewmen felt before a patrol or mission, especially the aircrewmen when flying missions into "MIG ALLEY". Those sorties were real "Ball Busters". Reclaimed: 06/27/54. (Campbell Archives)

CAPT.SAM & HIS TEN SCENTS-, 19th B/G, 28th B/S, black stripes with red tips and trim. The crew adopted their name from the way they all smelled when they returned from a long mission. (via B. Davis)

COMMAND DECISION-, 44-87657, 19th B/G, 28th B/S, black stripes with green tips and trim. A B-29-85-BW, flew 121 bombing missions against the N. Koreans and shot down 5 Russian built Mikoyan- Gurevich-15 jet fighters (MIGS), becoming the only bomber in the Korean war to achieve ACE status. Dropped a total of 2,500,00 lbs. of bombs and logged 1500 combat flying hours in the Air War over N. Korea. The entire nose section is on display at the Air Force Museum at Wright-Patterson AFB, Dayton, Ohio. The two characters are from the Walt Disney Studio's production of "Sleeping Beauty". On the left is "Dopey", and on the right is "Doc", holding on to the 20th Air Force insignia. (Campbell Archives)

COMMAND DESCISION- 44-87657, shows a complete view of the "Mig Killer" ace B-29-85-BW. Except for a small area on the upper half of the fuselage, the B-29 is entirely semi-gloss black. This is before her history making record was achieved. The name is visible, but not the two characters from the Walt Disney film "Snow White & the Seven Dwarfs." (Campbell Archives)

A Russian "MIG-15" fighter, the same type as flown over North Korea against the U.S. and our Allies. This Soviet Air Force "Mig" has the same markings as seen in June of 1951 and August of 1953. The United States offered a bounty/reward to any N. Korean Mig Pilot or Russian Mig Pilot who would deliver an intact Mig-15 into American hands. There were many cases where, in documents just recently declassified, B-29 crews and F-86 Pilots who were downed in North Korea were transported to Russia and forced into revealing technologies about both the F-86 fighter and the B-29. Wanting to amass their own versions of our technology in an attempt to win. Many of these pilots and crews have never been repatriated or returned home to the U.S. Recent reports from former Soviet high ranking military officials have verified these claims. (Campbell Archives)

COMMAND DECISION-, 44-87657, of the 19th B/G, 28th B/S. Capt. L.E. "Red" Hensley, Jr., sits at the controls of Command Decision as she prepares to taxi out on another flight. Her mission scoreboard with 5-Mig kills and 86 bombing missions would indicate she is just departing on or returning from number 87. The look of confidence on Capt. Hensley's face says it all. (Campbell Archives)

DEAD JUG-, 19th B/G, 93rd B/S, black stripe with red tips and trim. While most of the artwork of the 19th B/G is fairly typical and alike in a lot of ways. there were of course clever exceptions. "Dead Jug" was a cryptic reference to the still troublesome R-3350 engines which powered the Superfortress. (via J. Heyer)

CREAM OF THE CROP-, 44-61657, 19th B/G,30th B/S, black stripe with blue tips and trim. Was reclaimed on 09/13/54. The lavish artwork on the B-29 was not to stay intact. The Group Commander ordered that the visible portion of this femme fatale's anatomy be covered, so with brush in hand they painted a black rectangle over just enough of her anatomy to be within the limits which were set. They also painted "censored" in the center of the rectangle in white. (Campbell Archives)

DIXIE BABY-, 19th B/G, 93rd B/S, black stripe with red trim and tips. The southern bell we see here is ready to take a bite out of one of the South's favorite fruits, Watermelon. Ideas and thoughts of favorite things back in the U.S., were inspiration for these murals. (via G. James)

DOUBLE WHAMMY-, 44-87734, 19th B/G, 93rd B/S, was missing and presumed lost on 01/22/52. She is one of three B-29s that bombed the Seoul Railroad station and Han River Bridges 24 hours before the official word came from the White House to start bombing operations against N. Korea. The character is an Al Capp creation named "Evil Eye Fleagle" from one of Capp's comic strips. She was on a night mission when lost. (via J. Heyer)

DRAGON LADY-, 44-61835, 19th B/G, 30th B/S, black stripe with blue trim and tips. Salvaged on 04/12/51. On her port side the bombs were stenciled in red and she carried five stencils for Mig kills, but the total of five could never be confirmed. (Carmichael)

FUJIGMO-, 19th B/G, 93rd B/S, the letters are a cryptic message, meaning F____ you Jack, I Got My Orders. Based at Kadena, Okinawa, in 1951, seen here prior to return to the USA. (J. Ethell)

42-94009, this B-29 of the 19th B/G, 30th B/S, black stripe with blue trim and tips, is being escorted by a F-80 or an F-84C. A B-29A-30-BN, she was built at Renton, Washington. (Campbell Archives)

ALL SHOOK-, 19th B/W, 19th B/G, 28th B/S. Black stripe, prior to having the black underside painted she had gone by the name SOFT TOUCH. Kadena, 1951.

AMERICAN MAID-, 42-24593, 19th B/G, 93rd B/S, black striped, also flew with the 73rd Bomb Wing during WWII.Was in the 93rd squadron in WWII and Korean war, reclaimed: Tinker AFB/OCAMA on 09/11/50.

APACHE-, 19th B/G, black stripes red trim.

BAIT ME ?-, 44-69802, 19th B/G, 28th B/S, black stripes with green tips. This B-29 was a combat loss in the Korean war, lost 09/12/52.

FOUR-A-BREAST-, 44-86323, 19th B/G, 28th B/S, black stripe with green trim and tips. Reclaimed: 07/14/54. This artwork and name shows another cryptic joke about the four engines on the B-29. (T. Carmichael)

HAD A CALL-, 19th B/G, 28th B/S, black stripe with green trim and tips. An excited little man on crutches gets a sudden burst of inspiration from the little lady as he feels his youth returning. Also, a little munchkin peers out a porthole behind the old geezer. (via Mike Hill)

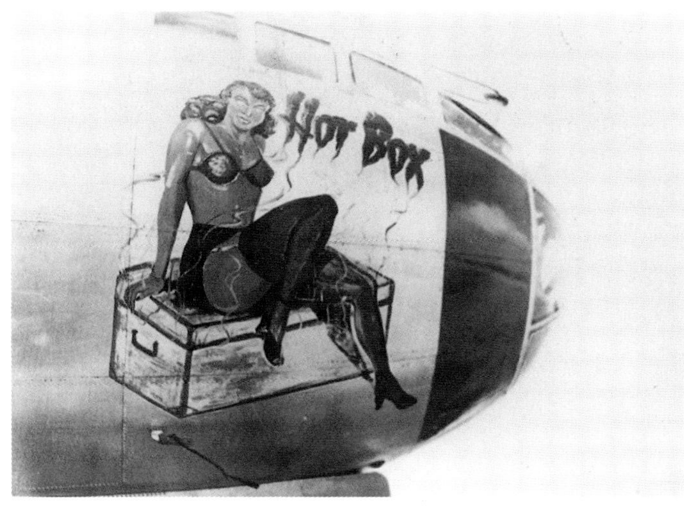

HOT BOX-, 19th B/G, 30th B/S, black stripe with blue tips and trim. Most of the pilots and crews preferred a female from of art as opposed to the cartoon characters because by popular opinion the crews thought more of the girls back home. (via B. Davis)

JITA-, (Jab In The Ass), 19th B/G, 28th B/S, black stripe with red tips and trim. A hostile and angered Jack Ass turns on a character of the devil in this clever piece of art. B-29A, Korea, 1951. (via J. Heyer)

JOHN'S OTHER WIFE-, 44-86349, 19th B/G, this image was shot while she was still assigned to the 22nd Bomb Group and had yellow tips. The ground crews and flight crew took time away from their daily routine to pose with this very unusual piece of artwork. While she was assigned to the 19th B/G she was attached to the 28th B/S, with green trim and tips. (Campbell Archives)

KOZA KID-, 44-97661, 19th B/G, 28th B/S, black stripe green trim and tips. Flew missions assigned to the 468th B/G during World War II with the name American Beauty III. Later the name changed to UGLY, and upon arrival at Kadena AB, Okinawa, adopted her present name, an insulting commentary on the women of a nearby village. (via B. Davis)

THE LEMON DROP KID-, 44-70042, 19th B/G, 28th B/S, black stripe, with green rudder tip and trim. B-29A, named for the Bob Hope movie character. The artwork is a caricature of the servicemen's most beloved entertainer. Bob Hope has contributed his talent and time from World War II and Korea, to Vietnam and Desert Storm. He is most certainly "The Best of the Best". (Campbell Archives)

LUCKY DOG-, 19th B/G, 93rd B/S, black stripe with red tips and trim. Based at Kadena AB, Okinawa, during Korean War. (via J. Ethell)

BOMBS AWAY-, B-29, 42-65361, 19th B/G, 30th B/S black stripe with blue trim and tips. Unloads her bombs on a target somewhere in North Korea. Seen from the Pilot's position of another B-29 on the mission, it is a sight to behold. The name of the B-29 is the "PURPLE SHAFT". She was salvaged at Davis-Monthan AFB on 05/16/54. (Author's Collection)

DOUBLE OR NUTHIN' 19th B/G, black stripe. Based at Kadena,1951.

HOT TO GO-, 19th B/G, black stripe./

HOUSTON HONEY-, 42-63475, 19th B/G, 28th B/S, black stripe, green tips and trim.

ISLAND QUEEN-, 19th B/G, 28th B/S, black stripe green tips and trim.

LUBRICATING LADY-, 44-61751, 19th B/G, 28th B/S, black stripe with green tips and trim. Forced to ditch off the coastline of Kadena on 10/31/52.

MISS MEGOOK-, 19th B/G, 30th B/S, black stripe with Blue tips and trim. Aircraft Commander/Pilot: Capt. Dick Thompson. This B-29A was one of the many B-29s that the base ordered to have clothes applied to all nudes painted on aircraft. (via G. James)

MY ASSAM DRAGON III-, 19th B/G, black stripe.

MY DRAGON-, 19th B/G, black stripe.

OPPOSITE: LUCIFER-, 45-21745, 19th B/G, 30th B/S, black stripe with blue tips and trim. Surveyed on 02/14/52. The cat named Lucifer is from the Walt Disney production of "Cinderella"—the evil feline was the pet of the wicked stepmother. This B-29 was specially modified to carry the TARZON bomb. Major revisions were made to the bomb bay and bomb bay doors. The forward gun turret was removed and radar moved forward. It was fitted with a Plexiglas nose from a B-50 to help improve visibility for the bombardiers. Lucifer flew 6 Razon bomb missions and 10 TARZON bomb missions. Tarzon was a 12,000 pound, radio-guided bomb usually dropped on heavily fortified structures such as the Yalu River bridges. (via W. Walrond)

MARGIE'S MAD GREEK III-, 44-61843, 71st Reccon. Group, 31st Strategic Reccon. Squadron. Was Reclaimed on 08/26/54. This B-29A flew up along the Soviet and Communist N. Korean Borders on patrol missions to gather essential information on troop and supply movements and any other significant buildups which could propose a threat to World Peace. (via J. Heyer)

MISS FORTUNE-, 19th B/G, 28th B/S, black stripe with Green tips and trim.(via W. Walrond)

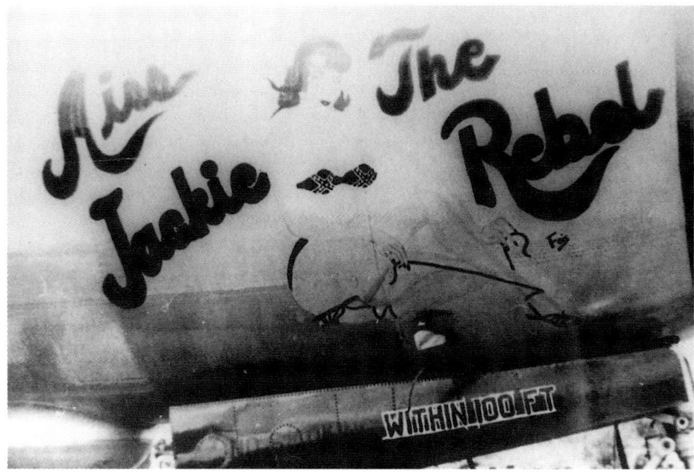

MISS JACKIE THE REBEL-, 19th B/G, 93rd B/S, black stripe with Red trim and tips. (via W. Walrond)

MISS N.C.-, 44-86376, 19th B/G, 28th B/S, black stripe with Green tips and trim. Reclaimed:07/14/54. Flew with 444th B/G during WWII. Photo in chapt. 3.

MISSION INN-,44-61669, 19th B/G, black stripe, now sits on display at March Field. Named for a famous hotel in Riverside, California, it was recovered from the Naval Weapons and Gunnery Range at China Lake, California, in the mid-1970s and was flown to the Museum in August 1981. (Veronico)

MISS TAMPA-, 19th B/G, black stripe. (via W./ Watts)

NEVER HOPPEN-, 44-61562, 19th B/G, 28th B/S, black stripe with Green tips and trim. The lady painted on this B-29-A-35-BN went through three types of dress before she was finally approved by the Kadena AB commanding officer. She flew ove 80 combat missions. (Campbell Archives)

NIGHT-MARE-, 44-87661, 19th B/G, 28th B/S, black stripe with green tips and trim. Also went by the names Koza Kid and Ugly. During World War II her name was American Beauty III. (via Mad Mike Hill)

No Sweat after running off of the hard deck and onto softer ground. This is not the ground accident which claimed her, though. The nose gear door and under nose trim is clearly seen in this image, as well as the rudder tip. She crash-landed at a fighter base and was later totally demolished when a P-51 Mustang fighter suffered engine failure on take-off and slammed into her. This B-29 had been equipped with blind bombing radar that had been mounted on the centerline. (Campbell Archives)

OUR GAL-, 19th B/G, black stripe.

NO SWEAT-, 44-87618, 19th B/G, 28th B/S, black stripe, with green trim and tips. Was destroyed in ground accident on 05/14/51. (via J. Heyer)

THE OUTLAW-, 42-65306, 19th B/G, 28th B/S, black stripe with green tips and trim. Based at Kadena AB, Okinawa, in 1950. Actress Jane Russell was the inspiration for this piece of artwork. This B-29 crashed on take-off on 10/02/51. (via G. James)

PEACE MAKER-, 44-86433, 19th B/G, 30th B/S, black stripe with blue trim and tips. Was based at Kadena AB, Okinawa, in 1951. B-29A-60-MO. Also flew with SAC while in the Korean war, assigned then to the 92nd B/G. (via J. Heyer)

PERSUADE-HER-, 19th B/G, 28th B/S, painted by Capt. Dick Thompson (via B. Davis)

PURPLE SHAFT-, 42-65361, 19th B/G, 30th B/S, black stripe, blue trim and tips, salvaged at Davis-Monthan AFB on 05/16/54. Flew numerous bombing missions over North Korea. (Mad Mike Hill)

RAZ-N-HELL-, 45-21746, 19th B/G, 28th B/S, black stripe, green tips and trim. Starting on her 2nd mission, she caught a flak burst. 124 missions later, ground fire ended her combat career. 126 total missions. The ground fire had started a fire in the no.1 engine. She made it safely back to Kadena, but extensive repairs were necessary. Wing ribs and longerons were burned away. After repairs she was returned to Sacramento AMA in May of 1952. She was reworked and sent back to Kadena, this time to the 307th B/W. At war's end she was reclaimed by Davis-Monthan AFB. In February of 1957 she was turned over to the U.S. Naval Weapons Range where she served as a target tug, and then as a ground target herself. She was also used in the movie "Enola Gay". In 1980 Castle Air Force Base procured her from China Lake for restoration and permanent display, as seen here in the 2nd photo.(Nick Veronico & Campbell Archives)

RELUCTANT DRAG'ON-, 44-62253, 19th B/G, also flew with SAC in the 98th B/G, 345th B/S, Salvaged: Davis Monthan AFB on 07/14/54. Flew over 90 combat missions while assigned to the Far East Air Forces, based at both Yokota AB, Japan, and Kadena AB, Okinawa—a B-29A-70-BN. (Campbell Archives)

ROCK HAPPY-, 44-62053, 19th B/G, 93rd B/S, black stripe, red tips, and trim. Salvaged: Davis-Monthan on 07/14/54. Many people mentioned Korea as the rock. There weren't too many trees there, and in the service man's career you can get a little nutty at times. Most of the time it's a little like cabin fever. This GI in the painting on this B-29 is tagged as "Rock Happy", playing with his yo-yo, and a vicious reptile in his right hand, not to mention the confused look on his face. (via John Heyer)

ROUGH ROMAN-, 19th B/G, 28th B/S, black stripe, with green tips and trim. (via W. Watts)

SHEEZA GOER-, 19th B/G, 30th B/S, black stripe with blue tips and trim. Also flew with SAC assigned to the 43rd B/G, 43rd Air Refueling Squadron. Was one of the first conversion KB-29 tankers. Seen in chapter 13 while assigned to SAC, ser. no. 44-69999. (via B. Davis)

SOUTH SEA SINNER-, 19th B/G, 28th B/S, black stripe and green tips and trim. Based at Kadena AB, Okinawa, in 1951. (via B. Davis)

NIP-PON ESE-, 44-87760, 19th B/G, 93rd B/S, black stripe with red tips and trim. Also flew when assigned to SAC's 92nd B/G while in the Korean war.(via J. Heyer)

PASSION WAGON-, 42-94043, 19th B/G, 93rd B/S, black stripe, with red trim and tips. Reclaimed: 04/06/49. Was assigned to the 314th B/W during WWII, 1st B/S of the 9th B/G. (See Photo in chapter six)

PEACE ON EARTH-, 44-61790, 19th B/G, 93rd B/S, black stripe with red trim and tips. Flew in WWII with the 73rd B/W 497th B/G. pictured in chapter 4. Reclaimed at OCAMA/Tinker on 07/14/54.

PUNCH BOWL QUEEN-, 19th B/G, based at Kadena AB, Okinawa 1951.

SOFT TOUCH-, 19th B/G, 28th B/S, black stripe, based at Kadena AB, Okinawa, 1941. Green trim, and tips. B-29A.

SPACE MISTRESS-, 44-86316, 19th B/G, 28th B/S, black stripe with Green tips and trim.

TARGET TONIGHT-, 44-70007, 19th B/G, 93rd B/S, black stripe with Red tips and trim.

SOUTHERN COMFORT- 44-61749, 19th B/G, 30th B/S, black stripe with blue tips and trim. Salvaged at Itazuke on 12/13/50. (via T. Carmichael)

STAR DUSTER-, 44-86254-, 19th B/G, 30th B/S, black stripe with Blue trim and tips. seen here in a bombing formation heading out to bomb targets in North Korea. The complete B-29 in the center of the photo is "PUNCH BOWL QUEEN", ser. no. 44-83974. (via B. Davis)

STATESIDE REJECT-, 19th B/G, 93rd B/S, black stripe with Red tips and trim. This B-29 crashed and burned at Kadena AB, Okinawa, in November of 1950. (via Mike Hill)

SURE THING-, 19th B/G, 928th B/S, black stripe with green tips and trim. (via Mike Hill)

THAT'S IT-, 19th B/G, 93rd B/S, black stripe red tips and trim. Salvaged/ Lost: on 11/30/50, at Kadena AB, Okinawa. (via T. Carmichael)

TOP OF THE MARK-, 19th B/G, 28th B/S, black stripe with green tips and trim. Named for a famous San Francisco night nlub and restaurant. (via Mike Hill)

VICIOUS ROOMER-, 19th B/G, based at Kadena AB, Okinawa, 1950. Little else in the way of information is known about this B-29A. (via J. Heyer)

A formation of four plus B-29s make their way for a target somewhere in North Korea. The blue tips and trim would indicate the 30th B/S, of the 19th B/G. (via B/Davis)

SIC'EM !-, another choice piece of art work contrived during the Korean war depicting a somewhat cowardly bulldog. (Hill)

Tail end Charlie's view of the low level formation departing Kadena AB, Okinawa. The target is somewhere up North. The trio of B-29s almost appear to be in a serene state of grace as they lumber on towards the target. (via John Heyer)

An End to the Korean War

FOR RESTRICTED WEAPONS EXPERIMENTS- one of the many uses for the old B-29s was gunnery practice, both as a ground target and a target for weapons of the U.S. Army. Whether it was for target spotting of mortar fire, artillery, or small arms, one will never know. These two obsolete B-29 fuselages, stripped of all parts and accessories, began the journey by truck to the Special Weapons Command, Gray, AFB, Camp Hood, Kileen, Texas. Supplied by Kelly AFB Reclamation Section, the "Giant Carcasses" required special permission of the State Highway Department (DPS) because of their enormous size. Here we see G.A. Merbeth, Chief of Supplies, Shipping and Receiving branch, talking with Floyd Mathis, the tractor trailer driver who will be responsible for the load's delivery. (Kelly AFB/ALC,HO)

The warm breeze blows over what remains of three B-29s in the Desert Boneyard at China Lake's Naval Weapons Center. These bombers, having fulfilled their purpose, sit as quiet reminders of a day long past. Birds make nests in openings and intakes, and the inhabitants of the desert—snakes, lizards, and other varmints—burrow under the discarded aluminum, fuselages, and cowlings.

Mother nature has long since taken her toll on the previously fabric-covered control surfaces of the rudders and horizontal stabilizers. Now only a few scattered remnants of these great bombers remain. A few fortunate individuals and groups have managed to salvage and restore a sorted few to their original beauty. You can close your eyes and almost hear the roar of the giant Pratt and Whitney 3350s as the B-29s would turn up their engines for take-off to a target in Japan or N. Korea. We dream back and think of our heroes of that day and that time in our history. Not so long ago as time goes, really. These men, like gods in their actions and likenesses, but in reality just men with a purpose, a just cause, and an honest belief that their actions were for the betterment of all mankind. (Johnsen)

OPPOSITE: This is a dramatic shot of the KEE BIRD as she sat for several years while the recovery team did their best to get work done to her in very short seasonal endeavors. In this photograph the missing rudder is clearly visible and the bare and naked tundra of Greenland is in the background. Sitting like the monument she was to all of the B-29s and their crews. (via Bob Vanderveen)

FIFI- a TB-29, now in the service of The Confederate Air Force, home based at the Confederate Air Force's Headquarters, Midland/Odessa, Texas. Seen here in a composite photograph of her reenactment of August 6, 1945. FIFI is the most photographed B-29 in the world. She has traveled to more airshows in the U.S. and abroad and stirred more nostalgia in recent years than all of her contemporaries. Not too bad for a 50+ year old. (via Fred Johnsen)

KEE BIRD-, 45-21768, B-29-95 BW recently restored in the last few years, but tragically destroyed by fire during a turn up for flight out of the barrens of Greenland, as seen here in the first of 5 photos. She is sitting close to where she bellied in, remarkably preserved and only slightly damaged to the naked eye. The rudder was torn off during a storm some years after the crash and blown a considerable distance. It was, however, recovered, reskinned, and remounted to the KEE BIRD. (via Bob Vanderveen)

Here is how the KEE BIRD looked just at the beginning of her restoration. All of her props were severely bent, and the rudder was gone. Greenamyer's team had worked 3 to four seasons on KEE BIRD, raising the B-29 off her belly and lowering the landing gear. They then moved her to a place were she is now sitting, in the middle of this shallow lake of near freezing water, her reflection in the lake her only companion for many years. She went down just after WWII in a remote area some two hundred miles from Thule, Greenland. (via Bob Vanderveen)

New propellers were just a little of the effort required in getting the KEE BIRD ready for a historic flight back to civilization. This B-29 had the Name "Ida" on the outboard port engine, and the name "Norma" on the port inboard engine. Perhaps named after a wife or sweetheart. The team had re-engined her and practically reworked the entire powerplant's system to ensure success. (via Bob Vanderveen)

One of the most critical steps in the resurrection of an old warbird is the running up of the engines to be sure that any bugs can be caught before the time arrives for take-off. This is one of the last few photos before the appointed time to depart. The departure day was met with tragedy, for one of the fuel cells ruptured and the KEE BIRD caught fire. The lack of any type of firefighting equipment spelled out doom for the B-29 as the only effort to quell the blaze was quickly exhausted when the fire extinguishers ran out of agent. The project had been funded by Darryl Greenamyer, a fine aviation enthusiast and air racing personality. The KEE BIRD, in a power test before the fire, had actually gotten up to 80 knots. (via Bob Vanderveen)

Boeing SB-29, was WB-29 seen on Guam in 1955. (Mikesh)

This B-29 had once been on display at the Florence, South Carolia, Air and Missile Museum. She had a Z on the tail, and like so many aircraft fell victim to the weather and was practically destroyed by hurricane "Hugo".

Tupolev Tu-4 "Bull" of the Chinese Air Force. Under the wing you can see the mounting point for the WZ-5 drone. (Griffeth)

Tupolev Tu-4 of the Chinese Airforce, ser. no. 2806501, but a red code "114" on the vertical. The Airborne Warning And Control Squadrons must have had a shock on seeing this Boeing variant. (Griffeth)

This Composite B-29 sits at the Air Depot entrance to Tinker Airforce Base in Oklahoma City. The reason she is referred to as composite is largely due to the fact she is not one but numerous B-29 airframes. Rescued from Aberdeen proving ground where her career had not been good to her, her sub assembly was loaded aboard air transport and taken to Tinker where the 2953 Combat Logistics Support Squadron reworked and reassembled her for generations to come and appreciate their efforts. (Campbell Archives)

FIFI- probably the world's most publicly visible B-29, seen here with her future beside her, the B-1B Lancer. Nowhere near the amount of Lancers will be built as was the case of the B-29. The aircraft today will be much fewer, due to a wider array of missions in their peacekeeper role. This photo was taken at Dyess AFB by Lt. Col. Kenny Wilkerson.

It is sad enough to close such an interesting subject knowing that the days of the flyable B-29 sorties are numbered. The Superfortress had a glorious history. Records were broken. Victories achieved, both in wartime and peacetime. Many men still alive today served on and in the mighty Superfortress, but never again will we see the conga lines and listen with deafened ears to the great roar as these giants take to the air, one right after another, their goal set firmly in their pilot and crew's minds and hearts. The few airframes that remain will have to serve as a rememberance to the literally thousands of B-29s that were built. This is their legacy. The pride of the builder, the designer, the pilots, and their crews, from a very grateful nation.

AMERICAN BOMBERS AT WAR
VOL.I
CONSOLIDATED B-24

John M. & Donna Campbell.

A superb photo tribute to the classic B-24, showing the variety of war fronts over which it served from CBI to Europe and North Africa. Most of the photos are published here for the first time.

Size: 8 1/2" x 11"   256 pages, over 700 b/w and color photographs, 10 color profiles; hard cover
ISBN: 0-88740-452-9 $39.95

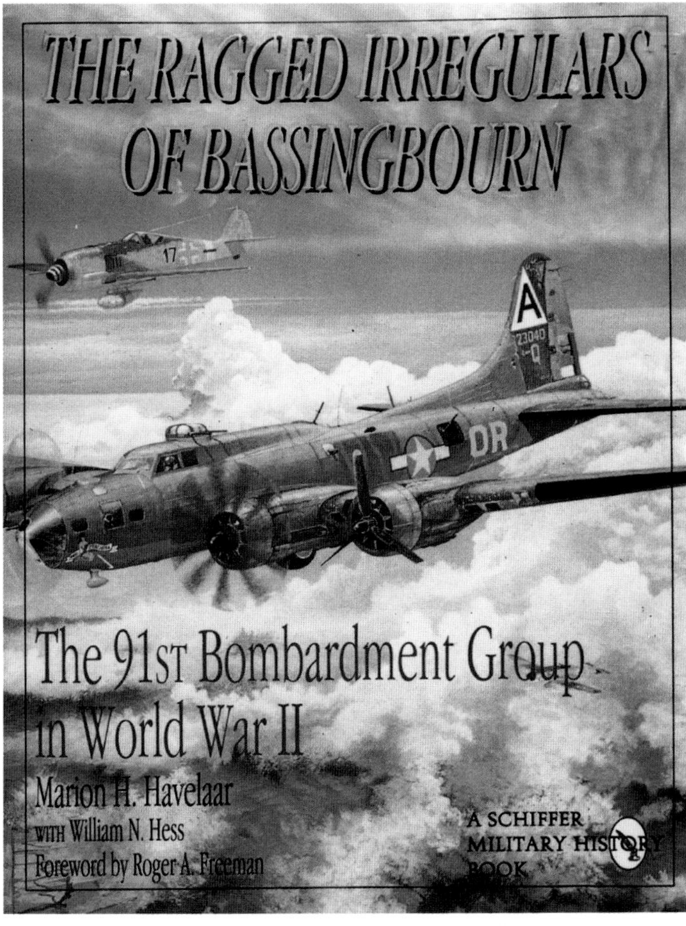

THE RAGGED IRREGULARS:
THE 91ST BOMB GROUP
IN WORLD WAR II

Marion Havelaar.

This new book is the first detailed history of the famed 91st Bomb Group.

Size: 8 1/2" x 11" over 300 photos
288 pages, hard cover
ISBN: 0-88740-810-9 $45.00

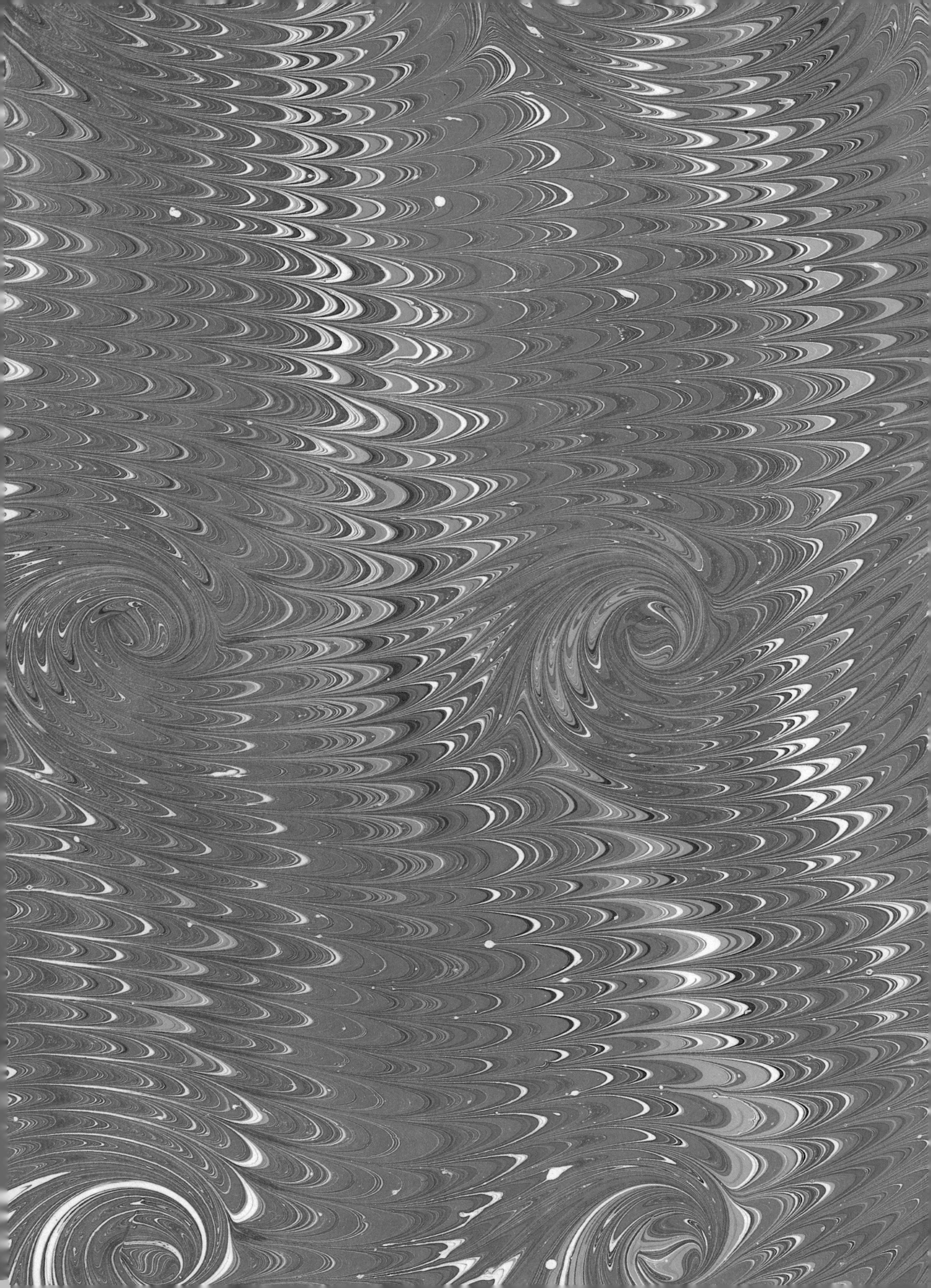